FINANCE
—*for*—
NON-FINANCIAL
MANAGERS

FINANCE
—*for*—
NON-FINANCIAL MANAGERS

AND SMALL BUSINESS OWNERS

LAWRENCE W. TULLER

ADAMS MEDIA CORPORATION
Holbrook, Massachusetts

Published by Adams Media Corporation
260 Center Street, Holbrook, MA 02343

ISBN: 1-55850-652-7

Printed in the United States of America.

J   I   H   G   F   E   D

Library of Congress Cataloging-in-Publication Data
Tuller, Lawrence W.
Finance for non-financial managers and small business owners / Lawrence W. Tuller.
p.   cm.
Includes index.
ISBN 1-55850-652-7 (pbk.)
1. Small business—Finance. 2. Finance. I. Title.
HG4027.7.T849   1997
658.15'92—dc20   96–27817
CIP

This publication is designed to provide accurate and authoritative information with regard to the
subject matter covered. It is sold with the understanding that the publisher is not engaged in ren-
dering legal, accounting, or other professional advice. If legal advice or other expert assistance
is required, the services of a competent professional person should be sought.
— From a *Declaration of Principles* jointly adopted by a Committee of the
American Bar Association and a Committee of Publishers and Associations

This book is available at quantity discounts for bulk purchases.
For information, call 1-800-872-5627 (in Massachusetts, 781-767-8100).

Visit our home page at http://www.adamsmedia.com

Table of Contents

Part I: Cash

Part II: Banks

Part III: Planning

Part IV: Financing

Part I
Cash

Chapter 1

Cash Management

Cash is the cornerstone of any business, large or small. Without cash, payrolls can't be met, materials can't be purchased, rent and utilities can't be paid, and dividends can't be distributed. It is unfortunate that current business practices cloud this truism, leading unsuspecting business owners and managers to disregard the criticality of managing in such a way as to ensure cash flows adequate to meet their company's operating needs.

For example, current accounting practices permit companies to show a profit on their financial statements even though they don't have enough cash to meet one week's bills. Governments levy taxes without regard to whether companies have the cash to pay them. Currently acceptable business valuation practices calculate the worth of a company on the basis of future earning potential, regardless of the company's ability to pay this month's rent. And banks frequently lend money against overvalued business assets without verifying that the borrower has the wherewithal to repay the loan on schedule.

There is nothing very complicated about cash management. In the simplest terms, cash management is a set of procedures aimed at maximizing the amount of cash available at any given time. Record keeping is one tool of cash management. Predicting future cash needs is another. Analyzing where our cash comes from and where it goes is a fundamental cash management procedure. So is analysis of the interaction between accounting reports and cash flows.

We all practice cash management in our daily lives when we keep track of checks we write and deposits we make. Only in this way can we be certain that we have enough cash in our checking accounts to cover tomorrow's checks. The same principle applies to cash management in a business. We have to make sure the company has sufficient cash in its checking account to pay its bills tomorrow, the next day, and the next.

That's all there is to cash management. And if we all followed this single, basic principle, a book like this would not be needed.

But we do not practice this basic principle. Instead, we are encouraged to buy on credit—to acquire inventory, to pay employees, to pay rent and utility bills. We pay our credit bills with money borrowed from banks and other lenders. Then, of course, we must use the cash generated by our business to repay bank loans, creating even more cash shortages and hence more borrowing. Eventually, when the business no longer generates enough cash to meet all these obligations, the bank forecloses and we lose everything.

This may seem to be a doomsday scenario. Yet an increasing number of small businesses face just such a dilemma. And that's the reason this book is so important to you as a business owner. It lays out a series of cash management techniques that you can follow to avoid the catastrophe of not having enough cash to run your business. Some of the basic precepts underlying cash management are reviewed, and then succeeding chapters will guide you through the basic mechanics of

- Getting bank loans
- Analyzing financial statements
- Forecasting future cash flows
- Constructing operating budgets
- Preparing business plans
- Developing strategic plans
- Raising venture capital
- Selling shares to the public
- Leasing hard assets

The last chapter in this book takes you through the mechanics of restructuring and refinancing your company when you need extra short-term cash that cannot be raised through normal banking channels.

You don't have to be an accountant to understand how to use these techniques. This book is specifically written for business managers with little or no knowledge of the niceties of debits and credits so beloved by the accounting profession. In fact, in many cases, managers can do a far better job of managing cash if they avoid the many pitfalls of current accounting jargon and practices.

Too often, accountants get caught up in the intricacies of generally accepted accounting principles and lose sight of the simpler, but more important, aspects of cash management.

The heart and soul of any cash management program is the *cash control plan.*

Controlling Cash

It always helps to have the right tools to change a tire or repair a leaky faucet. The same holds true for managing cash. The most fundamental tool available to business managers is the cash control plan.

I know that by this time you probably gag whenever you hear the word *plan.* Every business book you pick up pushes plans. Bankers insist on a repayment plan before they will grant loans. Most likely you are sick and tired of people telling you that you have to have a plan to run your business profitably, when you have managed very well over the years without one.

However, competition in every industry is increasing. To stay competitive, you have to make certain that every dollar counts. Therefore, it seems to me that using planning tools is a small price to pay for survival. For over thirty years I have worked with business owners and managers to make their companies and divisions grow. Of the hundreds of companies that I have provided consulting advice to, I have never seen one that was able to sustain long-term growth without using some form of cash control plan.

Some tool must be available to organize actions and to monitor the success or failure of business decisions. Any business, large or small, is too complex, too dynamic, for the business owner or managers to mentally keep track of every action that must be taken to improve cash flow. Six months from now, when competition has passed you, it's too late to change direction. With a cash flow plan and a cost-reduction program, you can see where you are heading and take corrective action before it's too late.

Without an architect's drawing that lays out a floor plan, a carpenter can't build a house. The same holds true for developing a cash management program. A cash control plan is similar to an architect's drawings. It establishes the ground rules for generating and using cash. It shows how much cash is needed to run the business and when it is needed. It establishes what the cash position of the business will look like when the plan is completely implemented. It summarizes, in quantifiable terms, how each aspect of the business contributes to the finished whole.

A cash control plan is a detailed, written document that identifies cash inflows and outflows that can be expected every month for at least twelve months into the future. Companies with longer production or sales cycles find a two- or three-year projection helpful.

A cash control plan is a working tool. It is an action plan, alive, dynamic, changeable. It should be used continually as the basis for tactical actions. It acts as a monitoring device so that you can be certain that the operating strategies you want to be followed are actually being followed. It is as different from the garden variety business plan as night is from day.

A well-thought-out cash flow plan serves as a road map for everyone in the organization. It lays out in clearly discernible terms how much cash will be coming in and going out as a result of every business action: from increasing an advertising program to laying off three employees; from leasing unused space to selling a piece of equipment; from implementing sales promotions to acquiring a new facility. Even more important, a cash control plan specifically identifies where and when you will be short of cash. If carefully prepared, it gives you advance warning of danger signals so that you can change course.

You don't have to be an accountant or a bookkeeper to construct a cash control plan. In fact, such backgrounds often confuse the issue. A cash control plan has little resemblance to traditional financial statements like balance sheets and income statements (although it depends on them for historical data and trends). It deals only with the cash result of business actions—how much cash comes in, how much cash goes out, and when these conditions are expected to happen.

If you are uncomfortable working with numbers, hire someone on a part-time basis to help—perhaps a public accountant or a retired bookkeeper. They don't charge that much, and they can save you a lot of valuable time. It usually doesn't work very well to have someone on your payroll do the calculations. Employees tend to have their own agendas to protect their jobs, and this invariably distorts the results of the plan.

A cash control plan is strictly an internal document. It won't be handed to bankers, employees, suppliers, or the IRS. It doesn't need to be bound in a fancy booklet. It can be done on a personal computer, a columnar tablet, or the back of a grocery bag. It certainly doesn't need to be typed. It's for your use in managing your business. The plan should include all expected cash receipts and expenditures. And it should be prepared in a format that can be easily used for monitoring daily, weekly, and monthly cash flow.

I won't bore you with forms. You can't use those appearing in books anyway unless you tear the book apart. And then the form will be the wrong size or have the wrong headings. It doesn't make any difference what the format is as long as it makes sense to you.

One important point to remember, however, is that the cash control plan should be structured to record expected cash coming in from all sources and cash going out for all types of payments. It should be divided into small enough increments to enable you to monitor actual results against it, preferably monthly and in some cases weekly.

Very small companies, or those selling only one or two product lines, can get by with a very simple cash control plan. If you have two employees and plan to lay off one, it's a snap to know how much cash you'll save, and you sure don't need a form to tell you. If you plan to sell that old printing press next month, once you get a bid price, you know exactly how much extra cash you'll have. And clearly, if you are the only employee, you can figure out in a few minutes what costs you can cut.

For slightly larger companies, however, a sound cash management program involves more complex, at times overlapping, procedures. Let's begin our journey by reviewing some basic approaches to maximizing the generation of cash.

Maximizing Cash Generation

Business cash generators are identical to those we use in our personal lives. As individuals, we can get cash from five sources:

1. Wages (earnings)
2. Investments (interest, dividends, royalties, capital gains)
3. Lenders (banks, relatives, friends)
4. Selling assets (a car, house, jewelry, etc.)
5. Gifts (inheritances)

Businesses get cash from

1. Earnings (from sales to customers)
2. Investments (interest, dividends, royalties, capital gains)
3. Lenders (business owner, stockholders, banks, government agencies, suppliers)
4. Selling assets (equipment, real estate, delivery vehicles, etc.)
5. Gifts (foundations, government agencies)

I can hear the purists now: "How can you call stockholders and business owners lenders? They are investors!" In a sense that's true. Interest is not paid on the money they put into a company, and in most cases there isn't any schedule for repaying principal amounts. However, investors, including business owners, expect a return on their invested capital, in the form of either dividends or capital gains from the appreciation in the value of their investment. In that sense, money obtained from investors must be repaid at some time in the future, and it is expected to earn a return during the period the company uses the money. It is no different from cash received from banks and other lenders.

From the recipient's viewpoint, the prioritization of the desirability of cash generators is also about the same, whether the recipient is an individual or a company. Most people would rather receive gifts of money than earn it; so would companies. Most people would rather receive cash from passive investments than work for it; so would companies. And most people would rather earn cash than borrow it; so would companies. Therefore, we can prioritize the desirability of business cash generators as follows:

1. Awards and grants from foundations or government agencies
2. Returns on passive investments—interest, dividends, royalties, rents, capital gains
3. Earnings from the sale of products or services to customers
4. Gains from selling unneeded business assets
5. Loans from banks and other lenders

Such prioritization is important because it focuses our attention on those cash generators that we should go after first, for two reasons: (1) to obtain cash at the least cost, and (2) to improve the long-term stability of the company. It may be that the type of business you have or the products or services you offer for sale preclude the possibility of obtaining grants and awards. Foundations may not be interested in giving money to a company manufacturing high-powered rifles. The Small Business Innovative Research (SBIR) program would be likely to stay clear of research programs aimed at developing more effective animal traps.

On the other hand, if you own a small business whose plans involve improving social conditions—such as establishing a manufacturing plant in a poverty-stricken neighborhood or implementing a training program to upgrade the skills of low-skill working mothers—it's quite likely that you could obtain cash grants from a number of different foundations. Similarly, small businesses engaged in research and development programs aimed at coming up with products that could be used by the U.S. Army, Navy, or Air Force could probably qualify for grants from the SBIR program or similar government programs, either state or federal.

Returns on Passive Investment

Second only to pure gifts, passive investments have become the preferred source of cash generation, especially for small businesses. Rental property, mutual funds, secured business loans, and royalties from patents, copyrights, and trademarks all provide a relatively steady source of cash while incurring no (or very little) expense.

Of course, to make such investments, you must have excess cash to begin with. If all your spare cash goes to build your company, clearly, generating cash from investments is not a viable alternative. On the other hand, one of the objectives of instituting a cash management program might very well be to squeeze enough excess cash out of the business to permit a long-term investment portfolio. More than one small-business owner has found it advantageous from both a tax and an estate planning perspective to set up an investment program through the company rather than as an individual.

Take the case of a two-partner advertising agency. An opportunity arose to invest in a real estate limited partnership. Shares were selling for $100,000 per unit. The partners could have drawn the cash out as a year-end bonus, but their accountant advised against it, explaining that personal income tax would have to be paid on the draws. And worse, the IRS might reclassify the draws as dividends. Instead, the partners chose to purchase two limited partnership units in the company's name.

Annual distributions from the limited partnership were then used by the company to liquidate part of its short-term debt. Moreover, the partners found this a convenient way to build their equity interests in the company and hence increase the value of their individual estates.

Another favorite strategy in many small businesses is to invest in rental property, either the property housing the company or a distant property, leveraging the investment with a high mortgage. The rental income flowing to the company increases the total cash flow available for running the business or for paying the owners extra draws. Of course, if you have patentable technologies or products, royalty income is probably the least time-consuming and least expensive way to generate extra cash.

Earnings from Sales to Customers

It goes without saying that the most common way for businesses to generate cash is to sell products or services to customers. To the extent that you operate a cash business, such as a retail store, accounts receivable never become a problem. You make the sale and collect cash. However, most companies aren't that fortunate and must abide by the market practice of granting customers credit. The main idea is to maximize sales—both sales volume and selling prices—in such a manner that cash flow also increases. Several tactics may be used to achieve this objective, depending on the nature of your business. Here are a few examples:

1. By pruning low-margin or low-volume products or services, you should be able to redirect current selling resources (e.g., sales personnel, advertising, sales promotions, etc.) to more profitable lines and customers.
2. Special pricing incentives may entice customers to buy higher-profit items as well as promotional goods.
3. Capturing new market niches should increase sales volume by expanding your customer base.
4. Advertising campaigns aimed at specific markets to promote one or more products or services should attract new customers.
5. A public relations program that puts your company's name on the map can bring in additional business.
6. Shifting a market mix may stimulate sales of previously dormant items.

Sales-promotion programs might actually allow you to raise prices on some items. Payment discounts and improved collection procedures move cash into the business faster. Incentive policies for customer returns coupled with same-day deliveries might stimulate a faster sales turnover. Special discounts in conjunction with COD terms for customer pickups inevitably improve turnover and speed cash flow. Perhaps an in-house training program for customer personnel would improve your company's image as an innovator.

Changing from a salaried to a commission sales force saves cash by matching personnel costs with sales. Direct selling efforts by yourself and other management personnel often improve customer service and simultaneously garner new orders. By redirecting other selling costs to productive channels, you could probably conserve cash while increasing the productivity of your sales force. Cooperative sales incentives and advertising campaigns with large customers, and even competitors, is another avenue for stimulating sales while simultaneously reducing selling expenses.

A wide range of possibilities for generating additional cash through sales channels exists. Frequently, all it takes is a little creative initiative on your part. In other cases, small cash investments can often bring substantial new sales.

However, much as we would all like to improve our cash flow by increasing sales, this may not be practical. Competition, market saturation, pricing barriers, or material shortages may prevent any significant increase in sales volume. Other, more creative means must be found. Perhaps you can increase cash flow by offering a discount for early payment. You might try factoring your receivables. Maybe you could reduce credit sales by offering reduced prices for cash sales. When credit sales make up a substantial part of your business, the main idea is to reduce, as much as possible, the length of time it takes to collect receivables.

Selling Unneeded Business Assets

Every business uses tangible assets of one type or another—production equipment, machinery, office equipment, furniture and fixtures, and so on. Many businesses own vehicles—cars, delivery trucks, forklifts, and so on. Perhaps you made a quick killing in the past and invested in an airplane, yacht, or lodge for entertaining customers. Manufacturing, retail, and distribution companies stock inventory. All businesses utilize office, warehouse, production, or sales space of some type.

The question is: How many of these assets are in constant use, and which ones could you dispose of without endangering the operation of your business? Psychologically, this is a difficult question to answer. It's human nature to feel that even if we aren't using that extra desk or delivery truck right now, we might need it in the future. We also enjoy the luxury of being comfortable with what we have and where we are. But sound cash management practices demand that we take a close look at what is really needed, right now, and increase cash flow by disposing of the rest. And that includes unused production, office, warehouse, and storage space. It may be convenient to have extra storage space, a file room, lunch tables, or meeting rooms, but such luxuries absorb cash and don't pay the bills.

In very small businesses, some owners go to the extreme. They subcontract out administrative functions, move their own office to their home, and lease out the entire office. Such was the case with the owner of a small advertising agency.

When business was booming, the agency turned annual sales of over $3 million. As clients began skimping on their advertising programs, business slacked off and office and staff personnel became luxuries that took too much cash to sustain. The owner talked his CPA into doing the bookkeeping chores, hired an independent contractor to prepare client billings from her home, moved his office furniture into a spare room in his house, and sublet the entire 4,000 square feet of office space previously occupied by his agency.

The added cash was enough to tide him over for three years, by which time he had added new clients. Rather than opening another office, however, this creative entrepreneur merely added an extra room to his house, hired a part-time secretary, and continued subcontracting the rest of the jobs. He is still operating this way today, and his annual billings have doubled.

Borrowing from Banks and Other Lenders

Certainly the least desirable way to generate cash is to borrow it. Although leveraging business assets has become a way of life in our business community—and without question has been a major force in allowing companies to grow faster than internally generated cash flow would permit—borrowing from banks or other lenders carries a high risk, and the trade-off may or may not be worth it. During market upswings, increased borrowings can fuel a company's growth, and, as long as the business grows, everyone benefits. Banks make profits, companies use bank money to buy additional inventory and production assets, and the concomitant increase in sales generates enough cash to meet debt service payments. In a market downturn, however, debt service payments can easily sink an otherwise salvageable business, as we see every time the country goes into a recession.

Companies that have borrowed heavily against inventory and receivables face a real problem in a business downturn. When inventory and receivables are increasing, a revolving line of credit brings cash into the business faster than normal. But in a downturn, when inventory and receivables both decrease, the reverse occurs; that is, the amount of cash used to repay loans each month frequently exceeds the amount of new inventory purchases and order shipments. Excess cash from sales, normally used for operating expenses, must now be returned to the bank.

Businesses saddled with fixed debt payments or a revolving line of credit can free up an enormous amount of cash if a way can be found to reduce or eliminate this outpouring to banks. This is never an easy task. In tough times, when banks become more obstreperous, credit dries up, and increasing loan defaults alert lenders to be especially watchful for potential delinquencies.

However, there are ways to reduce debt even in bad times. Given the right circumstances, you might exchange part of your company's debt obligations for equity shares. Or you might be able to convert a revolving line of credit into a term loan. You may be able to convert short-term loans into longer-term obligations, if your company has unsecured assets that it can pledge as security. Refinancing on more favorable terms with another bank is also a possibility. Regardless of the method used, restructuring a company's debt to increase liquidity always adds to the amount of cash available for operating needs. (See Chapter 15 for ideas about restructuring and refinancing your business.)

Once procedures are in place to maximize the amount of cash generation, the flip side of cash management comes into play—that is, the minimization of cash expenditures.

Minimizing Cash Expenditures

While increasing the amount of cash generated is essential in any cash management program, it is equally important to minimize the amount of cash expenditures—that is, to keep the amount of cash outflow as low as possible consistent with normal operating efficiencies. Although manufacturing, distribution, retail, and service companies all have different types of cash expenditures, for purposes of cash management they can generally be grouped as follows:

- Managerial and supervisory payroll
- Clerical and office payroll
- Direct labor payroll (manufacturing and construction companies)
- Sales payroll
- Payroll taxes and employee benefits
- Occupancy expenses—rent, property taxes, electricity, fuel
- Transportation expenses—autos, trucks, tractors, forklifts
- Maintenance and repair expenses—supplies, contracted labor
- Protection expenses—guards, insurance, alarm systems
- Selling expenses—advertising, public relations, printing, travel, entertainment
- Administrative expenses—data processing, office supplies, professional fees
- Material or supplies to make (or build) the product (manufacturing and construction companies)

The main tool for minimizing these expenditures is a flexible cost control system. A cost control system need not be complex—in fact, the simpler the better, as long as it can be used by everyone in the company and covers all expenditures. There are two underlying principles in any effective cost control system: (1) all costs (expenditures) must be planned and then measured against such plans, and (2) cross-checks must be built into the system to ensure that one or two people cannot by themselves make expenditures without prior approval.

The first principle is relatively straightforward. The operating budget is the basic tool for planning and then measuring costs against plan. Operating budgets have been around for many decades, and although the electronic age has made a variety of complex, sophisticated forecasting techniques available, nothing has yet replaced the cost-center budget as an effective and inexpensive way to control costs. Chapter 8 gets into the detailed construction of operating budgets.

The second element of a successful cost control system involves the assignment to different people in your organization of specific duties for requesting expenditures, approving such requests, signing checks, and reconciling bank accounts. For example, suppose a salesman requests authorization to buy a plane ticket to call on customers in a distant city. As general manager or business owner, you may approve such a request. The travel manager (or your administrative assistant) actually books the flight. Your controller prepares the check. And you, your general manager, or another executive actually signs the check. At the end of the month, when bank statements come in, someone in the accounting department (not the controller) reconciles the bank account. This might seem like overkill in a small company; however, the more people "get into the expenditure loop," the better your control will be. In addition to minimizing cash expenditures through a good internal cost control system, a well-conceived cost-reduction program can be a very effective weapon for reducing cash outflow.

Reducing Cash Outflow with Cost Reductions

Any business—large or small, manufacturing, distribution, service, or retail—has the ability to reduce at least some operating costs. A common rule of thumb is that any business, of any size, in any industry, can always reduce costs by at least 10 percent. A close look at payroll costs is usually a good place to start. Can you get by with fewer people? Trimming product lines should result in fewer production workers. How about personnel in sales, order taking, customer service, order expediting, shipping, and receiving? With realigned marketing strategies, at least some of these people could be let go.

Excessive administrative overhead is a luxury few companies can afford. Can you hire an outside bookkeeper or accounting firm at less cost than doing the work in-house? The preparation of tax returns—payroll, sales, use, property, or income tax—can easily be done on the outside. So can the preparation of financial statements and bank reports. Contracting for data processing services, janitorial work, deliveries to and from the plant, and building and equipment maintenance is nearly always less expensive than having employees do the work.

Do you really need all those managers and supervisors? How about subcontracting some of the personnel work, such as the management of employee benefit programs, pension administration, and workers' compensation compliance? In very small businesses, replacing employees with family members may be a viable alternative.

Although this won't necessarily reduce cash outflow, at least you can be sure that more cash stays at home. Company cars may be a convenience, or even a necessity in some cases. But how about subleasing them to employees? Or maybe you can reduce the number of cars.

There are always some costs that can be eliminated or curtailed. Every dollar that is not spent improves cash flow. Conserving cash is as valid a cash management technique as increasing sales or selling assets. In the next chapter we'll take a look at some methods for developing formal cost-reduction programs and then monitoring the programs to be sure of getting the reductions you plan.

Chapter 2

Developing a Cost-Reduction Program

Once the architect's drawings are approved, the next step in building a house is to develop the detailed construction plans and assemble the right tools to do the job. Similar actions hold for a business. Once you have defined how much cash is needed, what segments of the business will generate the cash, and when it must enter the company's coffers, the next step is to develop a detailed cost-reduction program and then assemble the tools needed to monitor progress.

As we saw in Chapter 1, the flip side of a cash-generating plan is a program for reducing expenditures. Such a program is often referred to as a *cost-reduction plan. Cost-center budgets* (a version of operating budgets) are the tools for monitoring the progress in meeting cost-reduction goals. This chapter offers ideas and recommendations for constructing a cost-reduction program. Chapter 8 looks at the construction of broader operating budgets.

Any company, large or small, can reduce operating costs by some amount. Leaving personnel layoffs aside, most companies spend money on luxuries and conveniences that could easily be eliminated without endangering the operation of the business. First-class air fares, second-shift janitors, redundant secretarial help, excess inventory, hour-long lunch breaks, overtime pay, routine bonuses, and noncritical travel are a few examples of conveniences that most companies can do without. For each dollar of cost reduced, an extra dollar gets added to the bank account.

Obviously, the manufacturing, distribution, service, and retail sectors each have certain types of unique expenditures. Some commonality does exist, however, among broad classifications of expenditures. Manufacturing companies always need materials and labor to produce products. Distribution companies must have space to stock products for delivery. Service companies, at a minimum, have an office and usually employ one or more technical or sales personnel. Retail operations employ salespeople and require a salesroom, store, or other facility from which to sell their wares.

Although it is impractical to tailor a universal cost-reduction program that meets the specific needs of all companies, a general format can be laid out. Ideas and suggestions can be proposed. Universal monitoring tools can be structured.

As we move through the preparation of cost-reduction programs, it's important to emphasize that the same comments that apply to cash control plans apply here. One format is as good as any other, as long as it meets the requirements of the business. However, even though the format differs for each company and the details that go into the program vary, the methodology and approach to cost reductions remain constant.

Setting up Controls

By their very nature, manufacturing and construction companies present opportunities for the most versatile, and usually the most complex, cost-reduction programs. To begin, you need some type of control form, a summary sheet of paper to record current actual expenditures by type of expense and expected results from cost-reduction actions. The more you can break down and categorize each type of expenditure, the easier it is to achieve reductions.

For example, assume that you have three supervisors, eighteen production employees, and an office staff of six, and you have one line on the control form called *payroll*. It's impossible to measure what the effect of laying off two production workers, one clerical employee, and two supervisors will be without making the detailed calculations for each class. Segregating payroll by type of employee makes the job much easier.

Although the relative importance of each expense classification varies with the type of business, they all play a role in keeping companies functioning. Quite naturally, nearly all expenses appear absolutely essential to the conduct of a business. No one intentionally spends more than is necessary to get the job done. Reducing essential purchases and payroll hurts as much as pulling teeth. However, sound cash management practices require that costs be controlled and in most cases reduced beyond current levels.

Manufacturing Costs

Since manufacturing costs usually represent the largest expenditures and are the most difficult to trim, this is a good place to start. Begin by listing those costs applicable to your business. The following groupings might fit your operation. If not, design your own categories.

1. Production materials
   a. Raw materials
   b. Product supplies—shipping containers
   c. Process/equipment supplies
   d. Finished product
2. Manufacturing payroll
   a. Direct workers
   b. Support/assistance workers
   c. Nondirect activities
   d. Supervision
3. Employee benefits
   a. Payroll taxes/workers' compensation
   b. Group insurance and pension
   c. Tools, meals, day care, other miscellaneous benefits
   d. Bonuses/incentive payments

Next, insert the amount of cash that was paid out for each of these categories last month and estimate the amounts for next month. On the "finished product" line, only cash expenditures for products to be resold (as a retailer) should be included. The cost of producing finished products is reflected in the purchased material and payroll categories.

Manufacturing payroll includes all employees directly associated with manufacturing the products. Only the total payroll for each category of employee should be inserted, not the amounts paid to individual employees. Be sure to include monthly amounts for those paid weekly, biweekly, or semimonthly.

Payroll taxes, workers' compensation premiums, and group insurance payments should be the same as last month's. Payments to a pension fund or retirement plan might be made semiannually or annually. In that case, note the time frame on the "pension" line.

Nonproduction Expenses

Payroll for nonproduction personnel should be grouped by major classification—supervisory, clerical, sales, and so on. It also helps to include payroll taxes and employee benefits under each caption. This makes it easier to judge the impact of cost-reduction actions. Your own salary and other compensation should obviously be excluded.

Cash payments for such nonproduction expenses as telephone, advertising, maintenance supplies, and legal fees will probably vary erratically month to month. If expenditures from last month do not reflect normal monthly payments, either an average or a reasonable estimate should be used as the starting point.

Clearly, if your business has a relatively simple cost structure, you don't need a complicated cost control sheet to know what is going on. Just record expected cost reductions on a piece of paper and have done with it. But do record them. This discipline formalizes the effort, and formal plans are always easier to implement than mental pictures of what you want.

Cost-Reduction Objectives

Once you have a handle on current actual expenditures, it's time to move on to structuring the cost-reduction program. Once again, every company is different, and no single plan works for everyone. The suggestions that follow are just that—suggestions. Obviously, you have to come up with those reductions that fit your business.

Certain rules should be followed to ensure the effectiveness of a cost-reduction program. These rules are:

1. Cost-reduction actions must be quantifiable. That is, the result of an action must be translatable into dollar reductions in one or more expense categories.
2. The cash savings from cost-reduction actions should be in reverse proportion to time. That is, the greatest savings should occur shortly after the action is implemented. As time

progresses, cash savings either disappear or continue at a decreasing pace.

3. Actions that will have a major effect on cash within six months should be given priority.

4. Projected savings from cost reductions should be formally recorded in a format appropriate for your business.

5. The cash savings resulting from cost-reduction actions must be measurable. That is, once a cost reduction is quantified, as in rule 1, a method must be implemented to measure whether or not the action resulted in the expected savings.

6. If cash savings are expected to be realized in increments over a period of time, or if the cost-reduction action itself will be implemented over time, a set of milestone achievement points should be established against which to measure incremental savings.

7. One individual must have responsibility for seeing that the action is implemented. In a one-person business, obviously this must be the owner. If you have several employees, then someone other than yourself should be assigned the responsibility, even though you manage the project.

8. Cost-reduction steps should be carefully chosen to inflict the least amount of real, long-term harm on the business and hurt the fewest people.

Several clients have tried to implement cost-reduction programs without following these simple rules. None of their programs resulted in the amount of cash savings expected. Most were abandoned before they were completed.

One reason these programs didn't work was that the planned cost-reductions were so general that they could not be quantified and measured. Milestones could not be set, and personnel responsible for implementing action steps became discouraged by the apparent lack of progress. Clients cited a more important reason, however: that the selected cost reductions did more harm than good to the business.

A perfect example involved a client who owned a farm implement dealership close to Waterloo, Iowa. For eight years sales had climbed, and the company had added several capable salespeople, field service personnel, a purchasing manager, and a bookkeeping department— twelve people in total. When the bottom fell out of the agricultural equipment market, the owner decided that a stringent cost-reduction program was the only solution for saving the business. He retained me to help structure the program.

We diligently set up the appropriate format to record existing expenditures. The owner, sales manager, purchasing manager, and bookkeeper came up with eighteen types of costs that could be reduced. I cautioned that this seemed like a lot for such a small business, but the managers were adamant. I also cautioned that they should set up a measuring system, such as an operating budget, to track each action as savings were realized. But they didn't have time for such a mundane administrative task.

Each of the three managers was assigned six action steps and instructed to go to it. In four months a total of three cost-reductions were implemented: a shelving of the company's effective advertising program, a cutback in sales personnel from four to three, and restrictions on long-distance phone calls. Within six months the sales manager quit, citing the disintegration of the customer base and blaming this on the cost-reduction moves.

Typical Manufacturing Cost-Reductions

When I propose to clients that a cost-reduction program be implemented as one means of increasing cash flow, they invariably ask the same question: "What costs can I cut that will make any significant difference without damaging the business over the long haul?"

Unfortunately, there is no simple answer. What works in one company will almost certainly not work in another. Your personal objectives, qualifications of personnel, the type and size of your business, market conditions, and many other factors are all unique to your company. However, although the details vary, the same approach can be applied in most businesses.

Aside from reducing the cost of borrowed money, nearly every business has one or more of the following categories of expenditures against which a cost-reduction program can be implemented:

- Expenditures for the purchase of materials, products, or supplies that will be either resold, converted to other products that are sold, or used in performing a service that is sold
- Expenditures for materials, supplies, and outside services that are not converted into sales but support other activities of the business
- Expenditures for people
- Expenditures to maintain a facility from which business can be conducted
- Expenditures to comply with government requirements

Let's look at a few cost-reduction ideas that might apply in each of these categories.

Materials and Supplies

Production supervisors always want to have plenty of material on hand so that they won't run short during the production cycle. The same can be said for store managers. They know that if the goods aren't in stock when a customer wants to buy, they will lose the sale.

In a booming economy, the tendency is to stock more than enough inventory. As everyone knows, you can't sell from an empty basket. But having enough material on hand to meet customer demand and having excess quantities so that you'll never run out are two quite different things.

In addition to the glowing reports we have all heard about the superior productivity of Japanese workers and their strong work ethic, one of the real contributions Japanese manufacturers have made to the producers and sellers of the world is a purchasing concept called *just-in-time* (commonly referred to as JIT) *deliveries*. This doctrine stipulates that a manufacturer, distributor, or retailer will not take delivery of materials until they are actually needed. Storerooms are stocked just in time to meet production schedules or to make the sale. JIT purchasing has grown in popularity over the past decade. Most giant corporations, including some of the largest—GE, the automobile manufacturers, the aerospace companies, AT&T, and Sears—now mandate the policy throughout their divisions and branches.

Shifting to JIT purchasing is an effective cost-reduction action. In some cases, I've seen a one-time cash saving of as much as 25 percent of purchased inventory. And any company can use JIT. The only requirements are that you (1) understand the exact amount of inventory you must have to maintain customer demand levels and (2) assign someone the responsibility of making sure that orders are placed and deliveries received to match this level.

Another potential cost-reduction step could be to reduce the amount of supplies and materials wasted. Even with the best inventory control system, employees tend to be careless about supplies. How often do we fill wastebaskets with computer paper, letterhead, and drafting paper to be carted off to the dump? Why not use the back sides for scratch paper and internal memos instead of buying more letterhead and paper tablets?

Machine oil, janitorial supplies, computer printer ribbons, and out-of-date catalogs and price sheets are other supplies that tend to be wasted. A conscientious effort to eliminate waste can result in substantial cost-reductions.

And what about manufacturing scrap? Many companies pay to have scrap removed from the premises to a local dump without realizing that, in general, everything has some value for someone. An effort to search out legitimate buyers for scrap could yield cash savings in two ways: by eliminating the cost of hauling it away, and by selling it.

Expenditures for outside services should also be examined closely. Do you really need equipment maintenance contracts, or is it cheaper to pay for repairs as they are needed? Relatively new equipment shouldn't break down. Why pay for expensive maintenance contracts when there is little likelihood of major repairs?

Legal fees are another cost many companies can reduce. Corporate lawyers love to have monthly retainer contracts to cover calls and advice on inconsequential matters, and then charge extra for preparing lawsuits or for court appearances. Do you really need to have a lawyer on standby? Try solving routine problems yourself and using lawyers only for major legal actions.

Accounting and audit fees fall into the same category. If a bank or other outside party doesn't require quarterly or annual audits, why go to the expense of certification when accounting reviews would suffice? If you have accounting personnel on staff and they are not included in cost-reduction layoffs, why not have them prepare payroll, sales, use, property, and other tax returns rather than paying extra for a CPA firm to do the job?

There are many other possibilities for reducing expenditures for operating expenses, purchased materials, and supplies. By putting a little effort into examining the internal policies for buying, storing, and using materials and outside services, you could probably come up with cost-reductions that are not recognized in the normal course of business.

Take, for example, the case of J & R Locknut Company. The president was thoroughly surprised at the results of the company's first try at a cost-reduction program. When cash grew tight during the last recession, this high-powered salesman who had risen to the company's top management post realized that with business turning down, he had to do something to keep costs in line. However, with only four people on the payroll, he was at a loss as to how to cut costs.

Five years earlier a consultant had set up a computerized inventory stocking system for the J & R primary warehouse. When the reserve stock of any part dropped below a predetermined level, an automatic purchase order was triggered. The company's accountant felt that this system resulted in excess inventory. But, realizing that the company had paid a sizable amount for the system, she kept her mouth shut. When I was called in to take a look at potential cost-reductions, I agreed with her assessment. We suggested that the company throw out the computer system and return to manually prepared inventory records on 3 X 5 cards.

I further recommended bringing the stock levels down another 20 percent. A new supplier ten blocks away could supply emergency parts within four hours. This reduction in inventory resulted in a one-time cash generation of nearly $20,000.

Personnel

Any company employing more than ten people can generally find a way to get by with at least one or two fewer. The 10 percent reduction rule of thumb is a good place to begin.

When considering employee layoffs as a method of cost-reduction, the tendency is to choose people who are not directly associated with either producing or selling products or services. This often damages a company over the long haul. Support personnel responsible for purchasing, accounting, quality assurance, advertising, data processing, engineering, and human relations activities may, in fact, perform activities that are crucial to the long-term health of a company.

Another mistake commonly made in companies with only a few employees is to assume that a manager, or the owner, can adequately perform additional activities. Therefore, laying off a bookkeeper, a salesperson, or clerical help will save money. Certainly one person can perform several different jobs. Owners of companies with no employees prove it every day. At the same time, by diverting your attention from selling or production to less critical activities, you inevitably hurt the business in the long run.

Exactly the opposite also happens—that is, making the assumption that all employees perform critical jobs, and therefore that no one can be laid off. This can be a fatal error, as a client in the auto repair business learned the hard way.

This client owned a string of three auto repair garages in suburban Philadelphia. The business had expanded from the original one-bay shop with no employees, and the company now employed twelve full-time mechanics and two administrative clerks. Normally, when a recession hits, people repair old jalopies one more time rather than buy new cars. But this time business fell off. Several mechanics spent two or three hours each day cleaning the shop rather than working on cars. I cautioned that if the business kept spending more money than it took in, cash reserves would soon dry up.

But the owner was obstinate. Good mechanics were hard to find. Rather than let them go, and then have to rehire when business turned, he preferred to keep his mechanics and spend a little money on nonproductive time.

Within four months the repair shop couldn't pay withholding taxes. In another two months the landlord threatened foreclosure. Within a year, the owner sold his rapidly declining business for substantially less than a profitable operation would have brought. A well-conceived cost-reduction program beginning with a reduction in employees might have saved the business, but the ex-owner will never know for sure.

A good way to determine the right number of employees for a business is to relate it to sales. Many trade associations maintain statistics compiled over the years from member companies. Most include ratios of the number of people to sales, or payroll cost to sales. These statistics are averages and are probably not specifically applicable to your company. But they serve as a good starting point to judge if employee cost-reductions should be seriously considered.

Possibilities for employee cost-reductions other than direct layoffs might include the following actions:

1. Do not replace employees when they quit; instead, assign their responsibilities to the remaining employees.
2. Encourage early retirement for older employees and then do not replace them.
3. Extend health care coverage or other benefits in exchange for an across-the-board reduction in wages.
4. Implement an employee cost-reduction suggestion system with noncash rewards.

Occupancy Cost-Reductions

Every company occupies some type of plant, warehouse, or office space from which to conduct the business. The space is either leased or owned by the company. In addition to rent payments or mortgage payments, property taxes may be paid separately. And every business pays for utility service—electricity, water, fuel. In addition, most businesses carry property and casualty insurance to protect against fire, wind, rain, vandalism, and theft.

At first glance it might appear that little can be done to reduce the cash expenditures for these costs. By applying creative ingenuity, however, you should be able to find cost-reductions in occupancy expenses as well as in purchases and payroll.

For example, electricity, water, and fuel costs can usually be reduced just by being more careful. Turn out the lights when a room isn't in use. Make sure water taps and toilets don't leak. Maintain thermostat settings within a wider band. Restrict air conditioning and heat to those areas occupied by people (as opposed to storage areas).

In a manufacturing operation, avoid repeated equipment start-ups and shutdowns, which require excess electric current. Shut down the company swimming pool (if you are fortunate enough to have one). Charge employees a nominal fee for using company exercise facilities, vehicles, and other conveniences requiring electricity, water, or fuel.

Property and casualty coverage is another area ripe for cost-reduction. Don't let your insurance salesman or broker determine changes in coverage. Insurance companies are notorious for increasing coverage, and hence premiums, at least annually, without first informing the policyholder. They justify this by claiming that inflation drives up the cost of replacing property, and therefore increased coverage is in your best interest.

Fine. Except that maybe it's more cost-effective to assume this risk yourself. Maybe even set up a self-insurance reserve. You can probably reduce insurance premiums either by cutting the coverage recommended by the insurance carrier or by going the self-insurance route.

Reducing building rental payments may not be feasible; however, it's certainly worth a try. In many markets, buildings go unoccupied for long periods, driving down rental prices. It's certainly possible that your landlord might be amenable to renegotiating lease terms in a depressed market, especially for an office or warehouse.

Regardless of how inflexible occupancy costs seem to be, an active cost-reduction program almost always nets cash savings. Once achieved, these cost savings frequently become permanent changes. As business conditions improve, don't go back to previous inefficient habits. Prove to yourself that your company can survive and prosper without the fat.

Clients have told me over and over again that they never realized how extravagant they had become until a stringent cost-reduction program was implemented. When they see how much extra cash can be generated, few return to their old ways.

Compliance Payments

Compliance payments to government agencies, banks, and other outside regulators are more or less immune to cost-reductions. Taxes of all varieties must be paid on time to escape penalties. Expenditures to meet safety or environmental requirements are difficult to avoid. Licenses, permits, and workers' compensation insurance must be retained to stay in business. It is difficult to dodge payments for imprinted bank checks, deposit lockboxes, and other charges mandated by banks.

On the other hand, at least you can try to keep these costs to a minimum. Challenging unemployment and workers' compensation claims can keep these premiums as low as possible. Negotiating with OSHA and EPA auditors to delay implementation of compliance programs might save cash in the short run. Changing banks, or threatening to change, could result in significantly reduced charges for bank services.

As with other operating costs, a cost-reduction program for compliance payments can effect real savings. They might not be as great as those realized with other expenses, but every dollar saved ends up as extra cash to work with.

Once a list of cost-reduction possibilities has been completed, the expected savings should be recorded on the cost-reduction control sheet. Be sure to include a complete description of what actions will be taken, and by whom, to achieve each cost-reduction.

The time frame within which the savings will be realized should also be established. If it's a one-shot cash savings, record the month in which it will occur. If it's a continuing savings, indicate over what period of time it will occur and in what monthly increments.

The criticality of formalizing a cost-reduction program by quantifying the expected results cannot be overemphasized. Totals from this time-sequenced program become integral parts of an overall cash management effort. Without a well-conceived, documented, and quantified cost-reduction program, your company will not maximize the amount of cash it has to work with.

All assumptions supporting how, when, and why each cost-reduction effort will be implemented should be documented. A looseleaf notebook works best because sheets can be added or deleted as the program progresses and assumptions change.

Cash management is dynamic. Strategies, tactics, plans, and programs keep changing over time as new information emerges and market conditions vary. Both the cash flow plan and its supporting cost-reduction program serve as the starting point. To become working tools, they must be adjusted as changing conditions become known.

Cost-Center Budgets

For more than fifty years people have praised the effectiveness of budgets on one hand and criticized them on the other. The debate has no end. Budgets work great for those who like to live their lives or operate their businesses according to a plan. Budgets don't work for those who prefer to fly by the seat of their pants.

Part 3 of this book covers three of the most essential plans: operating budgets, business plans, and strategic plans. Chapter 7 gets into financing plans. And Chapter 12 covers the offering prospectus needed for public stock issues. Why put such emphasis on planning? Because the essence of successful financial management is to predict what will happen to the business in the future and then to control the business to make sure these predictions come true. Without question, financial management also involves the accurate and timely recording of historical transactions and the regular preparation of balance sheets and income statements. But financial managers earn their keep by helping operating managers increase the company's profitability. And that can only be done by planning and control.

In one sense, budgets are plans. It would be easy to dismiss a budgetary system as too complex and therefore unworkable in a small business. As we will see, however, nothing could be further from the truth. (Be sure to check out Chapter 8 for a complete description of operating budgets.)

Cost-center, or operating, budgets are introduced at this point as a cash management tool that can be used to measure progress against the cost-reduction program. For this purpose, a brief explanation of their development and use will suffice.

Budgets come in a variety of forms. Although many are very complex, for purposes of measuring the cash savings resulting from a cost-reduction program, a very simple set of operating budgets does the trick. A separate budget should be prepared for each department (or cost center) in the organization that has responsibility for implementing a cost-reduction.

A larger organization might have one budget for each department manager and perhaps a subbudget for each supervisor reporting to a manager—although this tends to generate more paper than it is worth. In smaller organizations with fewer people and less formal lines of authority, three budgets should suffice:

1. One for the production activity (if any)
2. One for sales and marketing expenses
3. One for administrative, occupancy, and other supporting expenses

Figure 2.1 presents a simple budget format for administrative, occupancy, and other supporting expenses.

When preparing cost-center budgets for purposes of cash management, forget all you may have learned about bookkeeping. Only cash payments should be used. If invoices have been received but not yet paid, the amount doesn't get entered until they are paid. Every month the actual expenditures are entered in the "Month" column and added to the previous month's year-to-date balance.

Budgeted month and year-to-date figures should be taken from the cost-reduction control sheet. If a specific line item has no planned reduction scheduled for a given month, it should be left blank.

Figure 2.1
Operating Budget
Administrative and Occupancy Expenses
For the Month of January 19XX and Year to Date

| ___ Month ___ | | | | ___ Year to Date ___ | | |
Over (Under)	Budget	Actual	Expense	Actual	Budget	Over (Under)
			PAYROLL			
			Salaries/wages			
			Payroll taxes			
			Employee benefits			
			Other			
			Total payroll			
			OPERATING EXPENSES			
			Supplies			
			Telephone			
			Travel			
			Entertainment			
			Professional fees			
			Other taxes			
			Other expenses			
			Total expenses			
			OCCUPANCY EXPENSES			
			Rent—building			
			Rent—equipment			
			Property taxes			
			Insurance			
			Electricity			
			Water			
			Fuel—oil, gas, coal			
			Other expenses			
			Total occupancy expenses			
			Total Expenses			

As you begin working with these budgets, it won't take long to see clearly whether the cost-reduction program is working. If year-to-date actual amounts continue to run in excess of expected results, obviously the cost-reductions and the excess cash that you planned are not happening. Something is wrong. Corrective action must be taken.

Without top management's close and immediate attention to the progress of planned cost-reductions, the program won't work. Cash management is a continuous process, not a one-shot exercise. Measuring actual progress against expected results must be the responsibility of the person in charge of the business. Time and again attempts have been made to delegate this responsibility, and it never works. Here's an example of what can go wrong.

Before leaving for a six-week vacation in Europe, the CEO of Acelet Heating and Plumbing Distributors told the office manager to be sure everyone implemented the action plans agreed upon. When the CEO returned, expenditures were higher than when he had left. No cost-reductions had been implemented, and in fact, cash flow had deteriorated.

In another case, the owner of a flower and plant boutique developed a cost-reduction program to yield an additional $15,000 cash for the third quarter. When she took her annual buying trip to Mexico and the Caribbean, she put her bookkeeper in charge of implementing the plan. When she returned, the bookkeeper quickly pointed out that, although she had tried hard to follow directions, she couldn't figure out how to buy fewer cut flowers and still have enough on hand to sell.

Abdicating responsibility for the implementation of any part of a cash management program, especially one involving planned cost-reductions, just won't work. If you're not serious about doing it now, then postpone the actions until you have time to manage the program. Otherwise it's a waste of time and effort.

This chapter has reviewed the basics of setting up and managing the cost-reduction piece of the cash management puzzle. Once the total program has been laid out, the differences between the current expenses and projected monthly cash savings become the new planned cash expenditures. These monthly totals are then transferred, by expense category, to the cash control plan described in Chapter 1.

Chapter 3

Analyzing Financial Statements

It is indeed unfortunate that over the years the accounting profession has concocted rules and regulations so complex as to be virtually unintelligible, even to professional financial analysts. Small-business owners and non-financial managers have been left to fend for themselves while the accounting profession has devised ever more complicated measures of a company's performance and asset valuation. In large part such complexity is a direct result of defalcations and misrepresentations by financial people employed by publicly listed companies and Wall Street securities firms. In an effort to prevent misrepresentation of the earnings and future potential of listed companies, the Securities and Exchange Commission has foisted increasingly stringent requirements on auditors and the accounting profession. Nevertheless, small-business owners and managers have little choice but to follow the rules of the game.

This chapter should take the mystery out of financial statements, while at the same time giving a few pointers on how to analyze the performance of your company. When it comes to preparing pro forma projections for your business plan, financing plan, or strategic plan, the only way to create credible projections is to relate them to financial statements prepared according to the rules of the accounting profession. And to do that, you need to understand how financial statements are put together. But don't be put off. We will *not* get into the wearisome exercise of bookkeeping debits and credits.

Financial Statement Theory

The two basic financial statements applicable to every business, whether it is a corporation, a partnership, or a sole proprietorship, are the *balance sheet* and the *income statement*.

Balance sheets are snapshots in time; that is, they show the values in dollars of assets and liabilities as of a given date. These values will be different the day before this date and the day after. They are valid only for that specific point in time.

The income statement (at times referred to as the profit and loss statement), on the other hand, shows a series of transactions that have occurred over a period of time—specifically, the period between two balance sheet dates. This may be a month, a quarter, a year, or any other period, although typically, an income statement does not stretch beyond one year. All transactions that have occurred during this period show up in the income statement—sales, cost of materials and labor, operating expenses, taxes, and interest paid on loans.

A third report, called a *statement of cash flow* (or, in some cases, a *schedule of sources and applications of funds*) is not considered a financial statement in an accounting sense. Yet it probably tells more about a company's performance than either a balance sheet or an income statement. A properly prepared statement of cash flow shows the total cash receipts and cash disbursements of a company during the period of time covered by the income statement.

The relationships among the numbers in these three reports—balance sheets, income statements, and cash flow schedules—enable a reader to analyze the complete financial performance of any company. These relationships are usually expressed as ratios. Through comparative analyses of a wide range of listed companies, financial analysts have developed various standards based on these ratios for judging a company's liquidity, solvency, efficiency, growth prospects, and many other characteristics. Before we get into ratio analysis, however, it would probably be helpful to briefly summarize the makeup of balance sheets and income statements.

Balance Sheets

A balance sheet is sometimes referred to as a *statement of financial condition*, especially in banking circles. For our purposes, however, the term *balance sheet* will be used to describe the statement showing the financial position of a business as of a specific date. Although the formats of balance sheets in other countries differ from that used in the United States, our discussions throughout this book refer to generally accepted U.S. standards only.

The left-hand side of a balance sheet shows the dollar value of all the company's assets. Current assets are listed first, followed by fixed, or long-term, assets and then intangible assets. Current assets (which will be consumed within one year) are

- Cash
- Accounts receivable (also called *receivables*)
- Inventory
- Prepaid expenses (such as a lump-sum payment of insurance premiums that covers this year)

Fixed or long-term assets (which will be used over several years) include

- Land
- Buildings occupied by the business
- Machinery, equipment, furniture, and fixtures used in the business
- Vehicles used in the business
- Long-term investments

Buildings, machinery, etc., and vehicles are *depreciated;* that is, their cost is written off over their useful lives. The amount of depreciation to date is offset against the cost of these assets in a balance sheet. Land and long-term investments cannot be depreciated.

Intangible assets encompass a variety of expenditures for organization expenses, patents, trademarks, copyrights, and so on—that is, any expenditure that adds value to the company but cannot be touched or held (as with vehicles or machinery).

The sum of current assets, fixed assets, and intangible assets represents the total assets a company has at its disposal to generate income or cash.

The right side of the balance sheet shows the dollar value of all obligations or *liabilities* of the business. These liabilities represent the amounts owed to all creditors—banks and other financial institutions, investors in corporate bonds, suppliers, government agencies, and so on. The total amount owed to financial institutions and investors in corporate bonds is called *debt capital* or merely *debt*.

Current liabilities are amounts that must be paid within one year and include the following:

- Bank loans
- Portion of long-term debt due within one year
- Accounts payable (or payables), which are amounts due suppliers
- Accrued expenses (or accruals), which represent expenses incurred but not yet paid for, such as interest expense, wages, payroll taxes, utility bills, income and sales taxes, and so on

Long-term liabilities represent amounts due creditors after one year and include

- Long-term notes
- Mortgages
- Corporate bonds and debentures

The sum of current liabilities and long-term liabilities represents the total amounts owed by the company.

When total liabilities are subtracted from total assets, the remainder is called *net worth* (also referred to as *owners' equity* or *stockholders' equity*). Net worth can also be calculated by adding the accumulated earnings of a company since its inception (less dividends paid out to shareholders), preferred stock outstanding, and common stock outstanding. Net worth is also referred to as *equity capital*. Depending on the terms of the preferred stock agreement, outstanding preferred shares may be considered part of debt capital or part of equity capital for analytical purposes.

Income Statement

The income statement shows the dollar value of all transactions that the company has engaged in over a definable period, other than those involving the acquisition or disposal of assets and liabilities. An abbreviated income statement looks like the following:

Sales	xxxxxxxxxx
Less:	
Cost of sales	(xxxxxxxxxx)
Operating expenses	(xxxxxxxxxx)
Interest expense	(xxxxxxxxxx)
Income taxes	(xxxxxxxxxx)
Equals: Net profit	xxxxxxxx

Sales are all revenue-producing transactions and are recorded as they occur—not when customers pay for them. Cost of sales, operating expenses, interest expense, and income taxes are also recorded when they are incurred—not when the company pays its bills.

Cost of sales typically includes the dollar cost to the company of the materials, labor, and overhead that go into making a product, or the cost of purchasing products for resale. Operating expenses include all salaries, commissions, utilities, selling expenses, property taxes, and so on, that is, all expenses that are necessary to run the business.

Analytic Tools

Ratios that describe the various relationships among accounts in the balance sheet and income statement are the primary analytic tools of financial analysis. They are used to judge the financial health of a business, to project future earnings and cash flow, and to value a business. Investors and lenders use ratios to determine the viability of a business before lending to it or investing funds in it. Business buyers and sellers use ratios to determine a fair price for a company. And management uses ratios to prepare pro forma projections, to portray how a company is doing, and, in many instances, to arrive at amounts for incentive compensation.

Ratios yield relevant answers, however, only if they are compared with a standard. In and of themselves, ratios may be interesting from an academic perspective, but they don't provide new information to management, bankers, or investors unless comparisons can be made. Comparisons may be against other companies, stock market averages, industry guidelines, lender policies, alternative investment opportunities, widely accepted standards, or an investor's personal experience.

For example, the current ratio (current assets divided by current liabilities) is a measure of liquidity. One widely accepted standard holds that a current ratio of 2:1 indicates that a company has sufficient liquid assets to meet its current obligations. This standard has merit when applied to larger companies that must follow generally accepted accounting principles (GAAP). However, small businesses may have hybrid accounting systems that do not conform to GAAP. In that case, personal experience may indicate that a ratio of 3:1 or even 4:1 is necessary to ensure prudent cash management and adequate liquidity.

Ratios are a crucial ingredient for preparing meaningful pro forma forecasts. Receivables to sales, payables to inventory, accrued expenses to operating expenses, purchases to sales, number of employees to sales, and so on, are all useful ratios for the quantification of functional relationships that forms the basis of forecasting.

Although ratio analyses can certainly be helpful in analyzing a business, especially in the planning cycle, ratios are usually more valuable in avoiding inappropriate actions that may lead to losses than as a tool for increasing profits. Take lenders, for example. Banks frequently look to such ratios as days' sales in receivables, days' inventory in payables, the quick ratio, and the debt-to-equity ratio to provide early warnings of companies in trouble.

Despite their wide use by financial analysts, investors, and lenders to get a quick and easy fix on the health of a business, financial ratios can be very misleading, even when compared to valid standards. The reason is relatively simple. Ratios, like balance sheets, reflect the condition of a company at one point in time. Even income and expense ratios that span an entire accounting period reflect conditions during that period only.

Any number of events could cause a company's financial performance to go off track in a particular year. Floods, labor strikes, fires, significant R&D expenditures, the failure of a large customer, a leveraged buyout, and so on, could cause a deterioration in financial performance as reflected in ratios, even though the company as a whole has been and will continue to be a viable entity.

When using ratio analyses to measure a company's health, it's necessary to apply the same ratios to the same company over several years, dismissing extraordinary events that cause distortions. Such an analysis will yield trends—either favorable or unfavorable—and provide a reasonable beginning for determining future performance.

Many ratios are *quantitative* in nature; that is, the facts they portray lend themselves to numerical analysis. They can usually be derived directly from financial statements. Less common ratios are *qualitative*, requiring interpretation and further analysis to be useful. As this chapter explores several ratios that fall into each category, it's important to bear in mind the purpose for which you intend to use them.

Here are the major quantitative ratios that can be especially useful for measuring the health of a company:

1. **Profitability**
   - Gross profit/sales
   - Net income after tax/sales
   - Net income after taxes/total assets
   - Net income after taxes/equity
2. **Asset utilization**
   - Sales/average receivables (turnover)
   - Cost of sales/average inventory (turnover)
   - Sales/fixed assets
   - Sales/total assets
3. **Liquidity**
   - Current assets/current liabilities
   - Cash plus cash equivalents minus inventory/current liabilities
   - Current assets/short-term debt
   - Fixed assets/long-term debt
4. **Debt utilization**
   - Total debt/equity
   - Long-term debt/equity
   - Total debt/total assets
   - Income before interest and taxes/interest expense
   - Income before fixed charges and taxes/fixed charges

As many qualitative measures as possible should be translated to numeric quantities. To accomplish this, draw upon data from internally prepared reports as much as possible. The most common qualitative measures of a company's health involve three sets of measurements:

- Those that measure the effectiveness of cash management, as shown by receivables collections and payments to suppliers
- Those that measure production efficiency and labor utilization, derived from production reports and payroll records
- Those that measure the current status of customer relations, as reflected in allowances granted, complaints, and returns

The following sections make use of a fictitious company, MAPAX Manufacturing Corp. (MAPAX), to demonstrate the use of financial ratio analysis. This case study was used in my book *The Small-Business Valuation Book* to demonstrate the use of ratios and forecasting for business valuations. I strongly recommend that book for a fuller, more detailed analysis of financial statements and forecasting techniques. Chapter 4 also uses the MAPAX case study to illustrate the economic assumptions and cost/volume/asset functional relationships used to prepare pro forma financial statements and cash flow forecasts.

A manufacturing company has been chosen as a demonstration model because it tends to have a more complex cost structure than other types of businesses and therefore can be used to demonstrate a greater number of ratios. Identical ratio analysis techniques, however, apply to retail, distribution, and service companies, provided similar account classifications are used.

Although the MAPAX model is certainly larger than many small businesses, do not be put off by its size. This model was chosen because large numbers are easier to analyze and provide a much clearer picture than smaller ones. However, a company's size does not in any way change the usefulness of these ratios or the interpretation of their meaning. The identical principles and calculations apply to companies of any size—very small businesses as well as larger companies.

MAPAX Manufacturing Corp. manufactures two product lines, stoves and furnaces, both sold to the residential and commercial markets. The company also stocks a variety of resale accessories, some of which must be slightly modified to meet customer specifications. The stove and furnace business is a stable but growing industry. Although susceptible to both economic and industry cycles, its historical swings have been shallow, seldom more than 5 percent in either direction.

Figures 3.1 and 3.2 show MAPAX's balance sheets and income statements (respectively) for the years 1993, 1994, and 1995.

Figure 3.1
MAPAX Manufacturing Corp.
Balance Sheet
As of December 31, 1993, 1994, 1995
(in dollars)

	1993	1994	1995
Cash	622,852	121,691	1,000
Accounts receivable	1,364,344	1,392,188	1,406,250
Inventory	2,721,250	3,125,000	3,636,263
Prepaid expenses	5,000	5,000	5,000
Total current assets	4,713,446	4,643,879	5,048,513
Buildings	2,000,000	2,000,000	2,000,000
Machinery & equipment	6,000,000	7,100,000	8,000,000
Delivery trucks	50,000	50,000	50,000
Total fixed assets	8,050,000	9,150,000	10,050,000
Less: Accumulated depreciation	(2,200,000)	(2,668,000)	(3,200,000)
Net fixed assets	5,850,000	6,482,000	6,850,000
Other assets	100,000	100,000	100,000
Total Assets	10,663,446	11,225,879	11,998,513
Bank note payable	500,000	250,000	200,000
Accounts payable	580,440	666,559	775,614
Accrued expenses	200,000	200,000	200,000
Other current liabilities	50,000	50,000	50,000
Total current liabilities	1,330,440	1,166,559	1,225,614
Long-term debt	4,400,000	4,200,000	4,000,000
Mortgage loan	1,150,000	1,075,000	1,000,000
Total Liabilities	6,880,440	6,441,559	6,225,614
Common stock	100,000	100,000	100,000
Retained earnings—beginning	2,701,419	3,683,006	4,684,320
Profit/(loss)	981,587	1,001,313	988,579
Retained earnings—ending	3,683,006	4,684,320	5,672,899
Total Net Worth	3,783,006	4,784,320	5,772,899
Total Liabilities and Net Worth	10,663,446	11,225,879	11,998,513

Figure 3-2
MAPAX Manufacturing Corp.
Statement of Income
For the Years Ended December 31, 1993, 1994, 1995
(in dollars)

	1993	1994	1995
Sales	10,914,750	11,137,500	11,250,000
Cost of sales			
Material	5,588,352	5,702,400	5,760,000
Labor	849,430	866,765	875,520
Overhead	703,179	724,927	747,347
Total cost of sales	7,140,960	7,294,091	7,382,867
Gross profit	3,773,790	3,843,409	3,867,133
Percent of sales	34.6%	34.5%	34.4%
Operating expenses			
Selling expenses	584,788	596,722	608,900
Administrative expenses	520,297	530,915	541,750
Other expenses	20,000	20,000	20,000
Depreciation	468,000	532,000	585,000
Total operating expences	1,593,084	1,679,637	1,755,650
Net income before			
interest and taxes	2,180,705	2,163,772	2,111,483
Percent of sales	20.0%	19.4%	18.8%
Interest	597,500	548,750	517,000
Net income before taxes	1,583,205	1,615,022	1,594,483
Taxes	601,618	613,708	605,904
Net income	981,587	1,001,313	988,579
Percent of sales	9.0%	9.0%	8.8%

Profitability Ratios

Profitability ratios indicate a company's ability to earn a satisfactory return on sales, total assets, and invested capital. Of course, you must define "satisfactory" to meet your objectives. Every company is different, and it would be wrong to assume that a company that earns a 10 percent return on sales is outperforming one that earns a 5 percent return, or that a company with an 80 percent gross profit margin is run more efficiently than one turning a 30 percent gross profit. Comparison with industry standards or with companies of similar size in similar businesses is the only reasonable way to interpret the values derived from profitability ratios.

Two profitability ratios commonly used to measure the trend of a company's earnings potential are

- Gross profit margin as a percent of sales
- Net income as a percent of sales

These ratios can normally be read directly from financial statements without additional analysis. Obviously, increasing ratios indicate improvements in operating expense control, pricing, product mix, or competitive advantage—all positive signs. And, of course, the reverse condition indicates deteriorating earning power. The following shows that MAPAX scores high in terms of absolute ratios—34 percent and 9 percent, respectively, are very respectable for manufacturing companies in stable, mature industries. However, the trend is not so good and indicates that something negative may be happening to MAPAX's cost structure or market position:

	1993	1994	1995
Gross profit to sales	34.6%	34.5%	34.4%
Net income to sales	9.0%	9.0%	8.8%

Three other profitability ratios measure the return (i.e., net income) a company earns on invested capital:

- Return on owner's equity
- Return on investment
- Return on total assets

In the MAPAX example, these ratios were

	1993	1994	1995
Return on owners' equity	25.9%	20.9%	17.1%
Return on investment (adjusted for taxes on interest)	15.3%	13.9%	12.6%
Return on investment (unadjusted for taxes on interest)	17.9%	16.1%	14.5%
Return on total assets (adjusted for taxes on interest)	13.0%	12.3%	11.3%
Return on total assets (unadjusted for taxes on interest)	15.2%	14.1%	13.0%

Financial analysts will probably argue for the next two hundred years about which of these ratios yields the most accurate picture of investment return. The arguments run as follows:

- For *return on owners' equity*: The only true measure of a company is how much it returns to its owners.
- For *return on investment*: The true measure of a company is how much it returns to all investors, both debt holders and equity investors.
- For *return on assets*: The true measure of a company is the efficiency of its management, which can be measured only by the returns generated on assets employed.

Each argument has merit, and which ratio is appropriate in a given situation is related to the capital structure of a company and the purpose of the analysis.

Although the return on owners' equity ratio is straightforward, the return on investment ratios and return on assets ratios warrant an explanation. The theory behind return on investment is that long-term debt represents as valid an investment as common shares. Therefore, by definition, the term *investment* as used in these ratios represents the sum of the average outstanding balances of long-term debt and the average stockholder investment.

Furthermore, since debt is included in the ratio's denominator, interest expense must be added back to net income to arrive at the numerator. Arguments persist about the merits of adding back interest expense adjusted for the tax effect or total interest. The answer can only be a matter of personal choice. The final point to clarify is that practically speaking, only interest on long-term debt should be used. Theoretically, short-term interest should be included; however, since it is virtually impossible to obtain average interest expense for short-term debt, most calculations ignore the minor distortion caused by excluding it.

The return on assets ratio, sometimes referred to as the *asset utilization ratio* or *assets employed ratio*, uses average total assets as a denominator, on the theory that assets must be employed during the entire period to generate the income for the period. In addition, the same argument over using interest that has or has not been adjusted for the tax effect for the numerator applies here as in the return on investment calculation.

Asset Utilization Ratios

Asset utilization ratios measure the speed at which a company turns assets into sales, and hence cash. As with other financial ratios, to be meaningful, the trends of asset utilization ratios over several periods should be used. The speed with which inventory turns this year may be a relevant measure for evaluating purchasing and production personnel, but it has little meaning in the broader scope of analyzing the health of a business. Conversely, a trend might show that inventory turns are slowing, which could indicate an increase in obsolete goods, slowing sales, or errors in recording transactions.

Four major asset utilization ratios seem to receive the most use:

- Receivables turnover
- Inventory turnover
- Fixed asset turnover
- Total assets turnover

Receivables Turnover

Receivables turnover measures the number of times in a year that receivable balances are collected. Because it deals with the total receivables balance, distortions caused by individual customer accounts are ignored, except to the extent that they materially influence the total. The ratio may also be expressed as *days' sales in receivables*, meaning the number of days, on average, that it takes to collect receivables. The formula for receivables turnover is

$$\text{Turnover} = \frac{\text{annual sales}}{\text{average receivables}}$$

Since this ratio measures credit sales only, companies whose cash sales represent a high percentage of total sales will find it meaningless. A small percentage of cash sales won't make any difference in the average, however, and can be ignored. To get a true reflection of annual collection activity, *average* receivables should be used as the denominator. If possible, use an average of the monthly balances. When this isn't feasible, use the average of the balances at the beginning and end of the period.

The MAPAX receivables turnover ratios for the three years are

	1993	1994	1995
Receivables turnover	7.8 times	8.1 times	8.0 times
Receivables days' sales	45.6 days	45.6 days	45.6 days

In this case, the differences between years are so small as to be meaningless. Any one or all of the following conclusions may be drawn from these ratios:

- MAPAX management does a terrific job of monitoring collections.
- The stability of the industry permits very little creative pricing.
- A significant portion of sales are made with advance payments or down payments and do not show up in receivables balances.

Inventory Turnover

Inventory turnover is normally calculated by dividing the annual cost of sales by the average inventory at the beginning and end of the period. Virtually the same conclusions drawn from receivables turnover can be drawn from this ratio. That is, the faster the turns, the more efficient the company. Also, as with receivables, inventory turnover can be expressed as the number of times inventory turns during the year or the number of days' sales that reside in inventory at the end of the year.

MAPAX inventory ratios came out as follows:

	1993	1994	1995
Inventory turnover	2.8 times	2.5 times	2.2 times
Inventory days' sales	156.3 days	175.9 days	200.0 days

The MAPAX inventory picture is quite different from the picture shown by the receivables ratios. Inventory turns are definitely slipping, and days' sales are correspondingly increasing. This could mean (1) that the purchasing department is out of control; (2) that production schedules are slipping; or (3) that for some unexplained reason, inventory obsolescence is increasing. Clearly, any one or a combination of these reasons could be a serious problem, and management should determine the real causes as soon as possible.

Asset Turnover

Asset turnover ratios measure the efficiency with which a company uses its assets to generate sales; the higher the turnover, the more efficient the company. Although both fixed assets and total assets are used in separate ratios, fixed asset turnover isn't relevant for companies without a significant hard-asset base. MAPAX, on the other hand, has a fairly large hard-asset base, and therefore both ratios should be calculated:

	1993	1994	1995
Fixed asset turnover	1.9 times	1.7 times	1.6 times
Total asset turnover	1.0 times	1.0 times	1.0 times

The slight deterioration in the fixed asset turnover is probably caused by increased accumulated depreciation and therefore does not indicate a problem. Also, a constant total asset turnover indicates that very little change occurs year to year in assets other than those needed to directly support sales, such as receivables and inventory.

Liquidity Ratios

Liquidity ratios demonstrate a company's ability to meet its current obligations, that is, the payment of short-term notes, accounts payable, and accrued expenses. These ratios help to answer a question frequently asked by financial analysts and more astute bankers: "Does a company have assets in excess of those required to meet operating needs, or do its assets fail to meet its needs?"

The two most common liquidity ratios are the *current ratio* and the *quick ratio* (or acid-test ratio), expressed as follows:

$$\text{Current ratio} = \frac{\text{current assets}}{\text{current liabilities}}$$

$$\text{Quick ratio} = \frac{\text{cash and cash equivalents}}{\text{current liabilities}}$$

Traditionally, bankers have regarded a current ratio of 2:1 as satisfactory and anything less than that as suspect. History has shown, however, that many companies whose business requires a longer receivables turnover (as in a dating program) or a longer inventory turnover (as in advance purchases of scarce materials) produce much lower current ratios but are just as safe for creditors.

The quick ratio is used to indicate a company's ability to quickly convert assets to cash to pay off current obligations in an emergency. A quick ratio of 1:1 is normally regarded as satisfactory. Some companies carry marketable securities, bank certificates of deposit, or other highly liquid assets, which are regarded as cash equivalents. In the MAPAX example, no marketable securities are carried, but receivables tend to be relatively short term. Therefore, the assets used to calculate the quick ratio should be total current assets minus inventory. Over the three-year period, MAPAX's liquidity ratios were

	1993	1994	1995
Current ratio	3.5	4.0	4.1
Quick ratio	1.5	1.3	1.2

It should be noted that both the current ratio and the quick ratio measure liquidity at a point in time and do not necessarily reflect a company's true need to finance short-term working capital requirements with short-term credit. During the course of a year, short-term borrowings could escalate significantly to purchase inventory that may be liquidated before the year ends—as is usually the case in the toy industry, for example.

Debt Utilization Ratios

Debt utilization ratios measure the risk inherent in leverage financing. Too much debt impairs a company's liquidity because cash that could otherwise be put to productive uses is diverted to repay loans. Nonproductive interest expense damages a company's profitability. And during a business-cycle downturn, companies with heavy debt service obligations tend to be the ones that don't make it through the trough.

Three debt utilization ratios offer insight into the amount of leverage employed by a company:

Long-term debt to equity, expressed as $\dfrac{\text{long-term debt}}{\text{net worth}}$

Total debt to equity, expressed as $\dfrac{\text{total debt}}{\text{net worth}}$

Total debt to total assets, expressed as $\dfrac{\text{total debt}}{\text{total assets}}$

Companies with stable sales and earnings, such as utilities or railroads, can afford to employ more debt than those in cyclical industries, such as automobiles, consumer electronics, and residential construction. The reason is obvious: When cyclical industries turn down, a company's cash flow shrinks and may not be sufficient to cover fixed interest and principal payments, let alone pay dividends to equity investors. Referring to MAPAX's financial statements, these ratios yield the following results:

	1993	1994	1995
Long-term debt to equity	1.5:1	1.1:1	0.9:1
Total debt to equity	1.6:1	1.2:1	0.9:1
Total debt to total assets	0.6:1	0.5:1	0.4:1

Generally, healthy manufacturing companies try to keep the long-term-debt-to-equity ratio at 1:1 or less. Although MAPAX overshot the mark in 1993, the three-year downward trend to 0.9:1 in 1995 is a very healthy sign.

If your company uses high levels of short-term borrowings, you may find that the total debt-to-equity ratio is a better measure of leverage. However, for MAPAX, the amount of short-term borrowing is minor compared with long-term debt, making the ratios and the trends very similar. On the other hand, if the company's short-term debt were high relative to long-term obligations, and the total-debt-to-equity ratio trended upward over three years, it would indicate that cash shortages were occurring even though the income statement showed earnings.

The total-debt-to-total-assets ratio indicates how efficiently a company has used its debt. Although each company has different capital needs, a 1:2 ratio would indicate that a company has in fact used its capital to create a reasonable level of assets for future cash generation. Once again, the MAPAX ratio looks high in 1993, but is trending down to a reasonable level.

The ability of a company to cover its interest payments with earned income is measured by a ratio defined as income before interest and taxes to interest. In the case of MAPAX, this ratio yielded coverage of 3.7 times in 1993, 3.9 times in 1994, and 4.1 times in 1995. The greater the number of times income covers interest payments, the more protection afforded creditors. Ratios of three to four times show that MAPAX is probably not overleveraged and can easily support its debt service.

Qualitative Analytic Measures

In addition to ratio analyses that one derives directly from a company's financial statements, a series of qualitative ratios and data that use internal reports and records to measure management proficiency may be meaningful, especially for your top managers. The ability of department managers to control events, issue timely and accurate reports, and maintain solid relationships with customers and suppliers are a few examples of the type of information that can be derived from these reports. Examples of internal reports that reveal such information include

1. Measures of cash management effectiveness
    - Accounts receivable aging (a listing of customer accounts outstanding by due date, usually broken out by thirty-day increments)
    - Accounts payable aging (a listing of supplier accounts outstanding by due date, also detailed by thirty-day increments)
    - Payables turnover (annual sales divided by average accounts payable)
    - Ratio of receivables to payables (average receivables divided by average accounts payable)
2. Measures of production efficiency and the utilization of labor
    - Sales per employee (annual sales divided by average number of employees)
    - Employee turnover
    - Ratio of employee days absent to total days available for work
    - Ratio of labor hours lost because of accidents to total labor hours available for work

- Ratio of rework labor hours to total labor hours
- Ratio of scrap cost to total material purchases
- Sales per square foot of space (annual sales divided by total square feet of production and administrative space)
- Delivery promises kept

3. Measures of selling and customer service effectiveness
   - Unusual allowances
   - Ratio of customer complaints to sales
   - Customer returns compared to unit shipments

Measures of Cash Management Effectiveness

Average accounts receivable and accounts payable balances taken from financial statements provide an overall indication of how effectively a company manages its cash. But there could be wide variations between months or in the collection practices for different classes of customers. There could also be variations in payment schedules to different classes of suppliers.

Aged listings of receivables and payables—preferably quarterly—give an excellent picture of how consistent a company is in collecting accounts and paying suppliers. A slippage in the aging of either receivables or payables gives a pretty good indication that something is wrong with cash management procedures.

Measures of Production Efficiency and the Utilization of Labor

These measures are used primarily in manufacturing companies to get a handle on the effectiveness of controls on the production process and related personnel. Most industry trade associations maintain average statistics on sales per employee, personnel turnover, time lost because of accidents, and rework and scrap ratios. Comparing a company's performance over a three-year period with industry norms gives a good indication of whether managers can control the production process, or whether labor efficiency and productivity, as well as material usage, are out of control.

Delivery-promises-kept statistics can yield an especially provocative picture of customer satisfaction. If the lateness of deliveries increases, chances are good that customers have become dissatisfied, substantially increasing investment risk.

Measures of Selling and Customer Service Effectiveness

In addition to promises-kept statistics (which apply to most businesses, not just manufacturing companies), unusual customer allowances, such as price discounts, warranty costs, product returns, and so on, usually mean that either product quality has slipped or competitive pressures are becoming more intense. Not infrequently, extraordinary allowances indicate that the company cannot compete and is trying to buy the market. Increases in customer complaints and returned goods may also indicate something amiss in either the selling process or customer service.

That takes care of the ratios that are most relevant to most companies. A clear understanding of your company's ratios is a prerequisite to preparing pro forma forecasts—the topic of Chapter 4.

Chapter 4

Forecasting Cash Flow

The essence of any plan—whether it covers one year, five years, or longer—is the conversion of economic and business assumptions into quantifiable performance results. And a pro forma projection of a company's financial statements has become the accepted method for quantifying business transactions—at least in developed economies like the United States, Canada, Europe, and so on.

Although quantifying performance through the use of financial statements—balance sheets and income statements—is as far as many larger companies have to go in their planning cycle, this is not the case in small businesses. While financial statements satisfy the SEC, the IRS, and many other interested third parties, the only projection that can be used on a day-to-day basis by small businesses is the cash flow forecast. Without translating business decisions into cash, most small-business owners and managers would be unable to control their operation or make plans for future changes. As we saw in Chapter 1, cash is definitely king and cash management the basic tool for running a business. The cash flow forecast is the working tool of cash management. Without it, it's impossible to do your job.

With that as a fundamental principle, this chapter lays out the steps involved in constructing a detailed cash flow forecast, fully integrated with a company's historical and pro forma financial statements. Such integration is essential to give forecasts the weight of authority. Stand-alone projections whose cash receipts and expenditures do not flow directly from pro forma financial statements are nothing more than a guess.

The diversity of industries, ownership configurations, company forms, capital structures, and market conditions makes any general set of forecasting rules and formats subject to modification. However, experience has shown that the format and procedures described in this chapter can be used effectively as the foundation for forecasting pro forma financial statements and cash flow by virtually any size company in any industry. It should be noted that many of the analytic techniques, forecasting procedures, and descriptive elements in this chapter are proprietary; that is, I have personally developed them over a number of years. If you are interested in seeing the expansion of this forecasting method to a wide range of applications, pick up a copy of my book *Small-Business Valuation Book*, which is part of the Adams Business Advisor series. I strongly suggest that you add that book to your library as a complement to this one. If you would like me to assist you in applying this forecasting method to your company, I can be reached c/o ZYX-VU, LTD, P.O. Box 347, Southeastern, PA 19399.

The ten-step forecasting process can be summarized as follows:

1. Develop and evaluate a series of economic and business assumptions.
2. Prepare a sales forecast based on these assumptions.
3. Establish cost/production/sales functional relationships from historical accounting records.
4. Forecast personnel requirements.
5. Set up historical balance sheet ratios for payables, receivables, and accrued expenses.
6. Project fixed asset needs.
7. Develop an R&D budget and new product introduction forecast (if relevant).
8. Prepare pro forma balance sheets and statements of income.
9. Project new financing requirements.
10. Prepare a cash flow forecast.

The following sections make use of the fictitious company MAPAX Manufacturing Corp. (introduced in *Small-Business Valuation Book*) to demonstrate the types of economic assumptions and forecast techniques. These are applicable to nearly any company, regardless of industry or size. A manufacturing company is used as a case study because typically, manufacturing companies have the most complex cost structures and therefore are ideal for demonstrating the complete line of analytic techniques. As the forecasting process unfolds, however, it will become clear that the same procedures can be used by companies in distribution, retail, or service industries.

To briefly summarize the background of MAPAX, the company manufactures two product lines, stoves and furnaces, both sold to the residential and commercial markets. It also stocks a variety of resale accessories, some of which must be slightly modified to meet customer specifications. The stove and furnace business is a stable but growing industry. Although susceptible to both economic and industry cycles, sales volume seldom fluctuates more than 5 percent in either direction. New product development is not expected to be a major factor in the industry or at MAPAX during the forecast period.

Economic and Business Assumptions

Before developing economic and business assumptions, it's necessary to decide what period the forecast will cover. There are no hard-and-fast rules for choosing a forecast period. A period that is right for one company may be too long or too short for another. Macroeconomic cycles, market trends, product/customer configuration, and several other factors determine the most meaningful forecast period for any particular business. Industry cycles are especially important, since annual sales tend to dip as the cycle trends downward and accelerate as it heads up.

The typical forecast period for internal cash management covers one year; that for bank financing plans and business plans, at least one year (and often two or three years); strategic plans take a longer look into the future—perhaps five or six years. Most plans, whether used for internal purposes or for raising capital, should cover a period that includes at least one complete business cycle—peak to peak or valley to valley. Long-term strategic plans should include two or more cycles, assuming that the cycle is three years or less. Some widely known industry cycles are seven years for the aerospace industry, three to four years for residential construction, and ten years for nonresidential construction. Statistical compilations that track business cycles for your industry should be available from your trade association or the U.S. Department of Commerce.

Macroeconomic cycles also come into play. In the United States it's relatively easy to track cycles in gross national product, inventory and sales trends, money supply, and interest rates as indicators of economic slowdowns or growth periods. In the past, stock market averages also provided a key to national economic swings. Since the late 1980s, however, various changes in trading practices and the globalization of capital markets have practically invalidated this measure. On the other hand, average commodity prices have been an excellent leading indicator.

As a broad measure of the direction in which the economy is heading, it's hard to beat the three economic indexes published by the federal government—leading indicators, coincident indicators, and lagging indicators (see Chapter 10 for a definition of each index). Properly tempered with industry cycle indicators, these indexes can be helpful in assessing current and future national economic trends, particularly cyclical expansions and recessions.

The concept behind economic indexes is that recurring business cycles are caused by changes in the outlook for future profits (which is assumed to be the prime mover of the economy). Such an outlook is reflected in the index of leading indicators and in the ratio of the coincident index to the lagging index (which is itself a leading indicator).

In some industries, macroeconomic cycles do not have much influence on a given company's sales. In others, such as most consumer goods industries and both residential and commercial construction, they do. For the same reasons that pertain to industry cycles, the forecast period you choose should take into consideration macroeconomic cycles.

Unfortunately, trends in industries with long cycles are especially difficult to forecast. In fact, the further out one goes, the less reliable a forecast becomes. Typically, five years is about the maximum window for most companies. Even that can be too long for seasonal businesses or those subjected to erratic market forces, such as the toy industry.

Clearly, both the direction and the position of economic and business cycles are crucial to setting the forecast period. When a company can look forward to a lengthy upward trend in both its industry cycle and the much broader national cycle, it will inevitably forecast stronger earnings and cash flows than if one or both cycles are trending downward. When the economic cycle trends in one direction and the business cycle in another, either for the entire forecast period or crossing over midway through it, forecasting performance is not as straightforward. Further analysis will then be required to determine specific indicators and conditions that may affect a company's earning power.

In our case study of MAPAX, the following assumptions have been made:

1. The national economy as expressed by GNP will experience very slow growth during the balance of this decade. The year 2003 will be the beginning of the next boom period. European and Japanese GNP rates will lag behind the slow U.S. recovery by two years. The stock market will anticipate the next cycle and, in turn, draw new foreign capital to U.S. markets. The economic recovery will be spurred by (1) the success of the new Independence Party in winning the presidency and control of Congress in 1999, and (2) the new government's determination to immediately implement strong deficit-cutting policies. In anticipation of the next boom cycle, consumer confidence will begin building in 2001.

2. This slow-growth period of the 1990s will hold inflation in the range of 2 to 5 percent, with rates at the higher end beginning in 2001.

3. With inflation held in check, interest rates will remain stable. The prime rate will hover in the 6 to 7.5 percent range.

4. New commercial construction will hold relatively steady during the decade, spurting in 1999.

5. The commercial furnace industry, which experiences a five- to seven-year business cycle, is at its trough from 1996 through 1998, and will begin a slow upward climb in 1999.

6. The residential and commercial stove industry experiences a three-year cycle. It is already on the upward curve and will reach its peak in 1998–1999, after which it will decline for three years.

7. Unemployment in the stove and furnace industry will remain at about 7 percent throughout the decade, creating an adequate supply of technically qualified personnel.

8. Although foreign competition will accelerate in steel and cast iron material and components, the market will not be flooded.

With these assumptions in place, the first steps can be taken to assemble a forecast. Two extremely critical rules must be highlighted before we proceed, however. First, accurate cash flow forecasts depend upon realistic pro forma balance sheet and income statement forecasts.

To make a cash flow projection meaningful, and acceptable to third parties, it must interact 100 percent with related financial statements. If it becomes necessary to adjust financial statements that were initially prepared on a cash basis, a clear audit trail must be left to ensure that third parties can track the adjustments through the various steps to accrual accounts.

Second, pro forma financial statements must be based on functional cost/sales/asset relationships. Since these relationships are different for each company, no standard formulas can be created. However, the *principles* of interacting costs at different sales volumes are uniform. To establish and then work with these functional relationships, a computer-based spreadsheet program is strongly recommended. To arrive at reasonable results, it will probably be necessary to use *what-if* alternatives, plugging various data into the functional relationships. This is very time-consuming if done manually. All functional relationships used for the MAPAX forecast were generated with Lotus 1-2-3, and the mathematical equations used to express functional relationships were developed by the author.

Sales Forecast

The sales forecast is the starting point in any financial forecast. More often than not, you'll be tempted to take a shortcut, extrapolating future sales by applying an incremental growth rate to current sales. This approach can be very misleading, however, and you will obtain much better results by building sales trends over the forecast period based on the economic and business assumptions most applicable for your company.

In the case of MAPAX, stoves and furnaces experience conflicting business cycles. To recognize this situation and to reflect a projected improvement in the national economy toward the end of the decade, the decision was made to look at an eight-year period from 1996 through 2003, although the forecast period would be five years (through 2001).

The first step involved a forecast of unit sales for each of the three product lines: stoves, furnaces, and accessories. The sales trends shown in Figure 4.1 follow the assumptions about industry growth and economic cycles for stoves and furnaces. Accessories relate primarily to furnaces and echo that growth trend.

Since all product lines are in stable, mature markets, major new competitors are not likely to enter or introduce radically new products that would disrupt MAPAX's market shares. Therefore, the unit forecast can reasonably be assumed to reflect the general industry and national cycles. Accordingly, the growth rates used in Figure 4.1 were

Stoves
- 5 percent for 1996, 1997, and 1998, and level over the peak of 1998–1996
- 3 percent decrease for 2000, 2001, and 2002

Furnaces
- 1 percent growth through 1998
- 3 percent growth 1996 and beyond, reflecting the acceleration of the upward trend of a seven-year cycle

For accessories, the same growth rates as for furnaces were used.

Figure 4.1

MAPAX Mfg. Corp.   Sales by Product Line*

	Actual			Forecast			
	1995	1996	1997	1998	1999	2000	2001
Units							
Stoves	5,000	5,250	5,513	5,788	5,788	5,614	5,446
Furnaces	1,000	1,010	1,020	1,030	1,061	1,093	1,126
Accessories	7,000	7,350	7,718	8,103	8,103	8,103	8,103
Unit price							
Stoves	$920	$929	$938	$948	$957	$967	$1,015
Furnaces	$3,500	$3,535	$3,570	$3,606	$3,642	$3,679	$3,862
Accessories	$450	$455	$459	$464	$468	$473	$497
Dollars							
Stoves	$4,600,000	$4,878,300	$5,173,437	$5,486,430	$5,541,294	$5,428,806	$5,529,239
Furnaces	3,500,000	3,570,350	3,642,114	3,715,321	3,865,048	4,020,809	4,348,505
Accessories	3,150,000	3,340,575	3,542,680	3,757,012	3,794,582	3,832,528	4,024,154
Total sales	11,250,000	11,789,225	12,358,231	12,958,763	13,200,924	13,282,143	13,901,899

*Arithmetic difference due to rounding.

The next step involved projecting the changes in unit pricing. Beginning with the current product line price structure, it was reasoned that, given the absence of new competition and the unlikelihood of new products entering the market, current pricing should hold through the entire cycle. Accordingly, unit price increases for all three product lines were conservatively estimated on the lower end of the inflation spectrum. Annual price increases of 1 percent were included through 2000, and then prices were increased 5 percent for 2001, reflecting the expected strong economic recovery.

The final step was to multiply unit sales by unit prices for each year and lay out the totals in a product line sales forecast. Structuring the forecast with this much detail makes experimenting with what-if alternatives very easy: just substitute different product line growth rates and unit prices until the end result makes sound business sense. As will be seen in subsequent forecast segments, if functional relationships are clearly defined and forecast formulas set up to match these relationships, any number of what-if scenarios can be prepared with virtually no effort and practically instantaneously.

Purchased Materials Forecast

Once a reasonable sales forecast has been completed, the next step is to develop a purchased materials forecast. Retail companies may find it helpful to build in monthly or seasonal time lags between sales and purchases. When forecasting in annual increments, however, short-term lag times become irrelevant. For this reason, most retailers should forecast purchases based on a historical relationship to sales and at their standard markup.

Manufacturing companies don't have that luxury. They usually find it necessary to stock some level of raw materials or components inventory to meet production schedules, to take advantage of volume discounts, or to ensure supplies of scarce parts or materials. Most manufacturing companies must also deal with production cycles—the days, weeks, or months it takes to manufacture the product from beginning to end. Such is the case with MAPAX, which experiences a long lead time to get the materials into the plant and six- to nine-month production cycles.

To deal with these time lags, the MAPAX purchasing forecast in Figure 4.2 assumes that materials will be purchased in one year and converted to sales the following year—in other words, a one-year lag time. (The same relationships would exist on a monthly, quarterly, or other time frame basis.) Furthermore, using historical data, it was determined that, on average, purchased materials for stoves and furnaces accounted for 40 percent of the sales dollar and purchased accessories 80 percent.

Using these assumptions, annual material purchases for stoves and furnaces were forecasted one year in advance, at 40 percent of the following year's sales. Accessories were also forecasted one year in advance, but at 80 percent of the following year's sales. For instance, purchases of stove material in 1996 totaled approximately $2.1 million, which is about 40 percent of 1997 stove sales of $5.2 million.

Figure 4.2
MAPAX Mfg. Corp.
Purchased Materials
(in dollars)

	Actual	Forecast					
	1995	1996	1997	1998	1999	2000	2001
Stoves	2,009,860	2,131,456	2,260,409	2,260,409	2,106,377	2,145,345	2,185,034
Furnaces	1,442,421	1,471,414	1,500,989	1,592,400	1,656,573	1,791,584	1,937,598
Subtotal	3,452,281	3,602,870	3,761,399	3,852,809	3,762,950	3,936,929	4,122,632
Accessories	2,752,634	2,919,168	3,095,778	3,095,778	2,974,042	3,122,744	3,278,881
Total purchases	6,204,915	6,522,038	6,857,177	6,948,587	6,736,992	7,059,673	7,401,513

It was further assumed that, given weak competition among suppliers, purchase prices would not change radically and that foreign competition, though increasing, would not make a major dent in pricing until after the turn of the century. Therefore, the same inflationary pricing assigned to finished product selling prices was used for material purchases.

Since most of the materials and components will be put into production as soon as possible after arrival, the purchased materials forecast leads directly to a forecast of direct labor.

Direct Labor Forecast

Although nonmanufacturing companies do not have production direct labor, distribution and retail companies may employ storekeepers, delivery-truck drivers, maintenance personnel, or custodians. To the extent that (1) these employees are paid by the hour, (2) their work efforts are directly tied to the level of activity, and (3) they can be hired and fired as volume shifts, the same relationships used in manufacturing forecasts will probably hold.

As can be seen in the direct labor forecast in Figure 4.3, four elements are necessary to begin the calculations:

- Current number of direct labor employees.
- Approximate number of hours each employee works during a year (typically 1,944 hours after deducting holidays, vacations, and weekends).
- Average hourly wage rate. (If there are wide variations in wage rates between classes of employees, it might be better to segregate both the number of employees and wage rates by class.)
- Average annual gross payroll.

Figure 4.3
MAPAX Mfg. Corp.
Direct Labor

	Actual	Forecast					
	1995	1996	1997	1998	1999	2000	2001
Number of employees	51	52	53	53	53	53	53
Hours worked	1,944	1,944	1,944	1,944	1,944	1,944	1,944
Wage rate	$9,500	$9,785	$10,079	$10.381	$10,692	$11,013	$11,344
Payroll	$941,868	$989,146	$1,038,413	$1,069,566	$1,101,653	$1,134,702	$1,168,743
Percent of purchases	15.2%	15.2%	15.1%	15.4%	16.4%	16.1%	15.8%

Various approaches can then be used to forecast the out years. You can relate the number of direct labor employees to sales dollars; you can relate the number of hourly employees to total employees; or, as in the case of MAPAX, you can relate total payroll dollars to purchases and work backwards.

The first step for MAPAX was to determine a constant ratio of payroll to purchases. The second step was to forecast annual wage rate increases of 3 percent, consistent with inflation projections. The third step was merely to divide the payroll dollars by the product of average wage rate times hours worked, yielding the number of employees required.

Since this resulted in minor fluctuations that wouldn't be practical in a sustained workforce, it was assumed that once an appropriate employment level was reached—53 people—that level would be maintained until 2003, with overtime hours filling any gaps to meet increased production schedules.

Cost/Volume/Price/Asset Functional Relationships

As can be seen from the purchased materials and direct labor forecasts, functional relationships are the keys to forecasting. The amount and type of material purchased is a direct function of the sales forecast. The timing of those purchases is a direct function of the purchasing lead time and the manufacturing lead time. Material price increases are a function of changes in the prices of finished products.

Similar functional relationships hold for direct labor. The number of direct labor employees is a function of the work to be performed, which is a function of materials in inventory, which is a function of the sales forecast.

Further into the forecast, we'll see that nearly all costs and asset balances relate functionally to other costs, sales, or assets. (It is this relationship analysis that makes this forecasting technique unique.) For example, the number of shop supervisors is a function of the number of direct labor employees—more a *step* relationship than a direct one-to-one correlation. Depreciation is a function of fixed asset cost and useful life. Accounts payable relates to inventory. Accounts receivable is a direct function of sales dollars. Financing requirements relate to incremental sales volume, changes in fixed asset capacity, and profit margins (which relate to pricing decisions).

The final forecast schedule, the statement of cash flow, draws on all these functional relationships to determine cash inflows and outflows, which yield the net cash generated each year.

One note of caution: The biggest mistake you can make in pro forma financial statements, especially cash flow forecasts, is to underestimate the direct impact of various costs and balance sheet accounts on one another. Investors and owners of small businesses generally have an easier time establishing reasonably accurate business valuations than their counterparts in large corporations, mainly because functional cost relationships can be determined more directly than in larger firms.

The MAPAX gross profit schedule laid out in Figure 4.4 demonstrates the functional relationships between material and labor cost of sales and sales dollars.

Figure 4.4
MAPAX Mfg. Corp.
Statement of Gross Profit
For the Years 1996–2001
(in dollars)

	Actual	Forecast					
	1995	1996	1997	1998	1999	2000	2001
Sales	11,250,000	11,789,225	12,358,231	12,958,763	13,200,924	13,282,143	13,901,899
Cost of sales							
Material	5,760,000	6,051,920	6,360,364	6,686,310	6,798,203	6,845,868	7,170,421
Labor	875,520	919,892	966,775	1,016,319	1,033,327	1,040,572	1,089,904
Overhead	747,347	777,376	808,535	900,391	927,403	991,625	1,021,373
Total standard							
cost of sales	7,382,867	7,749,188	8,135,674	8,603,020	8,758,932	8,878,065	9,281,699
Gross profit	3,867,133	4,040,037	4,222,556	4,355,743	4,441,992	4,404,078	4,620,200
Percent of sales	34.4%	34.3%	34.2%	33.6%	33.6%	33.2%	33.2%

To construct the cost of sales forecast, the actual 1995 ratio of material cost of sales to sales for both stoves and furnaces was calculated to be 40 percent, with the ratio for accessories 80 percent. This yielded a combined material cost of sales of approximately 51 percent of sales. The material cost of sales was then forecasted for each product line—stoves, furnaces, and accessories—for each year. The result was a combined ratio approximating the 51 percent achieved in prior years.

The next step involved calculating the ratio of labor cost of sales to material cost of sales that was actually achieved in 1995. This turned out to be about 15.2 percent. Labor cost of sales could then be forecasted using this approximate ratio for each year. The percentage varied slightly in those years in which accessory sales were proportionately higher than normal.

The resulting gross profit as a percentage of sales held relatively constant for all years at 32.2 to 34.4 percent. It would have been more accurate to prepare a cost of sales forecast by product line, but for MAPAX's purposes the combined statement was close enough.

It should be noted that many companies include manufacturing overhead as a cost of sales component to reflect the true cost of producing the products. Certainly this is more accurate and results in financial statements that more clearly reflect true gross profit margins. For cash flow forecasting, however, the allocation of overhead to product costs achieves nothing. Here we are interested in expenditures, not accurate product cost accounting. Whether overhead costs are written off in the year incurred or reside in year-end inventory is of no consequence.

Inventory Forecast

After the cost of sales forecast comes the inventory forecast. This key schedule integrates expenditures for materials and labor (and overhead, if it is included in cost of sales) with financial statements prepared under generally accepted accounting principles. The model presented in Figure 4.5 can be used for any type of business that carries inventory, not just manufacturing companies. Of course, for nonmanufacturing businesses, labor would probably be written off as incurred and not passed through an inventory account.

Figure 4.5
MAPAX Mfg. Corp.
Inventory Forecast
For the Years 1996–2001
(in dollars)

	Actual 1995	1996	1997	1998	1999	2000	2001
Beginning inventory							
Material	2,093,750	2,538,665	3,008,783	3,505,595	3,767,872	3,706,662	3,920,466
Labor	1,031,250	1,097,598	1,166,852	1,238,490	1,291,737	1,360,062	1,454,192
Total	3,125,000	3,636,263	4,175,635	4,744,085	5,059,609	5,066,724	5,374,658
Additions							
Material	6,204,915	6,522,038	6,857,177	6,948,587	6,736,992	7,059,673	7,401,513
Labor	941,868	989,146	1,038,413	1,069,566	1,101,653	1,134,702	1,168,743
Total	7,146,783	7,511,184	7,895,590	8,018,152	7,838,644	8,194,375	8,570,256
Cost of sales							
Material	5,760,000	6,051,920	6,360,364	6,686,310	6,798,203	6,845,868	7,170,421
Labor	875,520	919,892	966,775	1,016,319	1,033,327	1,040,572	1,089,904
Total	6,635,520	6,971,812	7,327,140	7,702,629	7,831,529	7,886,440	8,260,325
Ending inventory							
Material	2,538,665	3,008,783	3,505,595	3,767,872	3,706,662	3,920,466	4,151,557
Labor	1,097,598	1,166,852	1,238,490	1,291,737	1,360,062	1,454,192	1,533,031
Total	3,636,263	4,175,635	4,744,085	5,059,609	5,066,724	5,374,658	5,684,589

It might be helpful to briefly review the flow of costs through inventory. From an accounting perspective, the cost of all purchased material, parts, and components used in the finished product, along with the cost of labor used to make the product (if applicable), should be charged to inventory accounts as incurred. The entry for purchases is a charge to inventory and a credit to accounts payable (accounts payable is then reduced when amounts are paid to suppliers).

A similar entry is made for direct labor. Gross payroll is charged to inventory. Payroll checks written are credited to the bank account, and withheld amounts are credited to accrued expenses (accrued expenses are then reduced when amounts are paid to government agencies, insurance companies, and so on).

If products that use these materials and labor are not sold, the costs remain in inventory. When products are sold, either the actual material and labor costs associated with the sold products or estimated amounts are deducted from inventory and charged to cost of sales.

Referring to Figure 4.5, it can be seen that forecasted material purchases from Figure 4.2 and direct labor payroll from Figure 4.3 are included as additions to inventory. Material cost of sales and labor cost of sales from Figure 4.4 are shown as deductions from inventory. The beginning inventory, plus additions, minus deductions yields an ending inventory, which is then carried to the balance sheet forecast in Figure 4.11. The additions or inputs to inventory represent cash expenditures, which carry forward to the Statement of Cash Flow in Figure 4.12.

Most of the errors made in cash flow forecasting result from mistaking the identity of material purchases and labor payrolls. It's important to reiterate that cost of sales does *not* represent cash outflows. Expenditures are made only for *inputs* to inventory. The only exception to this rule occurs in retail businesses with very high inventory turnover (less than one month). In this case, inventory accounts would not be used, and all monthly purchases would be charged directly to cost of sales for that month. These businesses do not include inventory accounts in their year-end balance sheets. If inventory accounts are used in the accounting records, regardless of the number of annual inventory turns, the cost of purchases should be recorded as inputs to inventory (and hence cash expenditures).

Operating Expense Forecast

Operating expense forecasts comprise several subforecasts: *personnel forecasts, fringe benefit forecasts, variable expense forecasts*, and *occupancy forecasts*. Since the more detailed the analysis, the more accurate the forecast will be, larger companies or those with a more complex array of expenses should compile each of these forecasts separately.

Smaller companies can get by with combining two or more, however, as in the MAPAX forecasts in Figures 4.6 through 4.9.

In addition to forecasting major expense elements (separately for larger companies and combined for smaller ones), operating expenses should be forecasted by department. Once again, larger companies may segregate expenses for many departments, whereas small businesses usually get by with three or possibly four groupings: manufacturing overhead expenses, selling expenses, administrative expenses, and R&D expenses (if relevant). Since MAPAX does not incur significant new product development costs, unidentified R&D expenditures are scattered throughout the other three departments. It usually works best to begin with departmental personnel forecasts. Figure 4.6 represents the personnel requirements for MAPAX.

Some companies prefer to forecast personnel requirements by job category—management, clerical, technical, and so on. Others prefer to list the actual names of people currently employed and identify new hires by job classification. MAPAX management plans to rehire people who had worked for the company in prior years, and so the actual names of new hires have been listed.

Bearing in mind the functional relationships between overhead employees, nonpersonnel overhead expenses, and sales volume, Figure 4.6 shows new hires in 1998 and 2000 to reflect increases in production activity. The payroll for both shop supervision and manufacturing administrative personnel (production control, inventory control, production scheduling, timekeepers, and so on) is considered a *step* cost that varies with production volume in incremental steps rather than directly (as with direct labor).

In the MAPAX case, it was assumed that salaries would increase 3 percent per year to keep up with inflation assumptions. Obviously, if merit increases are anticipated, they should be included. The same holds true for bonus or profit-sharing incentive programs.

As Figure 4.6 shows, sales personnel were added in anticipation of increased sales. This makes sense, because presumably they will be needed to generate these incremental sales. No new hires were anticipated for administrative personnel. This department should include office support employees, including those in accounting, engineering, and general management.

Figure 4.6
MAPAX Mfg. Corp.
Personnel Forecast
(in dollars)

	Actual			Forecast			
	1995	1996	1997	1998	1999	2000	2001
Manufacturing							
Shop Supervision							
Clem	38,000	39,140	40,314	41,524	42,769	44,052	45,374
Marge	32,000	32,960	33,949	34,967	36,016	37,097	38,210
Stan	28,000	28,840	29,705	30,596	31,514	32,460	33,433
Mike	27,000	27,810	28,644	29,504	30,389	31,300	32,239
Holly				27,000	27,810	28,644	29,504
George						28,000	28,840
Total	125,000	128,750	132,613	163,591	168,499	201,554	207,600
Shop Administration							
Mary	31,000	31,930	32,888	33,875	34,891	35,937	37,016
Roger	31,000	31,930	32,888	33,875	34,891	35,937	37,016
Harry	30,000	30,900	31,827	32,782	33,765	34,778	35,822
Joan	30,000	30,900	31,827	32,782	33,765	34,778	35,822
Sue				25,000	25,750	26,523	27,318
Total	122,000	125,660	129,430	158,313	163,062	167,954	172,993
Selling							
Mac	75,000	77,250	79,568	81,955	84,413	86,946	89,554
Roy	45,000	46,350	47,741	49,173	50,648	52,167	53,732
Mitsy	52,000	53,560	55,167	56,822	58,526	60,282	62,091
Ann	35,000	36,050	37,132	38,245	39,393	40,575	41,792
Clyde	30,000	30,900	31,827	32,782	33,765	34,778	35,822
Margaret				40,000	41,200	42,436	43,709
Ollie					50,000	51,500	53,045
Total	237,000	244,110	251,433	298,976	357,946	368,684	379,744
Administrative							
Bob	75,000	77,250	79,568	81,955	84,413	86,946	89,554
Marcia	75,000	77,250	79,568	81,955	84,413	86,946	89,554
Audrey	42,000	43,260	44,558	45,895	47,271	48,690	50,150
Gene	45,000	46,350	47,741	49,173	50,648	52,167	53,732
Barry	33,000	33,990	35,010	36,060	37,142	38,256	39,404
Ann	25,000	25,750	26,523	27,318	28,138	28,982	29,851
Pat	22,000	22,660	23,340	24,040	24,761	25,504	26,269
Clare	22,000	22,660	23,340	24,040	24,761	25,504	26,269
Ritchie	22,000	22,660	23,340	24,040	24,761	25,504	26,269
Dick	18,000	18,540	19,096	19,669	20,259	20,867	21,493
Total	379,000	390,370	402,081	414,144	426,568	439,365	452,546

The next step is to forecast fringe benefits and nonpersonnel operating expenses, as shown in Figures 4.7, 4.8, and 4.9.

Figure 4.7
MAPAX Mfg. Corp.
Manufacturing Overhead
(in dollars)

	Actual	Forecast					
	1995	1996	1997	1998	1999	2000	2001
Shop supervision	125,000	128,750	132,613	163,591	168,499	201,554	207,600
Fringe benefits							
Direct labor	376,747	395,658	415,365	427,826	440,661	453,881	467,497
Indirect labor	37,500	38,625	39,784	49,077	50,550	60,466	62,280
Shop administration	122,000	125,660	129,430	158,313	163,062	167,954	172,993
Fringe benefits	36,600	37,698	38,829	47,494	48,919	50,386	51,898
Operating supplies	5,000	5,150	5,305	5,464	5,628	5,796	5,970
Maintenance	9,000	9,270	9,548	9,835	10,130	10,433	10,746
Utilities	12,000	12,360	12,731	13,113	13,506	13,911	14,329
Telephone	3,000	3,090	3,183	3,278	3,377	3,478	3,582
Insurance	10,000	10,300	10,609	10,927	11,255	11,593	11,941
Property taxes	8,500	8,755	9,018	9,288	9,567	9,854	10,149
Miscellaneous	2,000	2,060	2,122	2,185	2,251	2,319	2,388
Total	747,347	777,376	808,535	900,391	927,403	991,625	1,021,373
Direct labor	941,868	989,146	1,038,413	1,069,566	1,101,653	1,134,702	1,168,743

Figure 4.8
MAPAX Mfg. Corp.
Selling Expenses
(in dollars)

	Actual	Forecast					
	1995	1996	1997	1998	1999	2000	2001
Salaries	237,000	244,110	251,433	298,976	357,946	368,684	379,744
Fringe benefits	59,250	61,028	62,858	74,744	89,486	92,171	94,936
Commissions	281,250	294,731	308,956	323,969	330,023	332,054	347,547
Telephone	12,000	12,360	12,731	13,113	13,506	13,911	14,329
Supplies	2,000	2,060	2,122	2,185	2,251	2,319	2,388
Samples	2,500	2,575	2,652	2,732	2,814	2,898	2,985
Auto expense	7,000	7,210	7,426	7,649	7,879	8,115	8,358
Sales literature	4,000	4,120	4,244	4,371	4,502	4,637	4,776
Advertising	2,900	2,987	3,077	3,169	3,264	3,362	3,463
Misc. expense	1,000	1,030	1,061	1,093	1,126	1,159	1,194
Total	608,900	632,210	656,560	732,001	812,796	829,310	859,721

Figure 4.9
MAPAX Mfg. Corp.
Administrative Expenses
(in dollars)

	Actual			Forecast			
	1995	1996	1997	1998	1999	2000	2001
Salaries	379,000	390,370	402,081	414,144	426,568	439,365	452,546
Fringe benefits	94,750	97,593	100,520	103,536	106,642	109,841	113,136
Telephone	12,000	12,000	12,000	12,000	12,600	12,600	12,600
Office supplies	4,000	4,000	4,000	4,000	4,200	4,200	4,200
Maintenance	5,000	6,000	6,000	6,000	6,300	6,300	6,300
Insurance	18,000	18,000	18,000	18,000	18,900	18,900	18,900
Professional fees	25,000	25,000	25,000	25,000	26,250	26,250	26,250
Misc. expense	4,000	4,000	4,000	4,000	4,200	4,200	4,200
Total	541,750	556,963	571,601	586,679	605,660	621,656	638,132

As previously mentioned, companies with a large number of employees or complex benefit structures should forecast fringe benefits in detail: payroll taxes, group insurance, pension cost, and so on. For most small businesses, however, the forecasting accuracy of annual cash flows will be nearly as good if the ratio of total fringe benefits to gross payroll is estimated. This should be done by department, not for the company as a whole. Although everyone may be included in the same benefit programs, departments with higher average salaries per employee will show a lower ratio of fringe benefits to gross payroll.

In the case of MAPAX, the forecast included ratios established from historical data. These ratios amounted to 30 percent for manufacturing overhead personnel and 25 percent for selling and administrative employees.

Nonpersonnel expenses should be forecasted based on actual current experience. If different types of expenses are expected in the future or if an extraordinary event will cause unusual swings, then of course these conditions should be forecasted. In the case of MAPAX, however, it was assumed that the current expense structure would hold during the forecast period. Most expenses reflect annual increases of 3 percent based on expected inflation rates. A few of the less variable costs (e.g., most of the administrative expenses) were forecasted as step costs.

Annual totals from the manufacturing overhead, selling expenses, and administrative expense forecasts then flow directly to the income statement in Figure 4.10. Since MAPAX does not consider manufacturing overhead as a direct product cost, annual totals of these expenses flow to cost of sales as period costs rather than to inventory. If your company absorbs overhead on direct labor, forecasted manufacturing expenses should flow to inventory (like material purchases and direct labor), not to cost of sales.

It should also be noted that companies using a standard cost system may record inputs and outputs from inventory at standard. In that case, variances between standard and actual costs are written off to cost of sales as variances. The material, labor, and overhead absorbed captions then reflect standard costs. To adjust a standard cost system to cash flow, it's necessary to add the variances to standard inventory input amounts for all three types of costs.

MAPAX does not use a standard cost system; therefore, forecasted operating expenses flow to the income statement as well as directly to the cash flow forecast.

Income Statement Forecast

The income statement (or profit and loss statement, as some companies prefer to call this schedule) summarizes the results of the previously described subforecasts, following the same procedures used in the company's accounting records. Although it is clearly not a cash expenditure, depreciation expense based on current guidelines must be included to correlate pro forma statements with historical accounting-oriented financial statements.

For simplicity, MAPAX's taxes were forecasted at a straight 38 percent of pretax income for all years (see Figure 4.10). To the extent that special exclusions or additions to income or expense are permitted, these should be estimated and included as increases or decreases to the normal tax base. Also, state income taxes should be included.

Figure 4.10
MAPAX Mfg. Corp.
Statement of Income
For the Years 1996–2001
(in dollars)

	Actual	Forecast					
	1995	1996	1997	1998	1999	2000	2001
Sales	11,250,000	11,789,225	12,358,231	12,958,763	13,200,924	13,282,143	13,901,899
Cost of sales							
Material	5,760,000	6,051,920	6,360,364	6,686,310	6,798,203	6,845,868	7,170,421
Labor	875,520	919,892	966,775	1,016,319	1,033,327	1,040,572	1,089,904
Overhead	747,347	777,376	808,535	900,391	927,403	991,625	1,021,373
Total standard cost of sales	7,382,867	7,749,188	8,135,674	8,603,020	8,758,932	8,878,065	9,281,699
Gross profit	3,867,133	4,040,037	4,222,556	4,355,743	4,441,992	4,404,078	4,620,200
Percent of sales	34.4%	34.3%	34.2%	33.6%	33.6%	33.2%	33.2%
Operating Expenses							
Selling expenses	608,900	632,210	656,560	732,001	812,796	829,310	859,721
Administrative expenses	541,750	556,963	571,601	586,679	605,660	621,656	638,132
Other expenses	20,000	20,000	20,000	20,000	20,000	20,000	20,000
Depreciation	585,000	585,000	585,000	585,000	585,000	585,000	585,000
Total	1,755,650	1,794,173	1,833,161	1,923,680	2,023,456	2,055,966	2,102,854
Net income before interest and taxes	2,111,483	2,245,864	2,389,395	2,432,062	2,418,537	2,348,112	2,517,346
Percent of sales	18.8%	19.1%	19.3%	18.8%	18.3%	17.7%	18.1%
Interest	517,000	485,250	453,500	417,500	390,000	362,500	335,000
Net income before tax	1,594,483	1,760,614	1,935,895	2,014,562	2,028,537	1,985,612	2,182,346
Taxes	605,903	669,033	735,640	765,534	770,844	754,533	829,292
Net income	988,579	1,091,581	1,200,255	1,249,029	1,257,693	1,231,080	1,353,055
Percent of sales	8.8%	9.3%	9.7%	9.6%	9.5%	9.3%	9.7%

Seeing how costs flow into an income statement, it's easy to understand why the accounting procedure that defines cash flow as net income plus noncash expenses (i.e., depreciation) does not yield an accurate cash flow:

- Material and labor cost of sales are determined through ratio analysis. Actual cash expenditures for purchases and direct labor payroll are recorded as inputs to inventory, not to cost of sales.
- When depreciation is added back to net income, the tax effect of the depreciation deduction is completely ignored.
- The actual tax rate may be more or less than a straight 38 percent depending on adjustments to income based on tax code provisions (although in the case of MAPAX such adjustments are assumed to be negligible).

One final point about the income statement. It may be that you'll use your business plan, financing plan, or strategic plan for several purposes, perhaps emphasizing future earnings rather than cash flow. Depending on the circumstances, forecasted earnings may be net income after taxes, before taxes, or before taxes and interest. With this in mind, it's easier to keep these different definitions of earnings separate in the pro forma financial statements.

Balance Sheet Forecast

From an accounting perspective, the income statement records transactions that occur over a period of time (in the case of MAPAX, over calendar years). Balance sheet accounts, however, reflect asset and liability amounts as of a specific point in time (in the case of MAPAX, on December 31 of each year). Income accounts are dynamic, balance sheet accounts static.

The cash flow forecasting procedure recognizes both, that is, cash flow created over a period of time by a series of income statement transactions, and positive or negative cash flow created by collecting the prior year's balance sheet assets or setting up new balance sheet amounts for the current year-end. This combination of dynamic transactions and static account balances yields the amount of cash remaining in bank accounts at the end of a period. Figure 4.11 shows the pro forma balance sheets for MAPAX.

The whole purpose of preparing pro forma projections for small businesses is to arrive at the amount of net cash flowing into (or out of) a company's bank accounts. Forecasts show the *flow* of cash receipts and expenditures over a given period that results in net cash balances. Therefore, the balance sheet bank account is a dynamically derived amount and is not the same as other static balance sheet accounts.

Figure 4.11
MAPAX Mfg. Corp.
Balance Sheet
As of December 31, 1995–2001
(in dollars)

	Actual 1995	1996	1997	1998	1999	2000	2001
				Forecast			
Cash	1,000	785,445	1,648,017	1,727,882	3,231,740	4,495,068	5,813,453
Accounts receivable	1,406,250	1,473,653	1,544,779	1,619,845	1,650,116	1,660,268	1,737,737
Inventory	3,636,263	4,175,635	4,744,085	5,059,609	5,066,724	5,374,658	5,684,589
Prepaid expenses	5,000	5,000	5,000	5,000	5,000	5,000	5,000
Total current assets	5,048,513	6,439,733	7,941,881	8,412,336	9,953,579	11,534,994	13,240,779
Buildings	2,000,000	2,000,000	2,000,000	2,000,000	2,000,000	2,000,000	2,000,000
Machinery & equipment	8,000,000	8,000,000	8,000,000	9,000,000	9,000,000	9,000,000	9,000,000
Delivery trucks	50,000	50,000	50,000	50,000	50,000	50,000	50,000
Total	10,050,000	10,050,000	10,050,000	11,050,000	11,050,000	11,050,000	11,050,000
Less: Accumulated depreciation	(3,200,000)	(3,785,000)	(4,370,000)	(4,955,000)	(5,540,000)	(6,125,000)	(6,710,000)
Net fixed assets	6,850,000	6,265,000	5,680,000	6,095,000	5,510,000	4,925,000	4,340,000
Other assets	100,000	100,000	100,000	100,000	100,000	100,000	100,000
Total Assets	11,998,513	12,804,733	13,721,881	14,607,336	15,563,579	16,559,994	17,680,779
Bank note payable	200,000	150,000	100,000	0	0	0	0
New bank note	0	0	0	0	0	0	0
Accounts payable	775,614	815,255	857,147	868,573	842,124	882,459	925,189
Accrued expenses	200,000	200,000	200,000	200,000	200,000	200,000	200,000
Other current liabilities	50,000	50,000	50,000	50,000	50,000	50,000	50,000
Total current liabilities	1,225,614	1,215,255	1,207,147	1,118,573	1,092,124	1,132,459	1,175,189
Long-term debt	4,000,000	3,800,000	3,600,000	3,400,000	3,200,000	3,000,000	2,800,000
Mortgage loan	1,000,000	925,000	850,000	775,000	700,000	625,000	550,000
Total Liabilities	6,225,614	5,940,255	5,657,147	5,293,573	4,992,124	4,757,459	4,525,189
Common stock	100,000	100,000	100,000	100,000	100,000	100,000	100,000
Retained earnings— beginning		5,672,898	6,764,479	7,964,734	9,213,763	10,471,456	11,702,535
Profit/(loss)		1,091,581	1,200,255	1,249,029	1,257,693	1,231,080	1,353,055
Retained earnings— ending	5,672,898	6,764,479	7,964,734	9,213,763	10,471,456	11,702,535	13,055,590
Total Net Worth	5,772,898	6,864,479	8,064,734	9,313,763	10,571,456	11,802,535	13,155,590
Total Liabilities and Net Worth	11,998,513	12,804,734	13,721,881	14,607,336	15,563,580	16,559,994	17,680,779

Referring to Figure 4.11, the following sections describe the functional relationships used to arrive at noncash balance sheet amounts, beginning with accounts receivable.

Accounts Receivable

Sales flow into accounts receivable as inputs, and collections flow out. During the course of a year the receivables balance will constantly fluctuate up and down based on these two flows. For forecasting purposes, however, we must arrive at a balance as of a point in time, namely the end of the year. Since it is impractical to forecast each sale and collection transaction for the entire year, an approximation of the accounts receivable balance at year-end can be calculated by assuming a functional relationship to sales expressed in terms of the number of days' sales that have not been collected. This relationship is referred to as *receivables days' sales* or *receivables turnover.*

In the case of MAPAX, historical data show that on average, the accounts receivable balance represents about fourty five days' sales. The forecasted year-end balance is then calculated as

$$\text{Accounts receivable} = \frac{\text{current year sales}}{365 \text{ days}} \times 45 \text{ days}$$

The simplified calculation translates to one month's sales times a factor of 1.5.

Inventory

As a subforecast inventory schedule including material purchases and direct labor payroll is used, no further calculation is necessary for the balance sheet forecast. Just bring in the year-end balances from the inventory forecast (Figure 4.5).

Prepaid Expenses and Other Assets

Generally the amounts in these accounts either are very small, and therefore immaterial in relation to total cash flow, or change very little from one year to the next. In either case, it should be safe to assume constant balances, as in the MAPAX forecast. If either of these conditions is not true in your company, then obviously a separate subforecast schedule should be used to track the ins and outs.

Fixed Assets

If major changes in facilities space or production/delivery machinery and equipment are not planned and significant disposals are not anticipated, these balances remain constant throughout the forecast period. Of course, major additions or disposals must be forecasted. For MAPAX, it was determined that furnace production would reach capacity in the 1997–1998 period. To meet the increased sales volume in 1999 and beyond, new machinery costing $1 million would have to be added in 1998.

Accounts Payable and Accrued Expenses

The majority of the transactions flowing through trade payable accounts relate to material purchases. This functional relationship allows the accounts payable balance to be forecasted as a percentage of purchases. In the case of MAPAX, material purchases make up the majority of inventory at any point in time, justifying the use of that functional relationship. This leads to a choice: Forecast payables either as a ratio of purchases or as a ratio of inventory. MAPAX chose the latter.

MAPAX's policy was to pay supplier invoices in approximately eighty days. For forecast purposes, it was assumed that payment terms would gradually be reduced from seventy-seven days in 1995 to sixty days in 2001, using the following formula:

$$\text{Accounts payable} = \frac{\text{inventory}}{365} \times \text{payment terms (in days)}$$

Accrued expenses usually include employer-paid fringe benefits, unpaid interest and property taxes, and various other items that have been booked as expenses but not yet paid. To the extent that the accrued expense balance varies significantly from year to year, the same functional analysis should be made as for accounts payable, only this time the balance should be calculated as a percentage of operating expenses. In the case of MAPAX, however, historical accrual balances varied slightly from year to year, but not enough to warrant a separate analysis. Therefore, balances were held constant over the forecast period. The same held true for other current liabilities.

Debt

Forecasting debt balances can be tricky, especially for companies with low profit margins or severely fluctuating cash needs. Of course, current debt service payments are easy to project and companies should plan to pay off current bank notes as soon as cash balances permit.

The determination of new debt requirements comes from the cash flow forecast. For those years in which sales volume does not generate sufficient internal cash to meet obligations, additional short-term borrowings should be forecasted. Large purchases of fixed assets may also be financed externally, necessitating the inclusion of additional long-term debt. To the extent that new short- or long-term debt is necessary, separate headings on the balance sheet forecast should be used to identify it. Interest expense on all outstanding debt should, of course, be included in the income statement forecast. And that brings us to the main forecast schedule—the statement of cash flow.

Cash Flow Forecast

All previous subforecast schedules and pro forma financial statements have been based on generally accepted accounting principles. This is not the case with the statement of cash flow. The format used in the MAPAX forecast in Figure 4.12 will not be found in any accounting literature and probably not in any business literature. Yet, through many years of experimentation with various formats, I have found this one the most useful in showing the cost/sales/assets functional relationships that generate or use cash and simultaneously interact with GAAP-prepared balance sheets and income statements. This format can also be easily adapted to computer-based spreadsheet formulas.

Cash Receipts

Cash receipts is probably the easiest place to begin. All cash receipts originate from one or a combination of six sources:

- Collections of prior period accounts receivable balances
- Current-period sales
- New loans or other debt financing
- Sale of business assets

- Sale of equity interests
- Settlement of claims or refunds

All current-period sales are assumed to be collected except those residing in accounts receivable at the end of the period, which is why ending accounts receivable are deducted from operating receipts. MAPAX does not need additional debt financing to reach its forecasted volume or to purchase new equipment, nor does the company plan to sell any fixed assets or equity shares. Of course, the amounts included as sales and beginning and ending accounts receivable flow directly from the income statement (Figure 4.10) and the balance sheet (Figure 4.11).

Figure 4-12
MAPAX Mfg. Corp.
Statement of Cash Flow
For the Years 1996–2001
(in dollars)

	1996	1997	1998	1999	2000	2001
			Forecast			
Cash Receipts						
Beginning receivables	1,406,250	1,473,653	1,544,779	1,619,845	1,650,116	1,660,268
Sales	11,789,225	12,358,231	12,958,763	13,200,924	13,282,143	13,901,899
Ending receivables	(1,473,653)	(1,544,779)	(1,619,845)	(1,650,116)	(1,660,268)	(1,737,737)
Cash receipts from operations	11,721,822	12,287,105	12,883,696	13,170,654	13,271,991	13,824,429
New bank loans	0	0	0	0	0	0
Other cash receipts	0	0	0	0	0	0
Total Cash Receipts	11,721,822	12,287,105	12,883,696	13,170,654	13,271,991	13,824,429
Cash Expenditures						
Beginning payables	775,614	815,255	857,147	868,573	842,124	882,459
Purchases	6,522,038	6,857,177	6,948,587	6,736,992	7,059,673	7,401,513
Ending payables	(815,255)	(857,147)	(868,573)	(842,124)	(882,459)	(925,189)
Material cash expenditures	6,482,398	6,815,284	6,937,160	6,763,441	7,019,338	7,358,783
Direct labor	989,146	1,038,413	1,069,566	1,101,653	1,134,702	1,168,743
Operating expenditures						
Beginning accrued expenses	200,000	200,000	200,000	200,000	200,000	200,000
Manufacturing expenses	777,376	808,535	900,391	927,403	991,625	1,021,373
Selling expenses	632,210	656,560	732,001	812,796	829,310	859,721
Administrative expenses	556,963	571,601	586,679	605,660	621,656	638,132
Other expenses	20,000	20,000	20,000	20,000	20,000	20,000
Ending accrued expenses	(200,000)	(200,000)	(200,000)	(200,000)	(200,000)	(200,000)
Total operating expenditures	1,986,549	2,056,696	2,239,071	2,365,858	2,462,590	2,539,227
Taxes	669,033	735,640	765,534	770,844	754,533	829,292
Machinery purchases	0	0	1,000,000	0	0	0
Financing expenditures						
Bank note						
Principal	50,000	50,000	100,000	0	0	0
Interest	12,750	8,500	0	0	0	0
Long-term loan						
Principal	200,000	200,000	200,000	200,000	200,000	200,000
Interest	380,000	360,000	340,000	320,000	300,000	280,000
Mortgage loan						
Principal	75,000	75,000	75,000	75,000	75,000	75,000
Interest	92,500	85,000	77,500	70,000	62,500	55,000
Total principal	325,000	325,000	375,000	275,000	275,000	275,000
Total interest	485,250	453,500	417,500	390,000	362,500	335,000
Total Cash Expenditures	10,937,376	11,424,534	12,803,831	11,666,796	12,008,663	12,506,045
Net Cash Generated	784,445	862,572	79,865	1,503,858	1,263,328	1,318,385
Beginning cash in bank	1,000	785,445	1,648,017	1,727,882	3,231,740	4,495,068
Ending cash in bank	785,445	1,648,017	1,727,882	3,231,740	4,495,068	5,813,453

Cash Expenditures

The steps in forecasting cash expenditures follow the sequence of account headings, first in the statement of income and then in the balance sheet. It is assumed that all payables outstanding at the beginning of the period will be paid during the period. The same holds true for material purchases, except for those amounts purchased in the last forty-five days, which are deducted as ending accounts payable. The amounts included as material purchases flow directly from the input section of the inventory forecast.

All direct labor payroll is assumed to have been paid during the period. Like material purchases, direct labor expenditures flow directly from the input section of the inventory forecast.

In the operating expenses category, any accrued expenses at the beginning of the period should be paid off during the period. Current expenditures for manufacturing overhead, selling expenses, and administrative expenses are shown as being paid, except for those incurred toward the end of the period, which are included as accrued expenses and deducted, just like ending payables. Each of the three classes of expenses flows from the income statement, which derived the data from the operating expense subforecasts. Taxes are shown separately and flow directly from the income statement.

If any fixed asset purchases are planned, they flow directly from the balance sheet and should be shown as a separate line item. The final class of expenditures includes all principal and interest payments on both short- and long-term debt. Principal payments flow directly from the balance sheet, and interest payments from the income statement. It usually works best to keep payments segregated for each category of debt (as in Figure 4.12). In this way, any prepayment or extended payment against a particular loan can be easily identified.

Net Cash

The final section of the cash flow forecast reconciles all receipts and expenditures for the period with the cash balance shown on the balance sheet. The net cash generated equals the total receipts for the period less total expenditures. Adding net cash to the bank account balance from the previous period results in the current cash balance on the balance sheet.

The beauty of this type of cash flow format is that not only can each element of receipts and expenditures be clearly identified, but every line item interacts directly with an account in the income statement, balance sheet, or supporting subforecasts. It's important to note the differences between this approach to forecasting cash flow and the traditional approach used by the accounting profession and securities analysts. Although when cash flow forecasts using both methods are properly constructed in sufficient detail, the net cash figures that result must, in fact, reconcile, the traditional method relies on accounting definitions of income and expense to shortcut the detailed flow of receipts and expenditures.

For example, instead of forecasting actual purchases, payroll, and operating expenditures during the periods in which the expenditures occur, the accounting approach merely considers total net changes in working capital accounts, that is, increases or decreases in accounts receivable, inventory, prepaid expenses, accounts payable, accrued expenses, and so on. Instead of forecasting actual cash collections from sales, operating cash receipts are derived by adjusting reported net income for noncash items such as depreciation and amortization.

That finishes the forecasting process. Although the MAPAX example represented a typical forecast for a manufacturing company and the numbers used in the examples were relatively large, the same format and procedure (with slight modifications) can be used for any type of company of any size.

To summarize the three major features of the cash flow forecasting technique introduced in this chapter:

1. *Economic and business assumptions.* Before beginning a forecast, it's necessary to set out the macroeconomic, industry, competitive, and specific company assumptions that underlie incremental changes in volume, product mix, selling prices, costs, and assets during the forecast period. Such assumptions should incorporate trends in the national economy as well as the current status of the relevant industry business cycle. Published leading and trailing indicators should be acknowledged. Conscious decisions should be made about inflation, interest rates, personnel availability, sources of supply, foreign competition, and the potential for new products or competitors entering the market. Assumptions about sources of supply, projected results of labor contract negotiations, and changes in

government regulations (such as tightened EPA restrictions) should be reflected.

2. *Cost/volume/price/asset functional relationships.* Using historical data, perhaps over several years, functional relationships should be established between each cost element and sales volume, prices, and asset employment. In any business, all income, expense, asset, and liability accounts are interactive. Each retains some type of functional relationship to another. The key to preparing meaningful cash flow forecasts is to thoroughly understand the relationships that are unique to your business. Although the detail necessary for each subschedule varies with each company and industry, most companies should have the following:

Sales forecast. A sales forecast should recognize both volume and price changes from historical periods. It should also incorporate probable variations in product mix, market trends, new product introductions, and potential competitor actions. Companies that manufacture products to customer order should forecast from the order book, order backlog, and production cycle rather than from historical shipments. However, historical receivables turnover ratios can be used to project cash receipts.

Purchase forecast. The purchase forecast should reflect the same variations in product mix as the sales forecast. It should also reflect inflationary changes in the pricing of at least major items and preferably all purchases. Companies that stock inventory for resale should base purchasing time lags on historical inventory turnover. Those that buy materials to customer order should incorporate the lag/lead time required by the production cycle.

Payroll forecast. Supervisory and direct labor payroll forecasts must include anticipated wage rate and salary increases. The projected number of employees should be used as the basis, in contrast to a straight extrapolation of historical payrolls. All fringe benefits should be included, recognizing expected increases in federal and state tax rates, workers' compensation rates, group health insurance rates, and potential new pension plans. All salaries to the owner/manager should be excluded.

Nonpayroll operating expenses forecast. The forecast of utilities, lease payments, telephone, operating supplies, insurance, maintenance, professional fees, and so on should be based on historical averages. Such averages can then be factored up for expected inflation rates. Obviously, if facilities are added or deleted, historical data must be adjusted accordingly.

Capital expenditures forecast. If additional space and production machinery and equipment are needed to meet the sales forecast, they should be forecasted in the appropriate years. The capital expenditures forecast should, where relevant, include backup analyses of lease-versus-buy decisions. If external capital is needed to finance capital additions, it should be included as both cash receipts and cash expenditures; however, such new financing should be segregated from current outstanding loans.

Taxes forecast. Income taxes may or may not be forecasted, depending on the structure of the company. For example, S corporations, partnerships, and limited partnerships do not pay income taxes. They pass income and losses directly to shareholders or partners for inclusion in personal tax returns. The same holds for proprietorships. C corporations, however, do pay taxes and should include a tax forecast based on expected tax rates.

Financing forecast. The forecast of payments against current financing (principal, interest, or dividends) should be treated separately from other expenditures. Financing expenditures may or may not be included as deductions to arrive at free cash flow, depending on the purpose of the forecast. For example, if you anticipate new financing to liquidate existing loans and/or preferred shares, forecasted payments against current financing have no meaning. Conversely, for minority investors, current financing expenditures are as relevant as any operating expense in determining free cash.

3. *Interactive financial schedules.* Despite the inaccuracies and variations among companies in applying generally accepted accounting principles, each element of the cash flow forecast must flow from another supporting schedule that has been prepared under the same accounting principles used in preparing

your company's financial statements. It is virtually impossible to make any sense out of pro forma cash flow projections without starting with historical income statements and balance sheets. To be believable, future cash flows must be derived from verifiable accounting records as expressed in financial statements.

Part II
Banks

Chapter 5

Banks and Bank Terminology

Banks have been and are likely to continue to be the cornerstone of our business community. Without banks, we couldn't pay our bills with checks, deposit our cash in a safe place, or borrow money when we run short of cash.

We trust banks. After all, doesn't the federal government guarantee that we'll get our money back, regardless of how inefficiently a bank may be managed? When we borrow money, the loan agreement we execute clearly spells out how much we must pay back on specific dates. What could be simpler or easier to understand?

But all is not as it appears in the banking industry. Banks are not in business to promote society's well-being, to help people and businesses in need of cash, to be a secure custodian of our family and business fortunes, to bail out the federal government, or to assist in the growth of our nation. Banks are in business to make money. Pure and simple. Just like every other private-sector business. And when banks don't make money, they fail. The big difference between bank failures and other business failures is that the greater the number of banks that fail, the harder it is to get loans at a reasonable price and the greater the risk of locking up our deposits for an indeterminate length of time.

The business community is rife with misconceptions about banks. Yet, because banks remain the cornerstone of business finance, it's difficult to make intelligent financial decisions without a basic understanding of the banking industry and some of its problems.

The Federal Reserve Board lists approximately 11,000 thousand banks in the United States, far and away the largest number of private-sector banks in any country in the world. Why so many? One reason dates back to the early Colonial period, when our nation was still rural. People from predominantly European heritage, fleeing oppression and rigid class structures, distrusted any large concentration of power—political, religious, or financial. In their new nation, our forefathers disdained the enormous financial power European banks held over political bodies as well as individuals. However, eventually the settlers needed a place to deposit cash and to borrow money for new businesses and farms, and rural banks were born. These small, locally owned banks dotted the American landscape for many years.

Gradually, as the federal government grew to need its own financing, and as businesses outgrew the capability of rural banks, large city banks developed. These city banks eventually blossomed into what today are referred to as *money-center banks*, with vast resources. These banks have now become more powerful than the European banks our forefathers disdained. The Federal Reserve estimates that nine money-center banks control over 50 percent of all U.S. banking assets. Moreover, most large American banks are holding companies. That is, they operate divisions and subsidiaries engaged in businesses other than commercial banking: credit cards, mortgages, asset-based lending, and so on.

Such a concentration of assets (and therefore power) in the hands of the few has a profound effect on small and midsize business borrowers. Any actions taken by money-center banks ripple down to regional, state, and local banks, as we saw happen in the early 1990s during our last major recession. Since many smaller banks already faced the same problems as their big-city cousins, the impact on the business community was double-barreled. Reasonably priced loans were next to impossible to come by. And it wasn't until these smaller banks got their own houses in order that they could cope with the severe restrictions placed on them by the big banks.

Like manufacturing, retail, and service companies, banks need capital (cash) to operate their business. In addition, however, they must satisfy federal regulators, who take orders from the Federal Reserve and the Comptroller of the Currency. Maintaining required capital ratios means that banks must hold a certain amount of money in reserve as a cushion against losses. This, in turn, determines how much they can lend. If a bank has insufficient capital, it has two choices: either get more capital or make fewer loans. And therein lies the rub.

When banks contract their lending activity to strengthen their own balance sheets, small businesses are left out in the cold.

In the early 1990s, bankers who in the past had been amenable to working with smaller businesses suddenly became adamant that loans be repaid on time. New loans became scarcer and more difficult to qualify for. Start-up businesses found that personal collateral had to be pledged against business loans. For all but the most secure businesses, leveraged buyouts dried up. The high-flying investment banks, asset-based lenders, and venture capitalists of the 1980s pulled in their horns.

Although the banking industry has, over the last few years, begun to examine new philosophies that would lead to more prudent business practices, billion-dollar errors in judgment (such as the uncollateralized loans to Latin American countries during the 1970s) cannot be rectified overnight. The likelihood of a lengthy period of easy business credit in the foreseeable future seems remote. Every indicator points to a continuation of bank demands for high levels of collateral and relatively tight credit for several years. This means that entrepreneurs, business owners, and managers must become smarter, tougher, and more creative in raising the financing they need to grow their businesses. You must learn how to play the financial game according to the rules laid down by the banking fraternity.

A Variety of Banks to Choose From

There are many different kinds of banks on the American business scene. The Federal Reserve Bank is the United States' version of a *central bank*. It acts as a bank for nongovernment banks and clears interbank transfers of funds. It processes checks written on banks throughout the country and debits and credits the accounts of both the payer and the payee banks.

Large money-center banks represent the private-sector equivalent of the Federal Reserve Bank. With banking deregulation, money-center banks branched out into a variety of financial services. Many now have separate divisions or subsidiaries engaged in investment banking, credit cards, and foreign lending. All money-center banks serve as clearinghouses for international money transfers. Most have branches scattered throughout the world. Their primary activities, however, haven't changed. They continue to act as depositories, lenders, and purchasers of government securities.

Large banks may be further divided between retail banks and wholesale banks. Retail banks, such as Citicorp and Chase, concentrate on deposits, loans, and short-term investments for individual and business customers. Wholesale banks, such as Bankers Trust and Morgan Guaranty, specialize in serving as banks for other banks. Although they also get involved in retail banking and investment transactions, they act primarily as wholesalers, borrowing and lending funds from other banks.

Next in line in the banking hierarchy, large regional banks such as Mellon, First Chicago, Norwest, and Crocker function on the regional level in much the same way that money-center banks function at the national level. Federal and state laws that prohibit interstate banking encouraged the growth of banks to meet the needs of large regional businesses. Although these banks were heretofore limited by city or county lines, recent legislation in many states has allowed them to expand statewide and to acquire banks in other states. Large regional banks have also become involved in foreign loans, and many have hired multinational personnel to handle international accounts. Money-center banks typically act as correspondents for regional banks.

Below the large regional banks, local federal- and state-licensed neighborhood and rural banks dot the landscape. In terms of pure numbers, these banks continue to make up the bulk of the more than 13,000 banks throughout the country. Most are strictly retail banks, lending money to individuals and smaller businesses and acting as depositories. Because smaller businesses find it much easier to establish personal relationships with banks of this size, most deal exclusively with them, leaving the larger banks to larger companies. Local banks use regional banks as correspondents. When a customer requires services beyond their scope, they merely funnel the transaction through their regional correspondent.

Specialized banks go by a variety of names: trusts, savings banks, savings and loan associations, thrifts, private banks, and so on. In addition, other financial institutions get involved in business finance to a greater or lesser extent: asset-based lenders, commercial and industrial finance companies, credit unions, and so on. Many money-center or regional banks incorporate these specialties as divisions or subsidiaries.

In addition to banks that are part of the U.S. banking system, many foreign banks now maintain branch operations in the United States. Many of these are full-service banks competing head-on with money-center, regional, and local banks. According to the Fed, all U.S. branches and affiliates of foreign banks (including those U.S. banks acquired by foreigners) account for less than 10 percent of total banking assets in the United States. Although that isn't a very high percentage, it continues to grow. By contrast, a much greater percentage (some estimates reach as high as 20 percent) of European banks are owned by foreigners.

Although the Federal Deposit Insurance Corporation (FDIC) insures deposit accounts up to $100,000 in all federally licensed banks, it does not insure deposit accounts in foreign-owned banks. Neither are foreign banks subject to the stringent new capital ratio requirements of the Fed, although they are obliged to follow capital guidelines established by their home-country central banks. Foreign banks also operate under different accounting rules than do their U.S. counterparts, giving them greater freedom and creativity.

The American Institute of Certified Public Accountants (AICPA), the Securities and Exchange Commission (SEC), and the General Accounting Office (GAO) make certain that U.S. banks abide by uniform accounting practices set down by these groups. Generally, U.S. banks follow the same conservative accounting principles as any publicly listed company. Assets must be recorded at the lower of cost or market, and liabilities must be recorded as soon as they are recognized. Off-balance-sheet financing instruments are frowned upon. Stringent audit procedures ensure that banks comply with these rules.

Foreign banks, on the other hand, follow the accounting practices dictated by their home countries. Certain U.S. standards of reporting must be adhered to, however, and when they are not, the foreign bank gets into trouble. Nonetheless, except for practices that endanger national security or that are clearly against U.S. public policy, foreign banks can do pretty much as they please. Many European banks handle letters of credit as off-balance-sheet transactions. Japanese banks are famous for recording certain assets at market value.

Many times a foreign bank will make a loan when an American bank won't. When U.S. bank regulators clamp down, a foreign bank might very well be the only place to obtain financing. When a bank opens its doors in a new city or neighborhood, new accounts are eagerly solicited. A newly opened branch of a foreign bank is no different. Very often you can get financing from one of these when the U.S. bank next door says no.

Foreign banks are accustomed to dealing with standby letters of credit (L/Cs) and other creative performance guarantees. For example, contractors often find a foreign bank willing to post a standby L/C against the contractor's performance when a normal surety bond is unavailable or too expensive. Foreign bank standby L/Cs can also be used as payment guarantees for third-party bank loans.

Choosing the Right Bank

With many types of banks competing for loan business and continual changes in bank portfolios and loan policies, it can be extremely difficult to find the right bank for a specific project. Yet that is exactly what you must do to be certain of getting the right financing for the minimum cost.

Shopping for a bank is no different from shopping for a car. We wouldn't think of buying the first car we see in the showroom, even if the dealer does happen to be located next door. We investigate, compare, evaluate, and finally choose the type of car we want. Then we search out and negotiate the best deal we can get, often talking to more than one dealer.

Probably because of the general mystique associated with banks and money, we seldom follow the same selection procedures when choosing a bank. Far too often we choose a bank because it is close, or because we know the name. More often than not, we choose a bank simply because we are happy to get a loan from any bank and jump at the first opportunity. Nine times out of ten, this results in higher costs and less desirable payback terms than need have been the case. Invariably, it also leads to disagreements with the bank and a falling-out. Then it becomes extremely difficult to interest another bank in making loans.

The following checklist/questionnaire, which I have used many times as a consultant for small businesses, shows the type of questions that should be answered satisfactorily before signing up with any bank:

Bank Ownership/Structure
1. Is the bank's stock publicly traded?
2. Who owns controlling blocks of shares?

3. Is the ownership foreign or American?
4. Is the bank licensed by the federal government or by a state?
5. Are deposits covered by the FDIC?
6. What is the current capital-to-assets ratio?
7. What is the current tangible common equity ratio?
8. What are nonperforming loans as a percentage of total loans outstanding?
9. What was the current year's loan loss provision?
10. What is the dividend record over the past three years, including the current year?
11. What percentage of outstanding loans are to foreign governments?
12. What percentage of outstanding loans are secured by real estate?
13. Will the bank provide financial statements for the prior three years?

Services Offered

14. Does the bank offer the following types of loans:
    a. Operating line of credit? Secured by receivables? Unsecured?
    b. Term loans for machinery, equipment, vehicles? For what period?
    c. Real estate mortgage? For what period?
15. What interest rates does the bank charge for each type of loan?
16. How much down payment is required for term loans and mortgages?
17. Does the bank handle leases for equipment and autos? For what period?
18. Does the bank have an international department?
19. Does the bank have a finance company or an asset-based-lending division?
20. Does the bank have an investment banking division or a Small Business Investment Company (SBIC)?
21. What short-term investment instruments are available? Overnight repos? Eurodollar accounts? Weekly certificates of deposit?
22. What are the monthly service charges?

Location/Correspondents

23. What branches are nearby?
24. Where are loan officers located?
25. What regional banks are correspondents?
26. What money-center banks are correspondents?

Loan Policies/Portfolios

27. Will the bank provide working capital loans for a business start-up? On what terms?
28. What is the smallest loan the bank will make for a start-up?
29. How much equity do you have to have for a start-up?
30. What type of personal guarantees are required? Cosigners?
31. How high will the bank go for an operating line?
32. Does the bank provide business acquisition funding?
33. Will the bank loan against an SBA guarantee? On what terms?

Customers/References

34. What other accounts does the bank have in the same industry?
35. What experience does the loan officer have in this industry?
36. What percentage of the loan portfolio is dedicated to small-business accounts?
37. Which other businesses in the area use this bank?
38. Will the bank provide three references from other customers?

Banking Language

The banking industry has its own vocabulary (apparently designed to confound nonbankers), adding a level of complexity to relatively simple transactions. Unfamiliar terminology often leads borrowers to agree to rules and conditions that they completely misunderstand.

Some of these terms are clearly necessary to describe instruments, situations, and conditions unique to banking. Others seem to have been concocted to encase banking in a cloak of mysticism, thereby elevating the industry above the mundane business world. Not dissimilar to special terminology devised by lawyers, physicians, and other professionals, many complex banking terms describe simple, everyday events.

As a starting point, bankers speak of four stages of business finance—*seed money, first stage, second stage,* and *third stage.* Funding the acquisition of a going business is often referred to as *acquisition financing*.

Seed money refers to the cash required in the preliminary stages of starting up a business. Typically, amounts run less than $20,000. Budding entrepreneurs require seed money to build a model or prototype of a new product, with the expectation of bringing it to market. Seed money buys materials, pays rent and utilities, and funds market research. Except in unusual cases, banks do not make loans for seed money without ironclad guarantees of repayment from a third party, such as the SBA.

First-stage financing is used to actually start a business. It may be used to meet payroll and other operating expenses, to purchase materials, or to acquire machinery, equipment, tools, and facilities for the production of products or services. First-stage financing occurs after a product or service has been selected and preliminary market research completed.

Second-stage financing relates to raising capital for expansion beyond the initial start-up phase. Perhaps a company needs an additional building for a new production line or inventory storage, or as a distribution warehouse. Second-stage financing also funds the purchase of additional equipment, machinery, or delivery vehicles. Rapidly increasing sales might necessitate a larger line of credit. Maybe a company needs financing to manage an export program.

Second-stage financing is frequently used to refinance original loans from the first stage, converting short-term debt to longer terms. Typically, second-stage financing occurs between the second and fifth years after a company begins business. Beyond five or six years, the company should be firmly established, and any further financing is then referred to as third-stage.

Third-stage financing usually involves larger amounts than either first- or second-stage. A company might decide to float a public stock issue to raise equity capital for liquidating debt. It could use third-stage financing for establishing an overseas facility.

Third-stage capital also finances the acquisition of another business, branch plants, or warehouses. It funds the replacement or upgrading of machinery and equipment. It provides the cash to make major facilities renovations. Third-stage financing is nearly always related to major expansions, refinancing, or very expensive purchases of hard assets. At this stage, a company should not have to go to the capital markets for additional working capital, except for overseas start-ups.

In order to intelligently assess the desirability of entering into bank agreements, and in fact to judge the advisability of even doing business with a specific bank, a person needs a basic understanding of banking vernacular. Literally hundreds of special bank terms will never be used by businesspeople and therefore should not be relevant. Some, however, must be used to communicate with bankers. The following sections define the most widely used, and the most widely confused, banking terms that you are likely to come in contact with when frequenting the mystical world of business finance.

Bank Instruments

A *bank instrument* is merely a document or agreement that evidences a specific indebtedness. U.S. Treasury bonds, preferred stock, common stock, corporate bonds, and corporate debentures are examples of well-known instruments of indebtedness used by the U.S. government and the business community. Here are descriptions of four bank instruments that may not be as familiar.

Demand Note

A *demand note* (also called a *promissory note*) is a document evidencing a company's promise to pay a bank a specific amount of money (principal) and interest. It may also specify the date or dates upon which such money principal and interest are to be paid. But in all cases, a demand note specifies that the entire loan must be paid back on demand by the bank. In other words, regardless of any mutually agreed-upon due date, the bank has the right to call for the entire payment of the note at any time it wishes, unilaterally, without the consent of the borrower.

Letter of Credit

A *letter of credit (L/C)* is a popular bank instrument used extensively in international trade. An L/C states that the bank has granted the holder of the document an amount of credit equal to the face amount of the L/C. In international trade, the holder of the L/C presents it along with other authenticating documentation to the drawer's bank and demands payment of the face amount.

Domestically, letters of credit may be used as a guarantee that the payee will perform an act or make a payment. An L/C used in this manner is called a *standby L/C*. The term *standby* means that the holder cannot draw against the L/C unless the payee fails to perform or pay as agreed upon by contract. The construction industry uses standby L/Cs in lieu of surety bonds. Standby L/Cs are also frequently used to guarantee a revenue bond issue or to secure loans from money-center banks.

Junk Bond

During the 1980s, many companies large and small raised capital for third-stage financing by issuing junk bonds in a public offering. The term *junk bond* identifies corporate bonds that credit rating agencies determine to be below investment grade. Such bonds represent a very high risk for investors. Junk bonds are seldom secured by any collateral. Because investors view them as a very high-risk investment, junk bonds normally must carry a very high interest rate to attract buyers.

Bankers' Acceptance

A *bankers' acceptance (BA)* is a time draft countersigned or *accepted* by a bank. Both documentary and clean BAs are used extensively in export trade as evidence that bank credit has been extended. Bankers' acceptances can be discounted. This means that when they are presented by the drawer, the bank actually pays less than the face amount of the draft. This reflects the market discount plus the bank's acceptance commission. In the past, BAs have not been used widely in the United States. However, given the increasing number of foreign banks doing business in this country that do use BAs, competitive forces undoubtedly will encourage American banks to use them as well.

Types of Loans

Once again, most businesspeople are very familiar with the standard types of bank loans, such as mortgages, lines of credit, installment loans, and so on. New terminology that has evolved during the past ten years that might not be so familiar includes *revolver, term loan, mezzanine loan,* and *nonperforming loan.*

Revolver

No, a revolver is not a gun—although many businesspeople believe that bankers use it as such! A revolver is a short-term loan secured by receivables and inventory. The term *revolver* was coined because as the loan secured by one customer's account is paid off from the collection of that account, another loan automatically takes its place with the next shipment, secured by a new customer receivable. Individual loans against shipping invoices and collections keep revolving, so that the outstanding loan balance continually changes. Exactly the same principle applies to loans secured by inventory.

Term Loan

Loans granted for a specific period of time, generally beyond one year, are frequently called *term loans*. When refinancing, short-term revolvers often get converted to three- to five-year term loans. Typically, term loans provide for monthly or quarterly payments of principal and monthly payment of interest. Interest rates on term loans generally run two to three percentage points above those on revolvers. Long-term assets secure term loans.

Mezzanine Loan

Used principally for financing the acquisition of a going business, *mezzanine loans* bridge the gap between term loans and equity contributions. Mezzanine debt is considered temporary, with terms of from one to three years. Within that time frame, the borrower is expected to either pay off the loan or refinance it with another term loan. Interest rates on mezzanine loans normally run one to two percentage points above those on term loans. The loan may be secured by a second position on long-term assets, or it can be unsecured.

Nonperforming Loan

The term *nonperforming loans* applies to a bank's balance sheet. A loan falls into this category if interest payments are more than ninety days in arrears. Federal regulators require that these loans be classified as high risk and provisioned against. Once a loan is classified as nonperforming, the bank may not accrue interest income from it.

Loan Security

Very few smaller businesses can borrow money without offering some type of collateral against the loan. After all, a bank's primary concern is to have the loan repaid. To ensure this, banks normally require borrowers to secure loans with assets whose value is at least equal to the balance of the loan, and in many cases greater.

Liquid or Soft Assets

A bank can readily convert *liquid assets* or *soft assets* into cash in the event that a borrower defaults. Such assets typically include current receivables, raw materials and finished goods inventory, cash in bank accounts, certificates of deposit and other short-term bank instruments, and marketable securities. Liquid assets secure short-term debt due within one year, such as revolvers.

Hard Assets

Machinery, equipment, buildings, land, automobiles, furniture, and fixtures are considered *hard assets*. Hard assets cannot be readily converted into cash by a lender. In the event of default, the lender must sell these assets to recoup a loan balance. Hard assets typically secure term loans, mezzanine loans, installment loans, and other long-term debt. Because hard assets can depreciate in value over time, lenders frequently demand that, at the execution of the loan documents, the market value of hard assets exceed the loan balance.

Cross-Collateral

The term *cross-collateral* applies to assets of one company used to secure a loan to another company. If the borrowing company defaults on its loan payments, the lender can seize the assets of the second company as satisfaction. This typically occurs when both companies have common ownership. In the case of small businesses owned by one or two shareholders, cross-collateralization may be used to tie up both the assets of the company borrowing the money and the personal assets of its shareholders. To perfect a claim, the lender files a lien against the assets of all parties under the Uniform Commercial Code (UCC).

Guarantees

Banks often insist on additional collateral for a loan in the form of *third-party guarantees*. If a borrower defaults, the lender looks to the guarantor to repay the balance of the loan. It is not unusual for a lender to file a UCC lien against the assets of the guarantor as well as those of the borrower. A third-party guarantor may be a business owner or shareholder personally, a spouse, a relative or friend of the owner, another company, or a third-party financial institution, such as the SBA or another bank. Obviously, to have any value, the guarantee must be supported by assets sufficient to liquidate the defaulted loan.

Interest Rates

In the United States, interest rates are usually based on the *prime rate*. The interest rate on short- and long-term loans is quoted as *prime plus so many points*. The rate may be fixed; that is, the interest rate established at the execution of the loan remains the same over the term of the loan, regardless of what happens to prime. The rate may also be variable; that is, it varies with prime, based on a point spread established when executing the loan.

Prime Rate

Bankers define the *prime rate* as the rate of interest they charge their best commercial customers. They claim that they base this rate on a complicated cost formula that takes into account the bank's cost of money (interest it pays out), its operating expenses (salaries, supplies, telephone, etc.), and its occupancy expense (rent, depreciation, and so on). Theoretically, this cost, plus a reasonable profit margin, equals the prime rate.

But this is not true. Money-center banks (and some large regional banks) establish a fictitious interest rate called prime, based on what the traffic will bear. All correspondent banks around the country then follow suit, regardless of what their specific cost structure may be. Obviously it doesn't cost a bank in rural Wyoming as much to operate as a bank in midtown Manhattan. Yet they both use the same prime measure to establish interest rates.

It should be clearly understood that the Federal Reserve Bank does *not* set the prime rate. The Fed has nothing to do with it. The prime rate is established by money-center banks as a measuring base against which to calculate customer interest charges.

Basis Points

One hundred *basis points* are equal to one percentage point of interest. Basis points are used to describe the market in corporate bonds. The phrase "spread over Treasuries" is used by bond issuers and traders to discuss the bond market. They measure the rate earned or charged by the number of basis points over a comparable maturity U.S. Treasury benchmark security. Companies utilizing municipal revenue bonds pay interest based on basis points plus or minus interest percentages against the prime rate.

LIBOR

The London Interbank Offered Rate, referred to as *LIBOR*, is the European equivalent of the U.S. prime rate, although it is not calculated the same way. LIBOR represents the base lending rate between banks in the London Eurocurrency market. With increasing frequency, the globalization of the financial system is forcing U.S. lenders to quote interest rates based on LIBOR rather than on prime. Generally, LIBOR runs slightly less than prime. Borrowers approve of LIBOR because it represents an actual rate charged by one bank to another bank, not a fictitious estimate.

Other Banking Terms

A few other banking terms might cause confusion. Since the financial community continually originates new phrases, words, terminology, and concepts, it is impossible to stay current with the entire spectrum. Some terms, however, are so universally used that it helps to have a basic understanding of what they mean.

Leveraging

Everyone has heard of leveraged buyouts, or LBOs. A business or an individual uses a small amount of equity as a down payment to buy a company. Using the target company's assets as collateral, loans make up the difference in the purchase price. The theory behind an LBO is that the company's earnings can then be used to repay the loan, thus *leveraging up* or increasing the value of the owner's equity contribution. Most of us practice leveraging when we buy a house or condo with a small down payment and a mortgage. As the mortgage gets paid down and the value of the dwelling appreciates, our equity multiplies geometrically.

Working Capital

Accountants define *working capital* as current assets less current liabilities. In business finance, a working capital loan is used to fund increases in receivables and inventory purchases as the business grows. Cash must be expended before sales can be collected, and working capital loans provide the bridge. Working capital loans can be revolvers or lines of credit.

Globalization

Globalization is a relatively new term in banking circles that has come into use as a result of the growth in international trade. Money flows freely across national borders. As companies expand overseas, they need to finance this expansion with local funds. Globalization provides the means to do this. In simple terms, globalization is the process of linking financial markets in different countries into a common, worldwide pool of funds to be accessed by both borrowers and lenders. Foreign banks operating in the United States bring globalization to our doorstep.

Debt-to-Equity Ratio

One of the favorite ratios used by banks to judge the safety of a loan is a company's *debt-to-equity ratio*. The higher the debt-to-equity ratio (that is, the more debt a company has relative to its net worth), the less secure the loan. Smaller companies should try to keep this ratio at no more than one dollar of net worth for every three dollars of debt. Although lenders prefer a lower ratio, most will consider a loan if the resultant ratio hovers around 3 to 1. In the past, LBOs frequently created debt-to-equity ratios closer to 9 to 1!

That covers the most confusing bank terminology that you are likely to run into. The next two chapters deal with the mechanics of getting a bank loan.

Chapter 6

Getting Through the Bank's Door

The first lesson a prospective borrower must learn is that there is nothing magical or mysterious about banks or bankers. Banks are businesses, just like General Electric, Ford, IBM, and Kmart. Banks are in business to make a profit, just like any company in a market economy. They have shareholders who must be satisfied with their investments. They have boards of directors who set bank policy. They have strategic growth objectives, just like other companies. And the officers and employees of banks make good and bad business decisions, just like anyone else in the business community. There is nothing unique about the banking industry, except that it must operate in a regulated environment under rules laid down and monitored by federal agencies.

Because this is a regulated industry, bankers are not free to make business decisions based on judgment and experience as officers in other industries do. In fact, bankers have unique ways of judging the viability of a business transaction that differ markedly from those used in other industries.

It seems ironic that we spend days, maybe weeks, researching the best deal when buying a car and then fall apart when it comes to negotiating a bank loan. The self-professed mystique created by bankers tends to throw us for a loop, and we end up taking any loan amount and terms offered. Yes, bankers do use a different set of criteria for making a business decision from those used by other business managers, but if we understand where bankers are coming from and the criteria they apply, we should be as tough when negotiating a loan as we are when negotiating for the purchase of a car.

This chapter should take the mystery out of dealing with banks by laying out the major criteria bankers use to evaluate loan applications. We will also sort out the level of importance that banks attach to each criterion and identify specific sales tactics that bring the best results. Chapter 7 explains how to prepare your loan application package to ensure the greatest success when you apply for a bank loan.

Loan Criteria

Every bank weighs the merits of a loan against its current portfolio requirements and against other elements peculiar to that specific bank at that specific time. However, all banks attach a high priority to the following eight factors:

1. Relationship between the bank and the applicant
2. Management ability of the business owner
3. References from other banks
4. Collateral to secure the loan.
5. Amount of equity capital
6. Cash flow to repay the loan
7. Credit history
8. Economic trends

If each of these elements is positive, you can be assured of getting practically any amount of capital you need from virtually any financial institution in the country. Conversely, low scores in more than one category nearly always mean rejection.

Relationships

Even though banks rent a product, money, and therefore are not strictly a service business, most bankers like to think of themselves as selling services. This mentality is relevant to a borrower because, as in any service business, personal relationships between the buyer and seller often determine whether a business transaction closes.

Make no mistake: Your company is not a buyer when applying for a bank loan. It is a seller. A sales campaign must be mounted early

enough to lay the groundwork for the loan. And as in any sales campaign, direct, one-on-one relationships between seller and buyer usually result in the best opportunity for making the sale.

Of the eight primary loan criteria, the strength of the relationship
between borrower and lender stands head and shoulders above the rest.
Irrational as it may appear, if a banker likes you and feels comfortable
with you, shortfalls in other criteria are often overlooked, or at least
minimized. That being the case, it makes sense to get on the good side
of bankers long before you need their money.

Romance them. Take them to ball games. Ask them out for lunch.
Show interest in and compassion for their personal lives. Bend over
backwards to make the relationship a positive force.

Other tactics can be just as powerful. The following have been
used successfully time and time again, but they must be done long
before applying for a loan.

Borrow When You Don't Need the Money

We all know the common maxim: *When you don't need money,
banks are eager to lend it. When you do need it, they are nowhere to be
found.* That being the case, establish a record before you need the
money. If you plan to start a business, take out a small loan at least six
months before the start-up. Use a car, CDs, or some other personal
asset as collateral. If you are already in business, borrow against your
company's assets.

In either case, be sure to pay the loan back in full before you need
a legitimate loan. This establishes a lender/debtor relationship and
gives a banker confidence that you do, in fact, fulfill your obligations.

Give the Bank Financial Statements

Bankers love to look at balance sheets and income statements.
Volunteer your company's financial statements from last year or last
month. Explain any unusual items. Clarify any apparent problem areas.
A forecast for next year also helps.

If your business is relatively new, volunteer a personal financial
statement that shows your assets and liabilities. Giving a banker financial statements well in advance of needing a loan accomplishes two

purposes: It shows that you have nothing to hide and are in fact a solid citizen, and it demonstrates that you know the value of financial statements and how to read them.

Hire a Public Accountant and a Lawyer Known by the Bank

Hiring outside accountants and lawyers when you really don't need them costs money. On the other hand, it clearly demonstrates that you value professional assistance, and bankers love to see that. Ask your banker for recommendations; it will boost his or her ego. Try to ferret out which CPA or lawyer the bank feels comfortable with. Conversely, find out from CPAs and lawyers what they think of the bank. If you are already in business, a certified audit increases a bank's confidence that you care about good internal controls—which they also love to see.

Management Ability

Although finance companies know how to liquidate assets and seldom hesitate to foreclose when borrowers default, commercial banks are different. They are not equipped to liquidate a company's assets and therefore avoid foreclosure whenever possible. For this reason, bankers regard the strength of your background and that of any management personnel in your company as crucial to the decision process. Banks want to be as certain as possible that the people in charge can, in fact, manage the business and do everything in their power to pay back the loan.

If you are a capable manager with years of experience, I'm sure this won't pose any problem for you. Company financial statements, market acceptance of products or services, and competitive position provide good indications of your managerial capabilities. The bank can rest assured that your technical and managerial acumen has already been proven.

Starting a new company or acquiring a going business requires a different tack. Prior employers may be asked to verify your management abilities. If you have owned other businesses, customers or suppliers may be asked to substantiate your credentials. If you are coming from the professions or the education field, proving technical proficiency should be a snap. Professional recognitions such as engineering or accounting certification or scientific awards provide concrete evidence.

Regardless of how you do it, you must satisfy the bank that your business will be professionally managed, and that therefore the loan will be repaid. References carry more weight than any other element for verifying management ability.

References

Without solid references, you won't get to first base with a bank. The best ones come from other bankers. References from business associates and professionals are also helpful, especially if the bank knows them. References are especially important for building relationships with a bank that you haven't done business with before. References don't have to be elaborate—just enough to show the banker that you are reliable, honest, and, hopefully, a capable manager. The best references come from other banks with which you have done business, preferably by borrowing money and paying it back. This gets tricky, however, and invariably raises the question, Why not get the loan from the bank with which you already have a good relationship?

Bankers are sensitive to loan shoppers. They like to feel that once a relationship has been established, you will never seek loans elsewhere. Soliciting a new bank raises a red flag. A loan officer immediately assumes that something went wrong with your first relationship. This can easily kill any chances for a new loan.

You might try one of two possible approaches to get around this problem, depending on your relationship with the first bank. The best way is to ask the first bank to explain in the reference letter why it cannot consider your new loan request. An explanation such as a full portfolio, different location, or the wrong type of loan satisfies most bankers.

A second, but less preferable, way is to explain to the new bank why you would rather do business with it than with the first bank. This can backfire, however. Solid relationships still get top billing, and bankers are suspicious of anyone who is changing banks because of personality clashes or policy disagreements.

Reference letters should also be obtained from owners of other businesses, business partners, or anyone known to the bank or whose reputation can be verified. These are basically character references. References from CPAs, lawyers, investment advisers, or anyone in a financial services business or a profession carry the most weight.

Collateral

Collateral is next in order of importance. Banks always look first at the security of their loans. They want to be certain of getting their money back. Federal bank examiners regard adequate collateral as a top priority in judging a bank's financial stability. Liquidity problems in the banking industry can be directly attributed to nonperforming loans to foreign governments, commercial real estate developers, and leveraged buyouts that were made without sufficient collateral. It stands to reason that banks that have been burned once won't let it happen again.

However (and this is something no banker will admit), once interest rates paid on certificates of deposit and money market accounts plummeted, and the spread between bank lending and borrowing rates widened significantly, many banks accumulated a substantial amount of cash reserves. Since banks would rather earn 10 percent or more on commercial loans than 5 or 6 percent on U.S. Treasuries, bank coffers once again opened wide. In their haste to lend their vast cash reserves, many banks have granted loans based on the same kind of subpar collateral that they accepted in the 1980s. However, when inflation begins to pinch again, you can be assured that banks will repeat their performance of the early 1990s and tighten their credit reins.

Although banks earn a good portion of their income from loans, the profit motive takes second place to getting their money back. This is the primary difference between banks and other businesses in a free enterprise system. Profit motivates everyone else. Loan repayment motivates banks. Regardless of the profitability of your business, without adequate collateral, forget about getting a loan from a commercial bank. This more than any other factor spawned the venture capital industry and the junk bond market, and allowed foreign banks to gain a strong foothold in the United States.

What does a bank regard as sufficient collateral? For working capital loans, banks accept receivables less than ninety days old, easily resalable raw material inventory, and marketable finished products. For term loans, they require hard assets—machinery, equipment, vehicles, buildings, and land. Banks make loans based on a percentage of the cash that they estimate they can recover from an asset sold during a forced liquidation.

For instance, banks commonly lend 80 to 85 percent of the face amount of qualified receivables and 20 to 40 percent of the resale value of qualified inventory. Against hard-asset collateral, the amount of the loan is based on approximately 60 to 80 percent of the cash banks could get if forced to sell the collateral at an auction.

Capital

Banks regard capital as the amount of equity an owner or shareholders have in a business. This capital compared to the amount of the loan results in the debt-to-equity ratio described in Chapter 3. During the last decade, many financial institutions made acquisition loans against very little equity, frequently without any equity from the buyer. Now times have changed. Today, most commercial banks lend a maximum of three times the amount of capital in a business.

The more capital you commit to the business, the more amenable a bank will be. Bankers believe that if, and when, the business gets into trouble, a significant amount of personal capital committed to the business will prevent the owner or other shareholders from walking away and defaulting on the loan. Banks also believe that significant capital in a business makes the filing of a bankruptcy petition much less likely.

Banks frequently require additional capital for first-stage and very often for second- and third-stage financing. This usually takes the form of personal guarantees or pledges of personal assets. Of course, banks hope they will never have to collect against these assets. But they also believe that, psychologically, an owner or shareholder is more committed to repaying the loan if personal assets are in jeopardy.

If you don't have sufficient personal assets to satisfy the bank, co-guarantors or pledges of personal assets by relatives or other third parties may be necessary. Banks want as much of a commitment as possible, regardless of the source. The more they can get, the happier they are. And, of course, the more collateral they can show the bank examiner, the less criticism they endure.

Cash Flow

The projected cash flow of the business is the third area a bank looks at in determining the likelihood of repayment. Even though a bank has liens against all assets of the company, personal guarantees from the owners and perhaps others, and liens against an owner's personal assets, a loan will not be made unless the bank is comfortable that the company has enough free cash to repay the loan and interest when due.

A bank defines free cash as *the amount of cash remaining in a company's bank account after all expenses and obligations are paid*, excluding salaries or draws to owners/shareholders and debt service payments. Compensation to owners and shareholders is excluded because banks expect to get paid before anyone else takes money out of the company. If cash flow projections show sufficient free cash to make debt service payments, banks don't care what you do with the balance.

Cash flow projections come from a formal set of financial statements—balance sheets and income statements—projected into the future over the term of the loan. When you apply for a loan, a cash flow projection becomes an integral part of the financing plan, as described in Chapter 7. Of course, projections always change. Therefore, after granting a loan, banks expect borrowers to furnish updated versions of cash flow projections periodically to enable constant monitoring of the progress of the business.

Banks are extremely conservative when judging the likelihood of loan repayments. When applying for a loan, don't expect a bank to believe your projections. Banks always reduce projected cash flow by some factor, ranging from 20 to 60 percent. The best way to keep this discounting to a minimum is to base your cash flow projection on the current cash being generated. From this base, assumptions can be made concerning increased volume or improved margins that should result from the new loan.

Regardless of the procedure used, banks rarely believe what loan applicants present. Therefore, always ask for more money than you really need. Banks need some point to negotiate down from. Recognizing this in the beginning saves a lot of time and increases the chances of getting what you need.

Credit History

Assuming that you can provide sufficient collateral, have enough capital committed, and can show a significant cash flow, and assuming that your banker feels that you can run the business according to your projections, the next hurdle will be credit history. Credit ratings play second fiddle to the other criteria—unless you have been through a personal or business bankruptcy. Then, all of a sudden, credit history becomes the dominant criterion.

Although a primary objective of bankruptcy laws is to restructure a company's debt to give the company a second chance, banks don't look at it that way. From a bank's perspective, there is no such thing as a second chance for borrowing money. If a person or company has defaulted once, banks assume that it could happen again. Even though bankruptcy laws give secured creditors precedence over all others (including wages owed employees and taxes due the U.S. government), and even though adequate collateral ensures that banks very seldom lose a penny in a bankruptcy filing, the stigma still exists. This stigma is very difficult, if not impossible, to overcome. If you have a bankruptcy blemish on your personal credit history or on your company's, don't even try to get a loan from a commercial bank, regardless of how successful you may have been since it happened.

One way around this hurdle is to transfer the ownership of your company to outsiders—friends, business associates with a clean record, distant relatives, even a trust. Taking this route also means placing the official management of the company in other hands, although from a practical perspective, you still run the company. To be honest, however, most business owners, or entrepreneurs just starting out, who have endured a bankruptcy have more success raising capital from sources other than commercial banks.

Unless you have a bankruptcy on your records, credit history doesn't mean too much. You can be a slow payer to suppliers and government agencies and still get a loan, provided you have good explanations. The only nonbankruptcy stigma that is impossible to overcome is a previous default on a bank loan, regardless of which bank held the paper. Once again, banks believe that if you defaulted once, you could again. Since prior bank reference letters are practically a necessity, defaults will be readily revealed regardless of what a credit bureau report shows.

Economic Conditions

The final bank criterion involves current and near-term projected economic conditions. Although bankers may not be astute economists, they do read the newspaper. They also listen carefully to prognostications from the Fed.

Three economic conditions affect a bank's willingness to loan money: the current status of the banking industry, the condition of the general economy, and the trend in the borrower's industry. The first set of conditions, the current status of the banking industry, takes precedence.

With the relaxation of federal regulations, banks expanded into a variety of financial services that they had previously avoided. Unfortunately, they expanded into these services without sufficient knowledge of the markets. Banks acquired or started asset-based lenders, Small Business Investment Corporations (SBICs), mortgage lending departments, international departments, investment banking divisions, credit card divisions, and a variety of other financial service offshoots from pure commercial banking. Some banks succeeded admirably in mastering the techniques and management procedures of these new ventures. Others have been notably unsuccessful.

One fallout of this expansion was not foreseen in most of the banking community: that economic factors affecting these new ventures differ from those influencing commercial banking activities. Strict federal regulations and the FDIC insulate banks from violent economic swings as long as they stay in their traditional businesses. But with expansion, economic curves affecting property values, business profitability, the stock market, international exchange rates, and a variety of other conditions that affect other businesses suddenly hit bankers where it hurt—in their balance sheets.

These new economic pressures, not the least of which was the increased emphasis by the Fed on capital requirements, had an enormous effect on bank loan policies. As unprotected loan losses resulted from businesses that bankers little understood, the industry scrambled to return to more traditional activities. Many banks have either closed or are in the process of selling the offshoot businesses they acquired over the past decade. Finance companies, investment banking divisions, and mortgage loan portfolios are rapidly finding new homes.

As this trend continues, the banking industry is once again becoming a protected monopoly. Nevertheless, it still behooves you to be careful to choose a bank that will survive and meet your long-term capital needs. Regardless of collateral, relationships, references, or other criteria, a bank in the throes of severe economic contraction will not be interested in extending small-business loans. Economic conditions in the general economy and in the borrower's industry are also important, but certainly not as critical as the economic vicissitudes of the banking industry. When the country or your region falls into a recession, banks become more choosy about loan collateral. They want a higher capital base and a tighter debt-to-equity ratio. And projected cash flow receives much closer scrutiny.

An industry on the skids has little chance of near-term growth. This makes borrowing from a bank practically impossible. You are much better off either waiting for the cycle to turn or raising capital from nonbank sources.

Approaching a Bank for a Loan

Regardless of how good relationships with a bank may be, it is always best to be totally prepared when first applying for a loan. First impressions are important when borrowing money, even more than in normal business activities. Knowing whom you will be meeting and the position the loan officer holds in the bank hierarchy makes a good starting point.

Know the Loan Officer

If at all possible, try to get an appointment with at least a senior vice president of the bank. If you use a branch bank, the branch manager will have to do. It's important to know what authority the loan officer has in the loan approval process. Lower-echelon loan officers merely shuffle paper. They meet with a prospective borrower, make sure all the paperwork gets completed, and then pass the loan application package further up the ladder for review and approval (or rejection). Some banks use loan committees to make the final decision. Others delegate this authority to a senior bank officer.

When you deal with lower-echelon bankers, all the work of establishing a good relationship is wasted. Decisions are made higher up by people you have never met who don't know you from the next applicant. Some bank officials estimate that under these conditions, more than 75 percent of loan applications get turned down. Without a personal relationship, loan decisions will be made purely on the numbers, and very frequently the numbers cannot tell the whole story.

A second problem arises when you have made efforts over a period of time to establish a good rapport with a banker, only to learn when you apply for a loan that the banker has moved on to a new assignment or to a different branch office. Personnel turnover in the banking industry is phenomenal. Six to twelve months in one job seems to be about the average tenure, except for top executives.

Bank executives argue that relationships should be established with a bank, not with a specific banker. That's great in theory, but it just doesn't work. How can anyone establish a personal relationship with a corporation? High personnel turnover and dealing with low-echelon loan officers without decision-making authority are two of the greatest drawbacks in trying to do business with a bank. There is no easy solution. If you plan to borrow from a bank, the best you can do is research the decision-making status of loan officers and then choose a bank that offers the best internal structure.

Documentation

Notwithstanding the difficulties of dealing with impersonal loan committees, come to the first meeting fully prepared with all the data and documents necessary to move the decision process along. You will have to complete a bank loan application form and probably translate your personal financial statement to the bank's format. Aside from these simple steps, you should have the following documentation on hand:

1. *Reference letters*—at least one from another bank that knows you
2. *Personal financial statement* showing both assets and liabilities
3. *Recent credit report* from a reputable credit agency for both the company and yourself
4. *Financing plan*
5. *Minutes from your board of directors* authorizing the borrowing (if you have a corporation) or a partnership memorandum executed by all partners (if you have a partnership)
6. *Certificate of incorporation and corporate seal* if you run a corporation, or a partnership agreement for a partnership
7. *Complete documentation of any other outstanding business loans*, including real estate mortgages

Questions Bankers Ask

Coming prepared with complete documentation shows the banker that you are serious about the loan, that you understand what information banks need to make a decision, and that you are, in fact, a professional manager with sound financial acumen. Right away the banker should be alerted that you are not interested in banking platitudes and that you want a quick answer, yes or no.

In addition, complete preparation forestalls a great many useless and time-consuming questions. Unfortunately, regardless of how well prepared a person may be, bankers seem obliged to ask the same questions over and over again. Invariably, bankers ask the following questions:

1. How will you pay the loan back?
2. When will you pay the loan back?
3. What assurances can you give that you will pay it back on time?
4. What evidence can you give that you know how to run the business?
5. Who is your competition, and what are they doing in the market?
6. Why is your business better than the others?
7. How much money can you put in?
8. Will you sign a personal guarantee?
9. What are the assets in your business worth?
10. What collateral can you provide?
11. What are your plans for growing the business in the future?

Will your relationship with a banker be sustained over a long period of time? That's hard to determine. Current bank philosophy stresses the need for and the desirability of long-term relationships, both for the bank and for the customer. Yet banks prevent long-lasting friendships from developing by continually moving personnel around and changing internal policies.

As silly as it might sound, sustaining a relationship with a banker over a period of time has virtually nothing to do with your business or the banker's bank. Sound relationships—those that endure for years and enable a borrower to rely on the banker (and the banker to rely on the borrower)—are based on personal synergy. Time and again, in those rare instances when a banker remains in the same job or at the same location for several years, borrowers fervently broadcast what a great bank they deal with and how wonderful the bank personnel are. Unfortunately, the reverse condition seems to be far more prevalent.

Several years ago, when the small-business segment of my consulting practice was at its peak, I took a poll of more than 275 past and present clients asking what they considered to be the most important elements for staying on the good side of their banker over a period of years. I was surprised at the answers, although I probably shouldn't have been. Overwhelmingly, they gave the following reasons, in this sequence:

1. Belonging to the same golf club, tennis club, or other athletic club
2. Belonging to the same religious denomination
3. Belonging to the same social or civic organizations
4. Having children in the same school
5. Graduating from the same college or graduate school
6. Originally coming from the same home town
7. Sharing the same political views

Monitoring a Loan

Getting a loan in the first place is only half the equation. Keeping your bank happy during the loan payback period is the other half. Because of a bank's preoccupation with recovering its money, expect one or more bank auditors and loan officers to keep close tabs on your business. Frequent audit reviews, meetings with loan officers, submission of financial statements, regular evaluation of cash balances on deposit, and a variety of other yardsticks enable a bank to monitor compliance with loan covenants and at the same time look for warning signals that your business is faltering. If these signals get too strong, count on your bank to get even more involved in your business.

Here are the major signals that raise red flags:

1. Failure to meet debt service payments
2. Being late or hesitant to provide financial statements and other financial data required by the loan agreement
3. Steadily shrinking bank balances
4. Overdrafts and returned checks
5. Turnover of key management personnel
6. Personal financial difficulties of the business owner or principals
7. Hesitancy in accepting or extending social invitations from or to bank officials
8. Inventory levels increasing without corresponding sales increase
9. Reluctance to permit bank auditors and other bank officials to view the property or to examine the company's record

10. Failure to make regular meetings with bank officials
11. Lawsuits against the company
12. A slowdown in accounts payable turnover
13. Slipping accounts receivable collections
14. Large equipment or facilities purchases without prior bank notification
15. Increasing debt-to-equity ratio

If one or more of these conditions occurs, it's best to inform your bank in advance, before it gets the information from other sources. By so doing, at least you have an opportunity to offer logical explanations before your banker forms personal, and often erroneous, judgments. Bankers hate surprises. If they form their own judgments without your input, regardless of the accuracy of their data or their perceived reasons, chances are very high that relationships will quickly deteriorate.

Pros and Cons of Bank Loans

Clearly, you are better off using internally generated cash to grow your business. Interest expense can be an enormous burden and can eat up funds that could be put to more profitable uses. On the other hand, the American free enterprise system has been built on credit. If your company is growing rapidly, chances are good that you won't be able to meet payroll and buy materials without using borrowed money. When that time comes, there are some definite advantages to choosing a commercial bank over other sources of capital. There are also some glaring disadvantages. Here are a few of the big ones—six on the plus side, six on the minus side:

Advantages in Using Bank Loans

1. Banks are conveniently located. Usually a branch will be located down the street from your business, or at least within an easy drive.
2. Banks normally charge lower interest rates than other financial institutions.
3. A good credit rating established through a bank is about as good a reference as you can get anywhere.
4. Banks are easy to locate and, with publicly available financial information, easy to research.

5. Once you are established with a bank, many other services become available (e.g., trust department, payroll preparation, customer credit checks).
6. A commercial bank must be used for financing export sales.

Disadvantages in Using Bank Loans

1. Bankers are notoriously poor businesspeople. Your banker probably won't know anything about your business. Bankers frequently give bad operating advice.
2. Long-lasting personal relationships are nearly impossible because of high bank personnel turnover.
3. Banks demand excessive collateral for loans, including personal guarantees.
4. Banks do not like to lend long-term money.
5. Nearly all bank loan agreements are unilateral. That is, the bank has the right to call the loan on demand, anytime it wants to, regardless of whether or not debt service payments have been made on time.
6. Banks are noncompetitive. With the FDIC in the background, a bank does not have to be managed efficiently to attract customers. Because of pervasive federal regulations, one bank cannot offer significantly different services from another bank.

Although commercial banks remain an important segment of the financial community, they are not the only, or necessarily the best, source of funds. Other financial institutions specialize in different types of loans for various purposes. One common element exists between banks and other financing sources, however: the need to establish and then maintain solid personal relationships. Dealing in money creates a natural distrust between parties. Though this can probably never be completely overcome, honest relationships between creditor and debtor can go a long way toward easing the pain of borrowing and repaying money.

Relationships with Other Financial Institutions

The eight criteria governing loans from commercial banks are not very different from those used by other financial institutions. Yet, there are distinct differences in emphasis. For reasons already stated, commercial banks continue to be the most conservative institutions in the financing spectrum. The responsibility for maintaining public confidence in our entire financial system falls, for better or for worse, on the shoulders of the commercial banking industry. With this responsibility comes a natural conservatism. Although it is not always practiced, it exists nonetheless. Free from this public responsibility, other financial institutions concentrate more on making a profit than on being repaid.

Asset-Based Lenders

Asset-based lenders (sometimes called finance companies), when freed from the yoke of commercial bank parents, fall at the far end of the risk-debt spectrum. These lenders, who are fully capable of foreclosing on and liquidating assets to recoup their investment, charge exorbitant rates for the risks they take. Asset-based lenders focus more intently on the underlying value of asset collateral. They are also more interested in the ability of the business to make money.

Managers of asset-based lenders tend to have a much stronger background in general business management than their commercial bank cousins. Because of this broader background, a different approach must be used to establish working relationships. These can be developed and nurtured only *after the fact*, not months or years *before* making a loan application. As businesspeople, these executives want the relationship to be on a purely business level. They expect to be kept regularly informed of how the business is doing—sometimes weekly. They don't care much for the romancing and the ball games. They don't want to be entertained, but they do want to be treated as professional businesspeople. Being heavy risk takers, asset-based lenders keep a close rein on the operation of the company. The relationship is more of a master/servant arrangement, with the borrower always the servant.

Venture Capital Firms and Small Investment Banks

Venture capital firms and small investment banks deal in equity investments, not loans. They expect substantial appreciation on their investment and a high average annual return. Venture capitalists and investment bankers are themselves businesspeople, not bankers. Most have had experience in a wide range of industries. Their primary interest is in seeing a company grow and eventually become profitable enough to go public.

In addition to making equity investments, venture capital firms and investment banks will, on occasion, provide mezzanine loans to bridge the gap between bank debt and their equity contribution. Because they concentrate on equity, these financiers actually become investors in the company. The relationship is more like a partnership than a purely debtor/creditor arrangement.

Unless a personal friend happens to be a venture capitalist or an executive of a small investment bank, the likelihood of forming a close relationship prior to negotiating a deal is very remote. Once the deal closes, the relationship becomes very close, including shared board decisions. At times, operating decisions will also be made jointly. These financiers know financial statements and pro forma forecasts and expect you to be equally knowledgeable.

Whether you are raising capital from a bank, an asset-based lender, a venture capital firm, or an investment bank, preparation remains the key to success. Those who take the time to prepare a professional-looking financing package and make the effort to anticipate the questions that are inevitably asked always stand a better chance of getting what they need. The following chapter takes you through the next steps of preparing and then presenting a completely documented loan application.

Chapter 7

Preparing to Borrow from a Bank

A bank's decision to accept or reject a loan application is based primarily on the borrower's ability to repay the loan. As a company grows, a clean record of loan payments causes banks to shift gears and place more weight on the business and less on your managerial capability. Although personal assets and individual financial standing remain important, as long as your company is healthy, banks expect it to generate enough cash to repay the loan, and look to you, the owner, and other shareholders only as fallback sources. Each year that a business improves its earnings and cash flow performance, owners and shareholders become further distanced from any repayment obligation. Nevertheless, management ability, personal integrity, and financial stability remain important ingredients for sound bank relations.

Regardless of the financing stage, banks want to see hard facts in addition to these personal attributes. This chapter examines the documentation and supporting evidence necessary to obtain a bank loan.

"The more money you need, the easier it is to get" is a general rule of thumb in the financing game. Naturally, there are exceptions. For example, the Small Business Administration (SBA) has maximum limits beyond which it cannot go. And collateral value must match any size loan. Experience has shown, however, that given the proper collateral, it's much easier to raise $10 million than $500,000, and it's easier to raise $500,000 than $50,000. So if you have an option, go for broke, even if you turn around and quickly repay the excess.

The Financing Package

A financing package consists of assorted documents that, when properly assembled, present a complete picture of the business, the business ownership, and the market. Although the degree of importance attached to each segment varies with the financing stage and with the proposed use of the funds, the same data must be included in all cases.

A financing package consists of two broad sections and several detailed segments within each section. The first section covers material related to the principal shareholders of a business or an entrepreneur who wishes to start or acquire a business. It presents the best possible picture and includes four subheadings:

- Personal background
- Business experience
- Financial status
- Reference letters

The second section covers information about the business under the following subheadings:

- Company structure and history
- Product/service characteristics
- Market status
- Financial performance

Business Owner's Qualifications

Management ability nearly always ranks at or near the top of the priority ladder, especially when the business does not have a track record. Because start-ups are such a high risk, bankers must rely almost exclusively on their perception of the entrepreneur's management ability to produce the product and capture a market. With this in mind, personal background and experience may, in the end, be the most important criterion for judging the desirability of making a loan. And all smart bankers know this.

Personal Statistics

The first item in this section should be a written description of the personal statistics of the business owner or principal shareholders—

residence address and phone number, education (including any academic awards), family status, condition of health, and, even though it smacks of discrimination, age. Whether we like it or not, the financial community continues to harbor traditional misconceptions that must be dealt with head-on at the first meeting.

Banks in different parts of the country and of different sizes hold different prejudices. Some feel that a woman raising children has no business applying for a loan to start a business. Or that an unmarried man or woman represents a higher risk than one who is married. Others feel that a man or woman past the age of fifty-five won't be around long enough to pay the loan back. Still others regard young applicants as lacking the experience necessary to make a business prosper. Even race and religion continue to play a part in some banks' decisions.

On the flip side, in an effort to remain unbiased, many banks have adopted antidiscrimination policies that effectively create reverse discrimination by giving minorities, women, young people, or the elderly preferential treatment.

Obviously, none of these practices are publicized. If they were, the public clamor would cause irreparable damage to the bank's image. Nevertheless, discrimination does exist. To pretend otherwise and try to accomplish something that can't be done only wastes time and money. We may not sanction discrimination, but the fact remains, prejudices do exist. We can't hide from reality.

To prevent wasted time and effort preparing and presenting a financial package, try to discreetly search out how a specific bank regards your unique situation. This is not particularly difficult. After you interview two or three bankers, you'll be able to sense underlying biases. If it looks like you're on a losing track, you might as well be pragmatic about it and search out another bank. Even if you do get a loan despite subtle prejudices, chances are good that you won't have much of a relationship with your loan officer. And, over the long term, that causes problems and a lot of heartache.

Business Experience

Banks also want to know what work experience you have that qualifies you to run this business. A banker looks at work experience from two vantage points: management experience and technical experience. Don't expect a banker to understand the specific talents required to operate your business. It would be pure coincidence to find one with firsthand knowledge of your specialty. However, that doesn't deter them from expecting you to have concrete work experience in the same or a similar type of business, as evidenced by previous jobs, technical certification, expertise in a hobby, or previous ownership of a similar business.

Regardless of the specific type of experience, you must demonstrate both managerial talent and technical capability. If a banker can't be satisfied that you can handle both the managerial and the technical aspects of your new business, you won't get the loan.

Banks also want to know your business objectives. Why do you want to get into this business? What do you hope to accomplish over the next five, ten, or fifteen years? These objectives should clearly reflect a long-term commitment to the business. Banks frown on short-term goals. Many business managers and entrepreneurs fail to attract a bank's interest merely because they misstate their objectives.

The proper answers to these questions are:

1. That you expect to build the business into a viable market competitor
2. That you expect to continue gaining market share
3. That eventually your company will be a major force in the marketplace
4. That you will stay with the company for the rest of your working career (this is the most important answer of the lot)

No banker wants to hear plans for eventually selling the company and reaping large capital gains. That may be a viable personal objective, but never admit it to a bank.

Financial Status

Banks are interested in two aspects of an owner's or a principal shareholder's personal financial status: (1) How much capital will be contributed to the business, and (2) what assets and liabilities the individual owns. The first question is easy. Every business must have some amount of equity capital. Maybe it's only $5,000 or $10,000, but regardless of the amount, banks want it to be a significant portion of your personal cash reserves. From a bank's perspective, the higher the proportion of personal cash and assets committed to a business, the less likely a person will be to throw in the towel and walk away when the going gets tough.

Full financial commitment to the business is absolutely essential. More than any other criterion, an owner's financial commitment determines the likelihood of getting a bank loan. As long as a bank, or any other lender or investor, for that matter, believes that you would suffer substantial personal financial damage if the business were to go under, it will look favorably at the other criteria. But if loan officers don't believe this, then the other criteria mean nothing.

Two types of documentation substantiate financial commitment: (1) a personal statement of financial condition, and (2) personal tax returns. A personal statement of financial condition lists all personal assets at their current market value, and all debts and obligations owed to nonfamily creditors. Later in the chapter we'll take a look at the steps in preparing such a statement.

Tax returns for the previous three years won't verify your cash balances, but they do show the bank how much income you should have coming in. From this, a bank can easily estimate what your cash reserves should be.

References

Although valid references are important for second-stage and occasionally for third-stage financing, they are crucial when you are going after your first bank loan. Include as many quality reference letters as possible from qualified, and preferably well-known, individuals and companies. It won't do any good to get a letter of commendation from your neighbor or friend stating what a great person you are. This goes straight to the trash barrel. On the other hand, reference letters from previous employers attesting to your honesty, integrity, and management acumen can be invaluable, as are references from partners in law firms or national public accounting firms.

Any reference letter you can get from a well-positioned executive in a bank or financial institution counts twice as much. Investment bankers, finance company executives, senior executives from other banks, and officers of securities houses rank the highest.

References from high government officials such as senators, congressional representatives, well-known officials from the executive branch, or governors are always impressive. These individuals may not know you too well, but the mere fact that you have their support adds political clout to your effort.

Establishing Credentials

With the exception of certain professional practices, the reputation of the owner or chief executive officer does not make a company successful. Rather, the company prospers and grows because the marketplace needs and wants its products or services.

Within the financial community, however, such is not the case. Especially in the banking industry, reputation means everything. Although thousands of people work in the industry without ever being recognized as outstanding citizens or possessing extraordinary financial acumen, those who rise to the top attribute their success in no small measure to their unblemished reputation. The same principle holds true when applying for a loan. Establishing a public reputation as an expert in a specific field nearly always eases the way toward favorable action. The big question for most of us is how to establish credentials as an expert in our field.

Certainly, reference letters from others in the same line of work help. But this is not the same as a public reputation. Although there is no sure-fire way to become publicly known, the following seem to work fairly well:

1. Run for public office.
2. Write a book.
3. Speak before a trade group.
4. Appear on a television talk show.
5. Publish articles in a professional journal or trade magazine.
6. Achieve recognition as a community supporter.
7. Teach at a university.
8. Hold office in a trade organization.
9. Start a business newsletter.
10. Speak before a banking or other financial group.

It doesn't seem to make much difference which path you choose. Just do something in the public sphere that attracts attention to your expertise. Even if you can't achieve instant recognition, a copy of a public review of your work included as part of the financing package carries significant weight with most banks, and with other lenders and investors, as well.

Personal Statement of Financial Condition

Every loan application from a company owned by one or a very small number of shareholders includes a personal statement of financial condition and a summary of income sources. Each bank uses a slightly different format, but the content remains the same. It helps if you prepare your own statement of financial condition in a format that emphasizes your best points and include it in the financial package. Most banks will want it redone on their form, but that's just a copying job. The inclusion of such a statement in the financial package immediately demonstrates an understanding of the loan process and impresses bankers.

Figure 7.1 shows the line items in a typical format for a personal statement of financial condition and the accompanying listing of income sources.

Figure 7.1
Statement of Financial Condition
As of date_____

1. **Assets**
    a. Cash in checking and savings accounts
    b. Cash-equivalent investments—CDs, money market accounts, etc.
    c. IRAs, Keogh plan accounts, SEPs, and other retirement accounts
    d. Marketable securities—traded stocks, bonds, mutual funds, etc. (at current market value)
    e. Cash surrender value of life insurance policies
    Total cash and cash equivalents

    f. Investments in privately held companies or public companies whose stock is not traded
    g. Investments in limited partnerships
    h. Investments in commercial or rental real estate (current market value)
    i. Collectibles—stamps, coins, antiques, jewelry, art, etc. (current market value)
    j. Investments in land (current market value)
    k. Other nonliquid investments
    Total nonliquid investments

    l. Residence (current market value)
    m. Second or vacation home, cottage, villa, etc. (current market value)
    n. Automobiles (current market value)
    o. Personal property at estimated market value
    Furniture
    Hobby equipment (e.g., woodworking tools)
    Library
    Boat
    Airplane
    Other personal property
    Total personal property
    p. Other assets
    Total Assets

2. **Liabilities**
   a. Notes and other loans payable to banks (list bank and amount)
      Note 1
      Note 2
      Note 3
   b. Loans against the cash surrender value of life insurance
   c. Current credit card balances
   d. Other bills payable
      Total current debt

   e. Mortgage on residence (current balance and monthly payment amount)
   f. Mortgage on other property (current balance and monthly payment amount)
   g. Loans from family members, friends, etc. (balance and due date)
   h. Other loans, debts, and obligations (list)
      Total liabilities

3. **Net Worth (Equity)** (subtract total liabilities from total assets)

4. **Income**   Monthly   Annual
   a. Interest
   b. Dividends
   c. Pension
   d. Annuities
   e. Rentals
   f. Other investment income
   g. Spouse's wages
   h. Other income   _____   _____
Total income   _____   _____

Note that any salary or drawing account for the business owner or principal shareholders is excluded from the income section. A banker wants to see how much income will be available independent of the business in the event it must be used to repay the loan. Also, the statement of financial condition should not be prepared in an accounting format. Asset values should be listed at their current market value, not at cost. Obviously, some market values will have to be estimated. In those instances, inflate the assets to a reasonable replacement cost.

This statement reflects only personal assets, liabilities, and income. It has nothing to do with the business. Financial statements for your company are included in the business section of the financing package. This section also includes a comprehensive explanation of the business being financed. This section of the package is referred to as a *financing plan*.

Financing Plan

The financing plan has four main sections, each dealing with a separate segment of the business:

- History
- Product/service
- Markets/competition
- Financial

In some cases, especially for third-stage companies, the financing plan incorporates the personal section described above. For first- and second-stage funding, however, banks prefer to keep the two sections separate.

A financing plan describes how the business loan will be used and how it will be repaid. It is also a commitment by the business owner or principal shareholders that the business will be operated in such a fashion that these results will be achieved. Finally, it serves as a documented promise to repay the loan on schedule.

Although a financing plan may be similar to a business plan, several important differences stand out. A financing plan emphasizes the financial performance of the business rather than product or market growth. It accentuates cash flow instead of profitability. A financing plan must be prepared in bank language. It must be conservative enough to ensure a high probability of its being achieved.

Banks, finance companies, venture capitalists, government agencies, and private financial sources each require slight variations in the format of the plan. Variations also apply for loans at different financing stages.

Although the many uses of financing plans preclude a uniform format, the following sections describe those elements that seem to be fairly universal. These elements appear in plans for first-, second-, or third-stage bank financing. If you plan to make a public stock offering, you'll have to use the format prescribed by the SEC.

Financing plans begin with a preamble, a description of how much money you need and what it will be used for. This introductory section highlights products or services offered for sale, market niches that the business serves, how the borrowed money will be used, and one paragraph describing when and how the loan will be repaid. The preamble should be short and succinct. It should give the banker a quick synopsis of the rest of the plan and should be no longer than one page. The next section of the plan, company history, introduces the company in greater detail.

Company History

For a start-up business, there isn't any history except the product development and market research phases. Presumably, however, a company has already been formed, and therefore a complete description of its ownership and capitalization should be set forth. For an S corporation, include the name, relationship, and ownership percentage for each of the shareholders. If the business has been operating for several years, describe any company name changes and variations in ownership percentages. Identify any outstanding debts to banks, to other institutions, or to individuals. Two pages should be more than adequate for this section.

Product/Service

The next section includes a brief description of a company's products or services. Avoid technical specifications, but include enough information to give the banker a reasonable idea of what your company sells. Also include enough market statistics to prove the market demand for the product or service. An elaborate market analysis looks like overkill. Simple statistical trends from government files or trade associations are sufficient.

The most important item in this section is a description of why your particular product or service is better than the rest; that is, why it is unique. Bankers are well aware of the number of new businesses that fail after one or two years. Many times failure results from trying to sell a product or service that does not offer the market anything different from or better than competitors. If you can't come up with a better mousetrap, don't borrow money to bring it to market.

Markets/Competition
Include three subsections in the markets/competition segment:

1. Market size, growth potential, and your company's market share
2. Current and potential new competition
3. Opportunities for export sales or other foreign market penetration

Market size will probably have to be estimated, especially if you are selling into one or more niche markets. Base your estimates on as many factual statistics as possible, however. Most trade associations maintain statistics compiled from member companies, and extrapolations to your niche market shouldn't be too difficult. In addition, the federal Department of Commerce stocks reams of trade information for virtually any Standard Industrial Classification (SIC) code. Don't guess. Base your judgment on statistics that can be verified by the bank.

Once you find a source of information about market size, this same source can usually furnish estimates and projections of market growth, at least at the national level. Obviously you will have to adjust these national projections for local or regional markets. Calculate market share from your sales forecast.

Research your competition very carefully. What companies sell into your market niche? How big are they, and how long have they been in the market? Can you compete on price, or must you rely on service or superior quality? What is the potential for new entrants over the succeeding five years? Don't get into elaborate explanations and analysis. Bankers will never understand it and probably wouldn't read it anyway. Limit the competitive analysis to a few simple and succinct sentences.

Bankers tend to get excited about foreign sales potential. Be sure to include a paragraph stating how you plan to exploit foreign markets over the next five years. Whether you actually plan to do so or not is irrelevant. It looks good.

Financial

The financial section is the part of the financing plan that bankers understand completely, or at least should. If your company has at least two years of operating results, include annual balance sheets and income statements for three years. Annual audits by certified public accountants carry a lot of weight with all banks. Even if you can only get the most recent year audited, it's well worth the money.

Business start-ups, of course, don't have this luxury. You can't do much about this except to include statements for current year-to-date results. Even those you prepare yourself are better than nothing.

Also include business tax returns for the past three years. For unincorporated businesses, this means Schedule C from your personal return. Corporations and partnerships, of course, have their own tax forms.

The second segment of this section is the most important in the entire financing plan. It lays out pro forma, or projected, financial statements for the next five years. This becomes the final proof that the company can generate sufficient cash to repay the loan.

Although you must include balance sheets and income statements, pro forma cash flow schedules are the most important. A start-up company, without history upon which to base projections, must use market size, market growth, and market share projections to arrive at the sales forecast. Other companies can extrapolate from historical data. (See Chapter 4 for a full description of forecasting procedures.)

Packaging the Plan

It's very important to package the plan in the most professional way possible. Showmanship is the essence of any successful sales campaign, and getting a loan requires the same type of sales tactics you use for selling your products. The "right" look goes a long way toward capturing the attention of even the most jaundiced banker.

The financing plan is an integral part of the total presentation but should be packaged separately. Most financing plans should not be more than twenty or twenty-five pages in length. The best and most convenient packaging is a plastic spiral binder of the type used for internal reports. The pages should be numbered, with a table of contents and section dividers. Be sure the front and back covers are laminated.

Quick-print shops have the capability to do this type of binding and lamination for a nominal price. Get about a dozen copies at the beginning. It's a lot cheaper than going back for more later on.

Regardless of the packaging technique, if the financing plan looks professional, it will be regarded with professional interest, and the reception a banker will give the total package will be immeasurably improved. Time and again, bankers peruse a professionally prepared plan cover to cover but immediately discard sloppily prepared plans or those that are poorly presented.

Variations to Financing Plans

The overall content of a financing plan remains the same regardless of the type of business or the amount of the loan. However, emphasizing particular sections can add impetus for certain types of businesses. Whether you are going after first-, second-, or third-stage financing also makes a difference.

Any start-up business should emphasize the uniqueness of the product or service to be sold. The more evidential detail included in this section, the greater the likelihood that a bank will understand why the loan is important to the growth of the business. Competition and marketing plans also carry heavy weight. If you have little or no financial history, it's difficult to convince a bank of the accuracy of pro forma forecasts. They are still an important piece of the plan, but they carry less weight than if the business has been operating for several years.

Conversely, the longer a business has been operating, the more important past performance becomes, and the greater relevance pro forma forecasts assume. Unless you are going after research and development funding, the uniqueness of the product has already been established in the marketplace.

Plans for second-stage financing should stress the need for additional capacity to handle increased business. This means placing greater emphasis on proving the assumptions used to forecast increased sales. Management structure and potential changes in the capability of supervisory and technical personnel also play more important roles.

Banks have a difficult time understanding the need for multiple or tiered corporations. If your business includes more than one corporation, or both corporate and partnership (or limited partnership) structures, take more space in the first section to describe the reasons for this hierarchy.

For manufacturing companies, emphasize employee efficiency, inventory control, and product costs. Service businesses need to stress the technical abilities and skills of both the owner/manager and key employees. If you have a retail business, concentrate on describing pricing, sales promotional efforts, and customer service.

The secret of preparing a winning financing plan is to keep in mind what banks do and don't know about your company and its markets and then emphasize those aspects that could be confusing or misunderstood. Bankers need all the help they can get to grasp the essence of any non-financial business. And, most important, they must feel comfortable that they understand your company well enough to monitor it, or you will never get the loan.

Personal Guarantees

When companies owned by one or a very small number of shareholders apply for loans, most banks insist on personal guarantees as additional collateral. Personal guarantees are always dangerous, but more often than not you won't have any choice. If you do have to execute a personal guarantee, remember that foreclosure procedures against personal assets fall under state laws, not federal. This makes collection against a court judgment significantly more difficult. Therefore, the chances that a bank will ever actually try to collect against a guarantee are very remote. On the other hand, personal guarantees do create a heavy psychological burden.

Personal guarantees come in a variety of forms, depending on the amount of the loan, the liquidity of business assets, and the type and amount of personal assets. Some personal guarantees cover the full amount of the initial loan balance for the entire loan period. Others decline with principal payments. Occasionally a bank limits the guarantee to the estimated liquidation value of personal assets. Some banks require cosigners, such as a spouse, relatives, friends, or a third-party financial institution or government agency.

Most states exempt certain assets from judgment in a default. Unless a spouse cosigns a guarantee, any asset held jointly between spouses—bank accounts, investment securities, automobiles, a residence, personal property, and so on—is usually exempt. Some states allow judgments against the borrower's portion of jointly held assets, but this is almost impossible to collect. Unless the item has substantial value, such as an art collection, jointly held assets tend to be immune. Of course, assets held entirely by a spouse who has not cosigned a guarantee can never be attached under any claim.

There are a few ways to protect your personal assets from banks and other creditors. Transferring title is the best way. Put your share of any jointly held assets exclusively in your spouse's name. Or transfer title to an irrevocable trust with children or other relatives as beneficiaries. Or set up a corporation and transfer assets to it, making sure that other persons—your spouse, children, relatives, friends, or anyone you can trust—have the controlling interest.

A less satisfactory way is to make it so complicated for a bank or other creditor to seize your assets that the cost of doing so would probably exceed the value of the assets. Four popular scenarios are used. Assets can be transferred to

1. Several corporations, each with a different ownership structure
2. Several corporations located in different states
3. Revocable trusts located offshore
4. Offshore corporations in a safe-haven country

If the judgment is large enough and the assets have a high enough value, these methods won't be foolproof. Corporate shields can be pierced by court action. Transfers of assets to revocable trusts can be invalidated under certain circumstances. Most owners of small businesses, however, find these methods sufficient to deter all but the most aggressive creditors.

Gaining the Edge with Banks

If bankers and banks all had the same capabilities and the same loan criteria, it would be a simple matter to come up with a list of action steps to ensure getting your loan. Such is not the case, however. Each banker comes from a different background. Each has different career aspirations. Each possesses a different intellectual capability. Each bank puts different emphasis on each of the criteria. Each bank stresses a different portfolio mix of working capital loans, term loans, mortgages, and other types of income-producing investments. And each bank's capital ratio faces different pressures from regulators.

When Applying for a Loan

Nevertheless, certain approaches seem to work better than others to give borrowers an edge. They are not sacrosanct, and I certainly won't guarantee that following them will ensure the success of your loan application. Generally, however, the following ten simple rules should permit you to be aggressive rather than defensive when dealing with banks:

1. Work hard at establishing a good rapport with a bank official high enough in the organization to have clout. Make the time to get to know your banker and to allow your banker to know you.
2. Build management and technical credentials. Develop a high profile in your industry or a recognizable technical skill.
3. Shop for the right bank. Interview bank officials, examine bank financial statements, and become familiar with bank loan policies.
4. Build a reputation for honesty and integrity with other financial institutions and in your community/industry. Try to get another bank to give you a good reference.
5. Come to the first loan application meeting prepared with a complete, well-documented, professional-looking financing package. Keep it as simple as possible.
6. Demonstrate that you understand your banker's concern about getting the loan repaid. Offer collateral, capital, and guarantees before the banker asks.
7. Know your own business well enough to clearly describe its uniqueness in the marketplace. Thoroughly understand competitors' positions.
8. Always play the "nice guy/gal" role. Be professional in appearance and demeanor.

9. Treat bankers with TLC (tender loving care). Bankers don't expect borrowers to care about their personal and professional well-being. Demonstrate that you are different.
10. Walk away from the deal if it doesn't feel right. Don't beg for a loan or argue with a banker.

Step 3 is especially important. Just as each bank is different, each borrower has different needs. Do enough research to be sure that the financial institution you choose makes the type of loan you need. A lot of time and effort can be wasted trying to get a loan from the wrong source. The right source may or may not be a commercial bank.

Closing the Deal

The second phase of getting a loan is making sure that the provisions of the final loan agreement are ones you can live with. All too frequently, with the euphoria of success clouding our minds, we gloss over the fine print in loan agreements. Invariably this leads to future disagreements with bank officials and major obstacles to sound bank relations. It's not overly difficult to read a contract, but if you don't understand the implications of each provision, get a lawyer to translate.

Over the years I have negotiated many loan agreements for my own businesses and for clients. I have found that abiding by three basic principles seems to be the best way to stay out of trouble:

1. Don't hesitate to state your objections to any of the terms in the agreement at the time they are being negotiated. Banks expect knowledgeable customers to take exception to some of their boilerplate language. Most are willing to make modifications if pressed. Once you execute the agreement, it's too late to disagree.
2. Insist that every condition you agree to be put in writing. When you have a very sound relationship with your bank, during negotiation it's easy to orally agree to clauses or terms. This invariably leads to misunderstandings and problems later on. Personnel turnover in the banking industry is high. Your very friendly banker will probably move on to a different job before the loan is fully repaid. The loan agreement is with the bank, not the banker.

3. Look at the long-term effect that loan provisions will have on your business and on your personal life. You will probably be living with this bank for several years. Even if you desperately need the cash right now, if the covenants might hurt your business next year or beyond, it isn't worth the gamble. Also, be aware of any provisions that affect you personally. Two provisions cause the greatest personal harm: (a) clauses that obligate you personally, or your estate if you die, to pay off the loan balance, and (b) those that restrict the amount of compensation you can withdraw from the business.

Purchasing new equipment, acquiring a going business, implementing a research and development program, or adding another facility can probably be financed more easily and at less cost by using nonbank sources, such as venture capital or public stock issues. Very often better terms and conditions, and higher amounts of capital, are available through these sources than through commercial banks.

Part III
Planning

Chapter 8

Operating Budgets

Strategic plans, business plans, financing plans, forecasts, and budgets all purport to do the same thing: assist you in planning and controlling your business. It's enough to make a person's head spin. Why so many terms for essentially the same thing?

Well, to begin with, the business community, the financial community, the academic community, and the U.S. government all tend to misuse these various planning terms. More often than not, people choose a term they are familiar with and then apply it indiscriminately to all plans. Unfortunately, this doesn't help the non-financial manager who is trying to make sense out of an apparent hodgepodge of financial terminology. Let me try to put this whole planning mess into perspective with some basic definitions that I use in this book (and, I might add, that are used by knowledgeable business planners and analysts), beginning with long-term plans and working down to short-term plans.

1. *Strategic plan.* A strategic plan is a long-term plan. Typically, it looks five years into the future—at times even longer, depending on a company's business cycle. If the cycle is seven or ten years, then the strategic plan should be seven or ten years. Strategic plans lay out a company's long-term objectives in narrative fashion, covering all major activities—markets, products, finances, human resources, and R&D. This narrative is supported by detailed financial forecasts of balance sheets, income statements, and cash flow schedules for each year of the plan. A strategic plan is primarily a working tool for top management and the board of directors to use to set and monitor a company's long-term business. Strategic plans are also

used in the preparation of offering prospectuses for public stock and bond issues.

2. *Business plan.* A business plan covers a shorter period than a strategic plan, typically this year and perhaps next year. It focuses on short-term tactics that can be implemented by middle management personnel. Often, business plans are used as the basis for financing plans given to banks and other financial institutions when applying for loans. However, the most important function of a business plan is as a working tool for top management to use to develop competitive tactics over the short term and then to monitor the performance of the company in achieving these objectives. A business plan includes a lengthy narrative, including the background of the company, marketing plans, operating plans, personnel plans, and financial plans. It also includes financial projections, prepared using the same forecasting techniques used for strategic plans.

3. *Financing plan.* A financing plan is used exclusively to project a company's ability to secure and then to repay loans (from banks and other financial institutions) and equity investments, such as those made by venture capital funds. Designed for readers with a strong financial background, financing plans have a minimum of narrative and focus heavily on financial projections. These projections typically cover three to five years and are prepared using the same forecasting techniques as strategic and business plans. Venture capitalists often ask for your strategic plans as well as a financing plan to give them a more thorough understanding of your objectives and potential for growth.

4. *Forecasting.* Forecasting isn't a plan in the sense of those previously described. It is a technique for projecting the most probable operating results of a company, in a numerical format, over future periods of time. The time periods may be months, quarters, or years. A forecast may be for one accounting period, such as a year, or for many periods, such as five to ten years. Forecasts nearly always include three basic documents: pro forma balance sheets, pro forma income statements, and cash flow schedules. Forecasts are used in all the previously described plans. Forecasts also form the basis for

quantifying business valuations when buying and selling entire businesses or shares in a business, for estate tax purposes, and for many other situations calling for a dollar value to be placed on a business entity.

5. *Operating budget.* An operating budget covers the shortest time period of any plan. It may be for a week, a month, or a year. Operating budgets seldom extend beyond one year, however. A budget is a formal, numerical expression of how a business, or part of a business, should operate over the planning period. Budgets are extremely useful as management tools for planning and controlling small segments of a business, such as departments, cost centers, or functions (like administration). The control feature is probably the most useful aspect of budgets. Actual results for this week, month, quarter, or year can be quantifiably compared with expected performance, allowing management to take corrective action in a short time frame. This is a critical feature of any cost-reduction program, as outlined in Chapter 2. Although some companies try to incorporate sales projections into their budgetary process, cost or expenditure budgets seem to be the most useful in smaller companies. These cost or expenditure budgets are often called *operating budgets* to differentiate them from more comprehensive planning documents.

So much for definitions. I hope that clears up any misunderstanding about planning terminology. Now let's proceed. This chapter covers the common techniques for preparing short-term operating budgets. Subsequent chapters deal with business plans and strategic plans. Forecasting is covered in Chapter 4.

The Budget Curse

It's fair to say that no one really likes to prepare budgets or to be held accountable for budgeted results. Too many times, a department head or supervisor—or even a clerk far removed from decision-making authority—is held responsible for spending that exceeds budgeted amounts. Such unwanted responsibility has, more than once, been the basis for firing or transferring an employee who was actually doing the assigned job properly. However, the fact that some managers misuse budgets is no reason to do away with them. You surely don't want to throw the baby out with the bathwater.

How then can we avoid the curse that budgets seem to inflict on employees at all levels? I have found that following three simple canons makes budgeting palatable to almost everyone:

1. Permit department heads, with input from employees reporting to them, to set their own budget goals.
2. Encourage monthly discussion periods with department personnel to analyze and explain variances from budget.
3. Let it be known throughout your company that no one will be fired, transferred, or otherwise disciplined if the actual performance of his or her department is worse than the departmental budget.

These rules do not imply that corrective action should not be taken when actual performance is worse than budget. It does mean that department personnel should have a hand in the decision-making process concerning what corrective action should be taken, when it should be taken, and how the action will be implemented.

Expense Budgets

Depending on a company's size and number of employees, expense budgets may be prepared by department or for the company as a whole. In Chapter 2, when examining ways to monitor a cost-reduction program, we looked at a typical layout for a budget that included the total company's administrative and occupancy expenses. Let's take another look at it in Figure 8.1, but this time with amounts entered for the month of March and year to date, and see what conclusions we can draw.

Figure 8.1
Operating Budget
Administrative and Occupancy Expenses
For the Month of March 19xx and Year to Date

Over (Under)	Budget	Actual	Expense	Actual	Budget	Over (Under)
			Payroll			
0	1,000	1,000	Salaries/wages	3,000	3,000	0
5	150	155	Payroll taxes	465	450	15
5	100	105	Employee benefits	315	300	15
(2)	2	0	Other	4	6	(2)
8	1,252	1,260	Total payroll	3,784	3,756	28
			Operating Expenses			
(44)	123	79	Supplies	390	360	30
12	50	62	Telephone	215	150	65
79	100	179	Travel	320	300	20
(13)	50	37	Entertainment	120	150	(30)
0	25	25	Professional fees	75	75	0
0	10	10	Other taxes	30	30	0
7	8	15	Other expenses	70	25	45
41	366	407	Total expenses	1,220	1,090	130
			Occupancy Expenses			
0	150	150	Rent—building	450	450	0
0	28	28	Rent—equipment	74	74	0
0	12	12	Property taxes	36	36	0
0	50	50	Insurance	150	150	0
10	75	85	Electricity	270	225	45
(2)	20	18	Water	61	60	1
(2)	34	32	Fuel—oil, gas, coal	85	90	(5)
(3)	10	7	Other expenses	30	30	0
3	379	382	Total occupancy	1,156	1,115	41
52	1,997	2,049	Total expenses	6,160	5,961	199

This report clearly shows that although salaries and wages kept to budget, and occupancy expenses were practically right on target, operating expenses had begun to slip. In March alone total operating expenses were more than 11 percent over budget, and for the first quarter they were almost 12 percent over budget. Looking at the individual accounts, it's clear that travel expenses for the month were much higher than expected, and for the first quarter, telephone expenses exceeded budget by 43 percent.

These variances from budget may easily have very rational explanations. However, the mere fact that you can see at a glance how these expenses match up with what was expected gives you a much better chance to take appropriate corrective action before any expense gets too far out of control.

The same principles that underlie total company expense budgets hold for departmental budgets. The number of accounts for any given department may be fewer than for the total company, and the amounts will certainly be less, but comparisons can be made and variances analyzed as easily as they are for total company expenses.

Fixed/Variable Budgeting

Fixed/variable budgets separate costs according to how they change in relation to other areas of the business. All operating costs are *fixed, variable,* or *semivariable* (sometimes called *step costs*). A fixed cost is one that is independent of other costs, sales, or asset changes. In other words, fixed costs will be incurred independent of other transactions affecting the operation. One such cost is rent held constant by a lease. Another is depreciation. A third might be product liability insurance premiums (at least for one year). Short of major changes, such as the renegotiation of a lease, actual and budgeted fixed costs should be identical month after month.

At the other end of the spectrum, variable costs are incurred in direct relation to other costs, sales, or asset changes. The demand portion of electricity expense goes up or down in direct relation to how much electricity is used each month. The same holds for the demand portion of municipal water charges. Travel expense relates directly to the number of trips made. The cost of material used in making a product varies directly with the number of products produced and sold. (If products are made for inventory, then material cost varies directly with increases in the inventory asset.) Sales commissions vary directly with orders booked (or account collections).

Semivariable costs are partly fixed and partly variable. They vary somewhat in relation to other costs, sales, or asset changes, but not in direct proportion. Most operating costs tend to be semivariable. (As an aside, don't confuse the distinction between fixed and variable costs with that between controllable and noncontrollable costs. The comparisons are entirely misleading, as we'll see a little later.) Examples of typical semivariable costs in a manufacturing company include direct labor, direct labor fringe benefits, payroll taxes, processing supplies, and equipment maintenance.

Practically speaking, most costs in small wholesale, retail, and service businesses (or manufacturing companies, for that matter) are either fixed for some length of time or semivariable. Very few costs of any significance are totally variable—other than sales commissions.

Before going forward, I should explain what I mean by *controllable* and *noncontrollable* costs. Controllable costs are those that management can control to a large extent. That is, business owners and managers have the choice of either incurring or not incurring these costs—a decision often made without regard for short-term sales volume or production-level fluctuations. For example, you have control over the number of people you want on your payroll, the amount of travel and entertaining to be done, the use of company automobiles, the amount of advertising and sales promotion expenditures, and the purchase of office supplies and new office equipment. These costs may be fixed or variable over the budget period, but you still have control over whether to incur them or not.

Conversely, some costs are beyond the scope of short-term decisions. These are called noncontrollable costs. They might include building rent, payroll taxes, property taxes, depreciation, and the base charge (nondemand charge) for telephones, electricity, and water.

Generally, noncontrollable costs remain fixed for a period of time; however, over two or three years, many can be negotiated to lower levels (such as building lease rental payments) or eliminated completely (by reducing the number of telephones, for example).

For demonstration purposes in preparing operating budgets, we will assume that all costs can be classified as either fixed or variable over the time period covered by the budget. However, it's important to note that the same principles used in these budgets apply to budgets incorporating semivariable costs or those defining costs as controllable or noncontrollable.

Case Study: Ultra Manufacturing Company

Ultra Manufacturing Company (UMC) makes gaskets of various sizes used in components of hazardous waste recycling equipment. Sales for the last three years have been $1.20 million, $1.50 million, and $1.88

million, a 25 percent increase each year. Because cash was getting scarce, the business owner decided to implement a budgetary control system. The company was too small to have clear-cut departmental responsibilities, and so it was decided to prepare a budget for the total company. On the advice of UMC's accountant, the budget was prepared by separating costs into fixed and variable. Figure 8.2 shows how the company performed against this budget for the second quarter and year to date.

This fixed/variable budget clearly identifies the impact that cost containment (or, conversely, noncontainment) has on profits. By eliminating any effect from changes in sales volume or pricing, fixed/variable budgets permit you to concentrate on keeping costs—and hence expenditures—under control. This, in turn, will improve your company's cash position.

In the case of UMC, the second quarter showed a 3.1 percent slippage in variable costs. This reduced profits by $11,000. Fixed costs remained about on budget. We can't determine the impact on cash flow, however, because some of these costs may be accounted for on an accrual basis; that is, they were recorded when incurred, not when paid for.

Year-to-date variable costs showed a slightly greater slippage compared with budget, coming in 3.6 percent higher. Although this is not significantly higher than second-quarter results, it does confirm that the first quarter was also over budget. By now the business owner realized that corrective action had to be taken or the upward trend in variable costs would soon have a severe impact on profits for the total year.

Let's go through the assumptions UMC used in preparing its budget. In a small company like this, production labor is likely to be a semivariable cost, changing with sales volumes in fixed increments or steps, rather than directly. However, to keep it simple, the owner opted to treat production labor and associated expenses (payroll taxes and other fringe benefits) as directly variable with sales.

The ratio of production labor to sales in 1994 was 25 percent, and this was also used in the budget. Payroll taxes and other fringe benefits each ran 15 percent of labor. Production materials used in UMC's gaskets had been running at about 10 percent of sales, and the owner saw no reason to change this for the budget. Demand electricity ran 5 percent of sales in 1994 and was budgeted to be the same. And the company paid its salespeople a commission of 6 percent of sales. These variable costs amounted to almost 54 percent of sales.

Figure 8.2
Ultra Manufacturing Company
Operating Budget
For the Second Quarter and Year to Date 1995
(in thousands of dollars)

| | 1994 | | Second Quarter | | | Year to Date | |
	Actual	Budget	Actual	Favor. (Unfav.)	Budget	Actual	Favor (Unfav.)
Sales	1887	644	644	0	1391	1391	0
Variable Expenses							
Production payroll	472	161	171	(10)	348	341	7
Payroll taxes	71	24	26	(1)	52	51	1
Other fringe benefits	71	24	26	(1)	52	51	1
Production materials	189	64	58	6	139	167	(28)
Demand electricity	94	32	37	(5)	70	78	(8)
Sales commissions	113	39	39	0	83	83	0
Total variable expenses	1010	345	355	(11)	744	771	(27)
Fixed Expenses							
Office supplies	45	12	13	(1)	23	25	(2)
Telephone	65	17	15	2	34	35	(1)
Travel	25	7	5	2	13	13	0
Entertainment	5	1	2	(1)	3	3	0
Professional fees	8	2	2	0	4	4	0
Rent—building	5	1	1	0	3	2	1
Property taxes	2	1	1	(1)	1	2	(1)
Insurance	6	2	2	(1)	3	4	(1)
Utilities (nondemand)	30	8	8	0	16	16	0
Other expenses	3	1	2	(1)	2	5	(3)
Total fixed expenses	194	50	51	(1)	101	109	(8)
Total Expenses	1204	395	406	(12)	845	880	(36)

Fixed costs were handled differently. Costs subject to inflation—office supplies, telephone, travel, entertainment, professional fees, non-demand utilities, and other expenses—were budgeted at a 4 percent increase over 1994 to account for anticipated price increases. Building rent and property taxes were budgeted at the same levels as 1994.

Fixed/variable budgets can be extremely beneficial for companies experiencing cash shortfalls resulting from increased inventory stocking or ballooning receivables. Month by month you can see clearly how reductions in costs that are presumed to be fixed or increased worker productivity can affect the bottom line. After you refine your fixed/variable cost analyses in operating budgets, it's relatively easy to expand these analytical techniques to an ongoing cost analysis program.

A Management Tool

Before we get into budgeting capital expenditures, it would probably be helpful to look at what factors make operating budgets effective management tools and some of the pitfalls to avoid when you implement your budgetary system. Many factors contribute to the effectiveness of operating budgets, and we certainly don't want to spend an inordinate amount of time going over minor points. With that caveat, here are the major elements that contribute to the effectiveness of operating budgets.

Realistic Goals

In one respect, at least, operating budgets are identical to all other types of plans in the business planning cycle: The goals that budgets seek to meet must be realistic and attainable within the planned time frame. To be effective management tools, operating budgets must not represent "blue-sky" dreams. They cannot be contrived targets aimed at motivating employees to reach for the moon. Modern-day employees do not respond to incentive goals unless they perceive the goals to be achievable. And when all is said and done, one of the main objectives in having operating budgets is to get your people to improve their performance.

Neither can goals be too soft. If operating budgets are meant to assist you and your managers in growing the business, you must have goals that make your people stretch. Operating budgets that do little more than keep expense levels where they are now will soon be recognized by everyone as a waste of time. Whether operating budgets are used mainly as a tool to reduce costs or as a mechanism to motivate employees to do better, the goals that budgets are built on must reflect improved performance at realistic levels.

Budgets Based on Accountability

To make operating budgets an effective management tool for controlling the business, you must be careful to hold accountable only those people who have the authority to control these costs. For example, you won't achieve anything but animosity by holding your marketing manager responsible for professional fees charged by your independent accountants and lawyers when the responsibility for negotiating those fees rests with you. Your controller will become very frustrated with a department budget that includes the costs of developing sales literature or sample catalogs. Your manufacturing manager cannot be held responsible for the costs of operating a computer system when systems and data processing report to your controller.

The secret to effective budgeting is to make sure that only those people who have the authority to commit to costs are held responsible for them. If someone else in the organization makes the decision about incurring or not incurring a cost, then that person should be held accountable. If no one other than you has the authority to commit to certain costs, then those costs should be excluded from operating budgets—unless, of course, your budgets are for the total company, not by department.

Playing Games with Budgets

The tendency of department managers (and business owners) seems to be to use budgets as weapons to prevent others from taking certain actions or from doing certain things—for example, "No, we can't buy new computers. The budget won't allow it!" when, in fact, you don't need or want new computers, or "The budget doesn't have enough money in it to take that nationwide trip to confer with sales reps" when, in fact, it would be easier, faster, and less expensive to ask your reps to meet in your office.

Using budgets in this way destroys their effectiveness. It doesn't take much for employees to see through such subterfuges, and when that happens, budgets lose their credibility. In that case, you might as well throw out the entire budgetary system. It will never be an effective management tool.

Participatory Budgeting

One of the tenets of successful budgeting is that, regardless of whether budgets are constructed by department or for the total company, they should be built from the bottom up, not from the top down.

As business owner or CEO, you have not only the authority but also the responsibility to establish overall company objectives consistent with a stated mission. Such objectives might be to

- Cut total costs 5 percent this year.
- Increase gross margin from 35 to 38 percent.
- Capture 10 percent more orders this year.
- Improve cash flow by 5 percent.
- Improve productivity by 15 percent.
- Pay off all bank debt.

These are top-level goals that affect the entire company and should not be set by anyone other than top management. But once company objectives have been established, turn over the preparation of operating budgets aimed at achieving these goals to your key employees or department managers. Along with giving them the authority to set their own budgets, make it perfectly clear that they should solicit input from everyone in their organization or who reports to them.

Once you turn your managers loose to prepare their budgets, make sure you also give them a timetable that includes your review. Ultimately, you have to pass on all departmental or functional budgets. That may involve give and take by everyone. And that can take a fair amount of time.

Capital Expenditure Budgets

As the term implies, *capital expenditure budgets* (or *capital budgets*) are operating budgets for planning and controlling capital expenditures for new hard assets—equipment, machinery, vehicles, buildings, and land. Although capital budgets look entirely different from the operating budgets we've looked at so far, they are an integral part of the budgetary process. In fact, for companies that rely on large investments in hard assets (capital-intensive companies), capital budgets probably contribute as much or more to improved cash flow as do operating budgets.

The idea behind capital budgeting is that if managers are forced to quantify the cost and timing of the purchase or lease of new assets, they will be more careful about frivolous additions. In other words, when managers must justify their wish lists with actual numbers and know that they will be held accountable for the actual benefits stated in their justification analysis, they tend to look twice at the possibility of getting by without the addition—at least for now.

Capital expenditure budgeting has two major objectives: to prove that the asset is needed in the operation of the business (and needed now), and to evaluate, after the fact, whether the result of the justification analysis was actually realized. The first objective relates to planning; the second, to control. In the broadest sense, capital budgeting involves the following steps:

- Determining that you do, in fact, need the proposed asset
- Searching out alternative sources, and possibly configurations, of the asset
- Determining the cost of the asset versus the benefits to be derived
- Considering alternatives other than purchasing or leasing the asset
- Controlling the budgeted expenditures as they are made
- Conducting a postacquisition audit to determine whether the results claimed in the justification analysis actually occurred (but only for capital asset acquisitions involving major expenditures)

Do You Need the Asset?

"Of course I need this machine (or computer, or truck, or forklift). If I didn't need it, I wouldn't have asked for it!" How many times have we all heard such comments from key managers? When I owned my Midwest screw machine company—which was a very capital-intensive company—I didn't get through one annual budget review without hearing this said by virtually every department manager. The fact is, however, that most companies that have been in business for a while really don't need new equipment, machinery, or other capital assets

unless a major change has occurred in customer orders or in the relia-
bility of operating assets (like a major breakdown or expensive repairs).

Nevertheless, it seems that operating managers always want some
new piece of hardware (or floor space), and they invariably use the
excuse that it will upgrade their performance. But no company can
afford to spend indiscriminately on capital assets. The amounts are too
large. Therefore, the first step in capital budgeting is to force your managers to come up with calculations and narratives that justify the
improvements that the new addition will bring to the *company*, not to
their own performance. Be sure to demand that the justification include
the quantification of both costs and savings. Otherwise, it's too easy for
managers to back down after the fact and claim that other factors
caused their poor performance. By then you have already committed
substantial funds.

Finding Alternative Suppliers

If you need a unique, made-to-order piece of equipment, that's
one thing. But in most cases, more than one supplier can furnish
exactly what you want, or something so similar that the difference isn't
significant. For this reason, it's important that the budget process force
managers who request new capital additions to come up with at least
three suppliers—and then get bids from each. This may take a while,
and no one likes to run around the countryside searching out equipment
suppliers. Still, if the budget process is an ongoing procedure, locating
alternative sources can be done well ahead of actually preparing a capital expenditure request.

Evaluating Cost Versus Benefits

This is probably the most difficult part of the justification process.
Cost is relatively easy to ascertain from alternative-source bids.
Quantifying the benefits to be derived from the asset addition is not as
straightforward. Yet, it is a crucial step in capital budgeting. Clearly, if
benefits don't outweigh cost, you shouldn't make the purchase (or lease).

Benefits must be quantified. The asset addition will save 500 production hours per year. It will reduce scrap by $5,000 a month. Repair
expenditures will be reduced 20 percent. Closing the books every month
can be done with three fewer people. Sales will increase 25 percent

because a company airplane will get sales personnel to customer locations three times as fast. New orders booked this year will increase at least 10 percent by entertaining customers on a new yacht. Regardless of the rationale, benefits to be derived from asset additions must be expressed in quantifiable, and hence measurable, terms.

To dispel a common myth, I feel obligated to comment briefly on the cost side of the justification equation. Accountants, financial analysts, and academicians, among others, advocate the calculation of a fictitious *cost of capital* that measures the present value of the asset expenditure against alternative opportunities. This is fine for large companies. Clearly, a dollar earned or saved today is worth more than one five years hence. However, even with the myriad ways to calculate cost of capital and its cousin *internal rate of return*, the only critical decision you must make is whether laying out $100,000 (or some other amount) now will bring greater profits next year, the year after, and so on. You certainly don't need a complex rate of return or cost of capital formula to make that decision—unless, of course, you have excess cash stashed away and are looking for alternative investments that will bring you the highest returns.

Alternatives to Acquiring the Asset

If the justification for adding the asset is to replace an existing piece of equipment, one must ask: Why replace it? Could we repair it for less money? Could we modify it to do what we want? Should we change the way we do things to eliminate the asset altogether? The answers to such questions should be included in any capital addition request. It may be that when you look closely at the rationale for adding an asset, you'll find that other options are available—at substantially less cost.

Assuming that the justification for adding the asset is reasonable, the next question to be answered is: Should we buy the asset or lease it? The lease-or-buy decision is one of the most difficult ones department managers have to make. There are no straightforward answers. However, rather than getting into a lengthy discussion about the pros and cons of leasing versus buying, I refer you to Chapter 14, which includes a thorough analysis of the factors involved in making such a decision.

Controlling Capital Expenditures

The same budget features that are used for controlling operating expenses can be used to control capital expenditures. Once the decision is made to acquire the asset at a specific cost, your internal controls should be sufficient to make certain that unauthorized expenditures are not made. Also, in those cases where payments are made over a period of time—as in the installation of a complex piece of machinery where progress payments are required—reviewing actual expenditures to date against budgeted amounts will give you assurance that overruns are not occurring.

Postacquisition Audit

The postacquisition audit is a relatively simple procedure, yet one that many companies either forget about or ignore. It is also one of the most important parts of capital budgeting. Here is a list of the items that need to be audited, preferably by your controller or someone who has not had a part in the preparation of the capital budget:

- Match the actual expenditures with those in the capital budget.
- Match the actual completion date (in the case of installed assets) against the date in the capital budget.
- Determine the actual payback period (if that was part of the budget).
- Verify the benefits from the addition that were used in the asset justification.
- Analyze the reasons for any difference in cost and benefits.
- Make suggestions for correcting insufficient or inaccurate budgeting procedures.

That finishes our discussion of operating budgets. Succeeding chapters cover business plans and strategic plans. These plans involve longer periods than operating budgets and serve significantly different purposes. Whether you actually implement these longer-term plans or not, I urge you to seriously consider putting operating budgets in place today. They are the best way to ensure that you have control over your day-to-day operations and that you will meet your objectives.

Chapter 9

The Business Plan

Business plans have many uses. One of the more common is for raising capital. In this respect, business plans are the foundation for financing plans. They are also part of the offering prospectus needed for an initial public stock offering.

Although business plans are not used as frequently as a management tool as they are for raising capital, it is as internal, working documents that they are the most valuable. They become an integral part of your annual planning process. They serve as the starting point for your long-term strategic plan. Business plans define the parameters for your operating budgets. Regardless of how business plans are used, however, the research and effort that go into the preparation of each segment of the plan help department heads, functional managers, and even top managers crystallize their understanding of your company's total operation, its business base, and its long-term future. This alone should be reason enough to go through the exercise of updating a business plan at least once a year.

It should be noted that, although the terms *business plan* and *strategic plan* are often used interchangeably, these plans serve entirely different purposes. A strategic plan is long-term. It outlines long-term objectives for market share, sales growth, return on investment, and many other aspects of the company's overall prospects. Business plans, on the other hand, cover a much shorter time period. They are oriented more toward short-term business tactics that can be implemented by personnel at middle management levels. Business plans focus on improving the performance of a company this year, and perhaps next year, but seldom for a longer period. And they include far more detailed financial projections than do strategic plans.

Business plans also tend to be confused with financing plans. Financing plans are restricted to raising capital. In the case of small businesses, raising capital often means applying for a bank loan. To meet bank criteria, financing plans are heavily oriented toward projecting a company's financial performance over the term of the loan. This can mean one year or longer. This type of plan emphasizes changes in the financial condition of a company. It is written in the language of bankers, using bank terminology.

Business plans, on the other hand, focus mainly on internal operations, with heavy emphasis on marketing, production, and organization changes aimed at reaching specific goals this year and perhaps next year. Although business plans are often used as the basis of financing plans, their main function is as a tool for managers to use to improve the performance of the company.

What then are the elements of a business plan that make it so valuable as a management tool? Regardless of a company's size or its business, a well-conceived business plan should include five distinct segments—a description of the company, a marketing plan, a production or operations plan, a personnel plan, and a financial plan. These segments are further divided into the following detailed sections:

1. The company
   - Mission statement
   - Background/history of the company
   - Capital and ownership structures
2. Marketing plan
   - Markets
   - Competition
   - Products/services
   - Pricing
   - Advertising and sales promotion programs
   - Distribution
   - Exporting, offshore sourcing, and other aspects of international trade
   - Warranties and returned goods policies
   - Customer service programs
   - Credit and collection policies
3. Operations plan

- The physical facility
- Equipment, machinery, and vehicles
- Operating systems and procedures
- New product development
4. Personnel plan
   - Management organization
   - Departmental organizations
   - Hourly workers/union contract
   - Benefits programs
5. Financial plan
   - Economic and business assumptions
   - Working capital requirements
   - Equipment and facility financing
   - Acquisition financing

In addition, a formal review process should take place on a regular basis, comparing actual operating results against this plan. The plan can then be updated for any major economic or market changes that occur during the year.

This chapter looks at the narrative part of business plans. Chapter 4 goes through the steps in preparing pro forma financial statements and cash flow projections, which form an integral part of business plans as well as of financing plans and strategic plans.

The Company

The first segment of the business plan is a statement of company mission. This may seem like a rhetorical exercise. After all, companies are in business to make money. Isn't that a self-evident mission? Not necessarily. Most companies have far more specific, or broader, missions than merely making money.

If you haven't broached the subject of company mission with your board of directors (if you have one) or your investors (if any) or even your spouse (for very small businesses), now is the time to do so. Without a definable mission, businesses of any size tend to wander aimlessly through a maze of daily transactions, swinging to and fro with the winds of change in customer demand, financial resources, and even the whims of the owner or shareholders.

If you already have a strategic planning procedure in place, your company's long-term mission should be included. It might be to achieve a constant 5 percent growth in sales per year. Or to expand into new markets every four years. Or to increase dividends every year. Or to dominate a particular market in five years. These are all long-term objectives and require close interaction of all facets of the company to achieve.

The mission statement in a business plan may incorporate some of your strategic goals, but it is primarily aimed at achieving specific objectives this year, or perhaps by the end of next year. This mission statement is oriented more toward operations than toward strategies. It might include such objectives as improving operating efficiency by 3 percent this year. Or pushing productivity up one or two percentage points. Or bringing a new product line to market. Or improving shareholders' return on investment over last year's. Or expanding a customer base to ten new customers. Regardless of the specifics, a business plan mission statement should be attainable within one or two years and should be definite enough to enable you to measure actual progress against it.

Background/History of the Company

This section should remain constant year after year, except for annual updates of the company's performance since the last business plan was prepared. Although there is nothing in this section that directly influences the character or the attainability of the plan itself, your company's history is a constant reminder of both wise and unwise decisions made in prior years. As such, it is a valuable reference for judging the likelihood of achieving the current year's objectives. In other words, if you haven't been able to increase efficiency in the past, for example, what steps will you take this year to make things come out differently?

Having the company's history readily available also has a psychological influence on your managers. Remembering the past tends to bring sobriety to the present. Also, and this point is seldom understood in today's frenzied environment, history usually repeats itself. That is, if you tried a certain tack in the past and it either succeeded or failed, the chances are pretty good that if you try the same approach again, you will have the same good or bad results.

Take the case of an export management company with a newly appointed marketing vice president. An eager beaver, the new VP proposed what seemed to be a revolutionary approach to gaining new customers in the Florida panhandle. His proposal included a door-to-door solicitation of all regional manufacturing and distribution companies that were currently exporting to Europe or Asia, guaranteeing them a certain percentage increase in their export sales by contracting with his company to provide representation in Latin America.

The other department heads were enthusiastic and applauded his initiative. However, the CEO, who had been around a few years, pulled out last year's business plan and asked everyone to read the history section one more time. It included a short description of the company's catastrophic experience selling in Central America eight years earlier. Suddenly, the VP's proposal lost its charm and was quickly dismissed as unworkable. Perhaps this supersalesman's idea would have worked for markets in Mexico or South America. But since the company's history showed that it had failed once, the likelihood of a repeat performance was too great to take the risk.

Capital and Ownership Structures

The capitalization of a company—that is, the structure of a company's debt and equity (net worth)—is more than an accounting nicety. It is the foundation upon which to build assets. Through the analysis of your company's capital structure, you can determine, within a very narrow range, how much money your company can borrow to leverage up its asset purchases.

Typically, a company's capitalization consists of two segments: debt capital and equity capital. Debt capital represents all short- and long-term loans outstanding, plus mortgages, debentures, and corporate bonds. Total debt capital reflects a company's indebtedness and how much cash must be paid out to creditors this year and in future years.

Equity capital represents ownership in the company and has two segments: amounts invested in the company by shareholders and earnings from prior years that have been retained in the company's coffers. Shareholder investments may be evidenced by *common stock* or *preferred stock* certificates. When a company buys back common stock certificates from shareholders, the stock changes its form and is called *treasury stock.* Treasury stock is shown as a reduction in a company's net worth. The amount of earnings a company has accumulated from prior years is called *retained earnings.*

The relationship between debt capital and equity capital—known as the *debt-to-equity ratio*—is a key measure of the solvency of a business and hence its ability to meet obligations and to add assets. The higher the debt-to-equity ratio, the less money is available for operating and growing the company.

The composition of a company's capital structure also shows how much cash must be paid out in interest payments, debt retirement payments, and dividends. These amounts are an integral part of the cash flow schedules developed as part of a pro forma projection of future financial results (see Chapter 4).

Disclosing the ownership of the various segments of a company's equity capital is also an important element in a business plan, especially for companies with more than one class of common stock or with both preferred and common stock outstanding. When pro forma financial statements are prepared, committed dividends (preferred and common) or other contractual distributions to shareholders must be included as reductions in future cash flow. Also, when more than one class of common stock is outstanding (say, for instance, one class of voting shares and one class of nonvoting shares) and one or a very small number of shareholders control the voting class, special provisions may have to be included in the pro formas to recognize the liquidation rights of the nonvoting class.

Marketing Plan

For most companies, the marketing plan is the heart and soul of a business plan. After all, without market demand for your products, you won't be in business very long. Without a thorough understanding of how the various features of markets interact with one another, you won't be able to plan your product lines, distribution channels, pricing policies, operation, financing, or virtually anything else related to the business. All effective marketing plans begin with a thorough definition of the various aspects of a company's markets.

Markets

Those segments of the business plan that deal with a company's markets are typically the most detailed of any. This part of the plan should be as inclusive as is necessary in order to clearly disclose all aspects of a company's market or markets. It should include—but not be restricted to—succinct descriptions by product line of

- Market size
- Market growth trends
- Market share

Each of these sections should have two parts: (1) one part describing the company's performance compared with the last update of the business plan, and (2) one part projecting future actions aimed at improving the company's market position.

Market Size

Many times market size can be difficult, if not impossible, to determine with any degree of accuracy. Especially in the globalized world we live in, foreign competitors with sales offices, distribution centers, or even manufacturing plants in the United States do not report or record shipping and order statistics the same way U.S. companies do. Yes, they must submit the same census data to the U.S. government as American companies, but their accounting procedures vary so much from U.S. standards that the information is often either misleading, inaccurate, or untimely. This tends to distort—at times severely—any industrywide measure of market size. Nevertheless, for most industries, sufficient market data are available to at least make a stab at market size.

While on the subject of market size, it should be noted that if your company is involved in exporting, market size for exported products relates to the country you're exporting to. Gathering enough data from foreign markets—especially markets in developing countries—can become very complex. Different tactics from those applicable to U.S. markets must be used. To get a thorough background in sources of market information for international trade, pick up my book *Exporting,*

Importing, and Beyond, which is also part of the Adams Business Advisor series.

Returning to U.S. markets, one of the best sources of market data could be your trade association. Many compile market statistics, as well as other data, that are free or available to members at minimal cost.

Probably the most important element of determining market size is to precisely define the market that relates specifically to your company. The total market for automobiles sold throughout the United States may be several million cars. But if you have a car dealership in Muskegon, Michigan, your market may be no larger than Muskegon and surrounding communities. If you run an auto repair shop, chances are good that your market should be defined as the auto population within, perhaps, a ten- or fifteen-minute drive of your shop. You couldn't care less about the market in other states, cities, or even neighborhoods.

Markets may be defined in terms of population, number of business customers, geography, previous buyers of similar products, or any number of other possible combinations of events, locations, and customers. Regardless of how you define your market, it should be specific enough so that your company's share can be measured with reasonable accuracy.

Market Growth Trends

Data on market growth trends can usually be obtained from the same sources that provide information about market size. When you prepare your business plan, historical market growth trends over the last three to four years should be used as a base for projecting market growth in pro forma projections. Be alert, however, to both cyclical and seasonal trends. Extrapolating historical growth trends to future periods nearly always results in a substantial over- or understatement of your projected sales volume.

Also, be alert to changes in industry pricing customs. The automobile industry is an excellent example of how changes in industry pricing standards can have a material impact on sales forecasting. Several years ago, in an attempt to get a quick boost in sales, Chrysler began offering cash rebates. It took General Motors and Ford several months to enact similar pricing policies. In fact, neither company recouped lost sales for that year.

Although there are many tactics a company can employ to increase sales, the growth, or in some cases the decline, of market demand has a larger effect on your company's sales volume than any individual policy you may enact. Therefore, it's crucial to spend whatever time and effort is necessary to formulate your estimates of economic indicators, industry cycles, and other assumptions that may affect the shape or direction of your market growth trend this year and next year.

Market Share

Once you have estimated market size and future growth trends, take a crack at projecting how your share of the market might change and what factors are most likely to cause this change. Of course, first you have to know what your market share is today. And for some companies that involves a fair amount of research and a lot of guesswork. Nevertheless, it's impossible to make your sales forecast credible without including changes in market share and the reasons behind those changes.

There are only three ways to increase sales of current product lines:

1. Keep the same market share in a growing market.
2. Increase market share.
3. Increase prices.

Since increasing prices may not be a viable alternative (the market may be resistant to higher prices or competition may prohibit increases), steps aimed at improving market share or, at a minimum, keeping your current market share in a growing market usually yield the best results. Of course, overt actions are needed to increase market share, and these actions probably have costs associated with them. The assumptions underlying new advertising, sales promotions, improved customer service, or other marketing tactics, and their related costs, should be reflected in your business plan sales forecast.

Competition

The section dealing with competition may be the most important one in the entire marketing plan. If you can't identify your competitors and estimate their market shares, it's practically impossible to determine your company's market position. Moreover, without a clear understanding of your competitors' pricing structures and customer service programs, how can you make intelligent decisions affecting your own pricing and service capabilities?

As a start, make a list of the names and estimated annual sales of all major competitors. This may be one company (for markets defined as small neighborhoods) or a lengthy list (as in national or international markets). Information about competitors that are listed on stock exchanges is readily available from the SEC, annual reports, or Moody's and Standard & Poor's directories.

Information about privately owned competitors is less readily accessible, although the references used for strategic planning in Chapter 10 should help.

Once you have a list of competitors prepared, contact these companies for price sheets (or test their pricing with small purchases) and information about their customer service programs. Most sales departments will be eager to relate their unique customer service policies; many will tell you their pricing policies on the phone.

With competitors' market shares, pricing policies, and customer service programs in hand, you have a much better chance of designing your company's strategies to meet or beat even the most aggressive competitors. These action steps should be described in this section of the business plan and then incorporated in your financial projections.

Products/Services

This segment may be very extensive or very concise, depending on how many truly different product lines you have. (When I speak of *products*, I also mean *services* for those companies in service industries.) Companies with many different product lines will need a separate subsection for each. Those with only one major line can get by with a brief descriptive narrative.

One note of caution: Do not go overboard in the technical description of your products. It's unnecessary to describe your products in detail when the plan is to be used as an internal document. When it is used as part of a financing plan, chances are good that no one outside your company would understand technical descriptions anyway. For each product line, comment on the following:

- What is the product used for (application of the product)?
- Who are the customers (or potential customers) that use the product?

- Is the product environmentally safe?
- What is the expected useful life of the product (for nondisposable products)?
- What materials is the product made of?
- Is the product proprietary or generic?
- If proprietary, do you hold patents?
- Does the product come with a warranty (and if so, how long does it last)?
- Are any new products planned for this year or next year?
- Do competitors plan to introduce new products that could make yours obsolete?

The main idea in the products/services section is to give readers as clear a picture of your products as possible. Include recent product photos from your sales literature if they are available. But stay away from technical details. If you feel bound to include technical data, insert product specification sheets rather than narrative descriptions.

Pricing

Pricing tactics may be part of the competition section, or they may be complex enough to warrant a separate section. Either way, current pricing policies and planned changes this year and next year should be clearly defined. The more succinct you can be, the more reliable your financial forecasts will turn out.

Advertising and Sales Promotion Programs

For some indeterminable reason, business planners tend to ignore advertising and sales promotion programs in the marketing plan. Perhaps they assume that advertising and promotions will be about the same in the future as in the past. Perhaps the company has done little or no advertising in the past and therefore does not consider it in the future. Perhaps the company's cash position is very weak and top management believes that advertising is the first expenditure that can be cut without harming the business. Who knows? Whatever the reason, this section is seldom given its due in business plans—unless, of course, a major new advertising or promotion campaign is planned. Then it receives a lot of attention.

To the extent that you plan to advertise or to initiate a sales promotion program, three elements need to be covered in this section. The first is a description of the type of advertising or promotion anticipated. Will you run ads in newspapers, on radio, on television? Will you start a direct mail campaign? Will you hit trade journals? Does a premium or a giveaway program make sense?

Second, it's important to identify total cost. How much can you allocate to each advertising campaign or promotion? Can you do any of the preliminary work in-house, or must you rely exclusively on an advertising agency? Will the campaign be local, regional, national, or international? And how much will each segment cost?

Third, no business plan would be complete without a description of what results the advertising campaign or promotion is expected to produce. How much increased sales can be anticipated? Will the programs be aimed at attracting new markets or expanding existing markets? When will results be realized (time-phasing the programs is necessary in order to forecast the proper time period in which increased sales, and hence increased cash flow, can be expected)?

Distribution

This section of the marketing plan may be very lengthy or very short—or you might not even need it. Clearly, companies that sell only services in a very restricted geographic market never have to worry about distribution. Conversely, companies that sell products nationally, or internationally, for that matter, will probably have to sell through distributors or dealers. They may have stocking warehouses in remote locations. They may sell partially from the home office with salaried sales personnel and partially from distribution warehouses with commissioned sales agents.

In this distribution section of the marketing plan, explain as specifically as possible the distribution system for each of your product lines. If distributors or dealers are involved, list their names, addresses, and territories. If company-owned warehouses or distribution centers operate in various locations, name the locations and the approximate sales percentage out of each center.

If some product lines are sold direct from the home office, try to elaborate on delivery schedules and on-time deliveries.

The main idea in the distribution section is to provide readers with enough information about how you get your products to market to give them a reasonable understanding of your overall business. Of course, as in so many other sections, when you circulate your business plan outside the company, you must take care to be inclusive in your narrative, yet not reveal proprietary trade secrets.

Exporting, Offshore Sourcing, and Other Aspects of International Trade

Obviously, if you are not exporting, sourcing offshore, or operating a foreign facility, and you don't plan to do so in the foreseeable future, this section would be omitted in its entirety. However, if you are involved in any aspect of international trade, this segment of the marketing plan could be the most important part of your entire business plan. Not only does it help your managers to clearly and succinctly describe their international activities, but if you expect to use the business plan as the foundation for a financing plan (of any form), readers from outside your company will spend more time on the plan's international section than on anything else. There is something about international trade that seems to pique the interest of almost everyone.

Begin this segment with a description of your export or sourcing markets. Bring in as many statistics about each country's political and economic conditions as possible, both as they exist today and as you see them developing over the next couple of years. Demographic data such as literacy rates, urban population, birth rates, age spread, and so on, are always appreciated by any reader not familiar with the country.

Be sure to include comments about local and multinational competition, pricing abnormalities (such as a high-inflation environment), advertising peculiarities, and so on. A separate description of distribution channels, agent relationships, and tariff/customs conditions is also a welcome feature.

Wrap up this segment with an explanation of future growth plans, including the possibility of establishing offshore manufacturing facilities or distribution centers. Don't be afraid to embellish your prose with as many statistics as possible. This not only forces you to thoroughly research the foreign market but also gives the reader a better feel for that market's future potential.

Warranties and Returned Goods Policies

In today's highly competitive environment, nearly every company warrants its products or services in one way or another. This section is the place to spell out precisely and inclusively all types of warranties you offer customers. This is also the place to elaborate on the number of warranty claims received during the past year. How were they settled? What were the complaints? Have corrective measures been taken to ensure that the same problems won't recur? This information is important as the foundation for estimating warranty costs in your pro forma projections.

Also comment on your company's returned goods policies. Are all returns accepted? If not, what criteria are used for accepting or rejecting? What has been the return rate as a percentage of gross sales during the past year? Have corrective measures been put in place to reduce returned goods in the future?

Customer Service Programs

As with warranties, every company has some type of customer service program in place. It may not be elaborate, or it might be, but at a minimum, you try to keep customers satisfied with your product and service and make an honest attempt to correct those conditions that seem to irritate customers. After all, without customers, none of us would be in business.

Try to be as inclusive as possible when describing the various facets of your customer service program. Do you grant full refunds when a customer is dissatisfied? Do you have technicians or service people to train customers in the use of your products? How about twenty-four-hour phone service to answer customer questions? Be sure to comment on your program compared with those of your competitors.

Credit and Collection Policies

This segment should describe your company's credit verification procedures and collection record during the past year. In contrast to other segments of the marketing plan, the discussion of credit and collection activities should be relatively broad. Stay away from too much detail that could either reveal your company's proprietary approach to credit verification or bring to light discrepancies in collection procedures (such as favoring one customer or class of customer over another). If the business plan is strictly an internal document, it doesn't make much difference what you reveal. But if it is to be the base for a financing plan that will be circulated to bankers and others outside the company, then it does make a difference.

Some companies like to include a summary of aged receivable balances. That's OK, if you feel it adds anything to the overall plan. However, it might be better to include an aging of receivables schedule in the backup to your pro forma forecasts.

Operations Plan

The operations plan details how your company makes its products (or furnishes its services), how and where it is housed, product engineering changes planned for the future, new product development programs, and anything else having to do with making, delivering, or storing your products. Manufacturing companies need to include descriptions of quality assurance programs and planned additions or disposals of equipment and machinery. Distribution companies should concentrate on facilities layout, inventory control procedures, and order-filling policies. Capital-intensive service businesses like hotels, resorts, and athletic clubs generally find it desirable to emphasize planned facilities renovations and the addition of apparatus or appointments. Retail businesses such as restaurants and bars should also concentrate on the physical plant and any planned innovations to it.

The whole idea in the operations plan is to elaborate on how and where you create the products you sell. Typically, regardless of the type of business, operations plans can be divided into four segments:

- The physical facility
- Equipment, machinery, and vehicles
- Operating systems and procedures
- New product development

The Physical Facility

This segment describes in as much detail as appropriate the type of facility that houses your business, be it a factory, warehouse, store, or lodging/eating establishment. Use narrative to give the reader a feeling for what the facility looks like (pictures are also helpful). It's usually not wise to include engineering or architectural drawings of the facility, unless they are absolutely necessary for a complete description. Be sure to include such features as

- Whether you rent or own the facility. If it is rented, then describe the main lease features. If it is owned, then cover the details of any mortgage. Also mention the amount of property taxes.
- Size. How many square feet of production, storage, and office space are available? How many floors do you occupy? How much parking space?
- How the facility is constructed—brick, concrete block, wood, etc.
- Location. Urban or rural? Near public transportation? Accessibility to rail lines, major highways, or airports?
- Anticipated changes. Are you planning to expand your existing facility? Add new facilities? Lease out unused space? Or sell unneeded buildings or land?

Equipment, Machinery, and Vehicles

This section should include brief descriptions of the types of equipment or machinery used in the production process. A list of major items might be helpful (but do not provide a complete list of all equipment and machinery—in a manufacturing plant, that could require a large number of pages and reveal very little about the operation). Of course, if you're in the transportation business, then include an explanation of your fleet of vehicles. The same holds true for businesses that lean heavily on delivery trucks, hauling vehicles, or other types of roadway or off-road equipment. Regardless of the type of hard asset, elaborate on its technical aspects relative to the state of the art, age relative to useful life, and planned replacements or additions.

Operating Systems and Procedures

Use this section to lay out your plans for new computer systems, the addition of local or remote networks, planned updates in inventory or production control systems, anticipated revisions in quality assurance procedures to qualify for ISO certification, steps that will be taken to upgrade compliance with EPA standards, and so on. Some companies use this section as a catchall; that is, they include everything about operations except facilities and hard assets. That's not such a bad idea if you have many planned changes in operating procedures.

You may be planning a new cost system to further enhance your pricing policies. Or a new order entry system to speed up reaction to customer needs. Or a new computerized accounting system to provide greater detail in your financial reports. Or a new inventory system to enhance control over high-value items. Or a labor reporting system to better control labor hours. Or any number of other changes to operating procedures that will be important adjuncts to the overall efficiency or productivity of the company.

New Product Development

You may not have any plans to design or introduce new products or services over the coming year or two. In that case, this section should obviously be omitted. On the other hand, this section may be the most important part of your entire operations plan. High-tech companies or those manufacturing products that face rapid obsolescence—such as toys—may have to devote many pages of narrative and pictures, and even drawings and sketches of planned new product introductions. Of course, if the business plan is to be distributed outside your company, you won't want to reveal any product or design secrets in it. In that case, general descriptions of the planned new products are more than sufficient.

This section should also include comments about methods for getting your new products to market. As we all know, it's becoming increasingly important for companies to shorten the design and development time span between product conception and market introduction. Business plans that are used exclusively as management tools could include budget-type goals, with measurable milestones, to assist department managers in monitoring new product development. Or it might be more meaningful to simply set end dates for market introductions that would serve as incentive goals.

Personnel Plan

To clearly identify the various policies and structures related to employees, the personnel plan should be divided into four parts:

- Management organization (including board of directors)
- Departmental organizations
- Hourly workers/union contract
- Benefits programs

Management Organization

Management organization should be given first because this section lays out the qualifications of your company's top management team. This can be done in several different ways, but probably the easiest method is to list each member of the team and give a brief description of background, tenure, and responsibilities. For business plans used exclusively for internal management purposes, such a listing can be very brief; business plans used for external purposes must include a much broader narrative.

Figure 9.1 shows one way to format a management organization chart that can be adapted for both internal and external use. Annual compensation can be blocked out when the plan is distributed internally and added for external review. Also, while initials are sufficient for internal use, full names should be added for external distribution:

Figure 9-1

Management Team	Title/Responsibility	Tenure	Annual Compensation
J. P. Tenor	President/CEO	10 years	$150,000
Previously CEO of LONOW Corp., $300 million mnfr. listed on NYSE Shares owned: 150,000			
S. F. Wingit	VP Marketing	8 years	$100,000
Previously headed marketing for East Coast region of Webster Machine Co. Shares owned: 42,000			
O. B. Right	VP Operations	8 years	$92,000
Started QBT Machine Co., subsequently sold to ITT Shares owned: 20,000			
L. H. Heavy	VP Finance	9 years	$75,000
Previously CPA with Arther Bright & Co., New York Shares owned: 10,000			
Q. A. Painly	VP Quality	5 years	$73,000
Seven years with Boeing Company as quality supervisor on 747 program Shares owned: 5,000			

Of course, you can get much more elaborate if you like. It usually isn't necessary, however, unless managers' egos need massaging. If any manager has an employment contract, it should be mentioned, but specific terms should never be disclosed.

Either before or immediately after the listing of top management, a narrative should explain the composition of the board of directors. For outside board members, describe company affiliation, title, and tenure as a director. For company officers who are also directors, mention only their name and title. Be sure to designate any open board seats reserved for future venture capital or other equity investors.

Departmental Organizations

The best way to display departmental structures is with organization charts. They don't have to be elaborate, but they should show enough detail so that any descriptive narrative can be kept to a minimum. In other words, draw the organization chart to show as much pertinent information as possible about reporting lines, tenure, and responsibilities. The chart should extend only through second-line supervision. Beyond that, organization charts tend to become unwieldy and therefore ineffective.

Internal-use-only business plans should not include compensation information—for obvious privacy reasons. Your controller will have all the payroll records for use in preparing detailed pro forma forecasts, and so such information here would be redundant.

However, when you circulate the business plan to outsiders, include the compensation of department managers and, if relevant, second-line supervisors. An informal departmental organization chart might look like this:

Marketing Department
S. F. Wingit
VP Marketing

S. Claus	R. Maudlin	I. Live	F. Boot
Manager	**Supervisor**	**Manager**	**Manager**
Order Entry	**Customer Service**	**Sales**	**Advertising**
9 years	3 years	4 years	5 years
Enter customer orders	Customer training	Sales calls	Manage
Maintain order backlog	Handle product claims	Book orders	advertising campaign
Initiate shop orders	Handle customer	Develop sales	Attend trade
Initiate change orders	inquiries	literature	shows
		Collect past-due	Develop sales
		accounts	promotions

If you have large numbers of personnel reporting to one department officer or manager, use your good judgment about how far down the organization to go. A general rule of thumb is, never display more than is necessary to present a reasonably complete picture of the key personnel in the department.

In addition to describing the current departmental organization, comment on anticipated employee additions (or reductions) during the next year. Since this information will be incorporated in your pro forma forecasts, it's important to allow sufficient time and effort to thoroughly think through personnel requirements in each department. This is also the place to comment on plans to use independent contractors for overload conditions or to replace current employees with outside services as part of a cost-reduction program.

Hourly Workers/Union Contract

For companies with unions, this section should divulge as much as is practical about the main features of the contract. It should also include comments about the historical relationship between the union and the company. Has it been amicable? Have grievances been handled promptly and to the satisfaction of both parties? Do union and management leaders work together to resolve disputes before they reach out-of-control proportions?

Whether or not you have a union, this section should outline the pay scale of hourly workers. A simple tabulation will suffice, such as the following:

Job Classification	Number of Employees	Hourly Wage Rate
Machinist	6	$15.95
Helper	6	7.50
Inspector	3	12.32
Driver	1	11.87

In addition, be sure to include explanations of overtime, vacation, and holiday policies. Some companies prefer to consider these matters in the benefits section. In that case, reference should be made to that section here.

Benefits Programs

This final section of the personnel plan can be very brief. Its main purpose is to outline the various benefits programs available to nonunion employees. (Union benefits should be described in the previous section when you list the main features of the union contract.) It can also provide background material for preparing your pro forma forecasts by showing the relationship of each benefit to employees or to salaries and wages. The following example is one format that can be used to do this:

	Amount per Employee
Federal payroll taxes	8% of payroll
State/city payroll taxes	7% of payroll
Medical insurance	$100/month
Life insurance	$75/month
Pension plan	6% of payroll

As mentioned previously, overtime, vacation, and holiday policies are sometimes considered in the benefits section. In that case, they should be added to this list.

Any anticipated changes in the types of benefits or their cost during the following year should be mentioned here. Don't guess. But if you plan to change insurance carriers to reduce medical premiums, say so here. If you plan to introduce a 401(k) pension plan to replace the retirement plan you have now, comment on that. Or if you anticipate including a broader range of employees in the life insurance program, comment on that.

This is also the place to elaborate on your current or planned incentive program. Explaining such programs is especially important if changes are planned in the way incentive compensation is calculated, the way goals are established, or the number of job classifications of covered employees.

Financial Plan

Do not confuse the financial plan with pro forma forecasts. Pro formas involve balance sheets, income statements, and cash flow projections based on historical trends, sales/cost/asset ratios, and business assumptions about future events. A financial plan relates projected cash requirements to internally generated funds and makes assumptions about the type and amount of external financing needed to fulfill the operating plan. The financial plan is in narrative form; pro forma projections are in numerical format.

The financial plan comprises at least three segments, and possibly more:

- Economic and business assumptions
- Working capital requirements
- Equipment and facility financing

In addition, if a business acquisition is in the cards, acquisition financing should be a part of this section.

Economic and Business Assumptions

Before you can make intelligent assessments of financing needs—or, for that matter, project market growth—you must decide what the economic climate that affects your business will be next year. Is the country heading into a recession? Is there increasing inflation or deflation, or will it remain at about the same level? Will your markets suffer from economic fluctuations in Europe, Japan, or other global locations? Will changes in federal taxes, environmental requirements, funding of government programs, or other policies create a more favorable or more detrimental business climate? Does your industry project an upward, downward, or flat growth curve? How about your city, state, or region—will there be any major changes in the economic base or in government policies that will affect your company or markets? And finally, to project the cost of any new financing, you must make assumptions about the trend of interest rates and possibly stock market trends.

These and many more economic and business assumptions will have material impacts on your company's ability to meet its objectives and should be carefully thought out simultaneously with the preparation of other sections of the business plan. Among the most helpful tools for estimating where the general economy is headed are the federal indexes—leading, coincident, and trailing—described in Chapter 10. Make sure you understand each of these before you write your financial plan.

Working Capital Requirements

As your business grows, extra cash will be needed to finance increased inventory levels and climbing receivables. Some of this cash will come from delaying payments to suppliers (as expressed in increased accounts payable). But most increases in working capital will probably have to be borrowed from banks as short-term loans. (See Chapter 5 for definitions of *working capital* and other financing terms.)

Before you can determine how much working capital will have to be borrowed, you need to prepare pro forma financial statements and cash flow projections as described in Chapter 4. From these documents you can determine how much working capital will be required and when it will be needed. Using that information, write a short narrative in this section describing the amount, timing, and source of new working capital.

Equipment and Facility Financing

When you develop the operations plan, it should become obvious whether or not you need to add major equipment, machinery, or facilities to meet production, storage, or other operating requirements. Although such hard assets may be purchased with internally generated cash, more often than not, companies opt for external financing. In almost all cases, this must be long-term capital, to be repaid over at least five years and maybe a longer period.

This section of the financial plan should detail anticipated acquisitions of new equipment, machinery, and facilities. It should estimate the cost of these assets. And it should clearly describe how these purchases will be financed. Will you apply for term loans from your bank? Lease the assets? Take out a mortgage on a new building? Rely on equipment manufacturers and real estate sellers to finance the purchases?

Not only should you explain the amount and source of new long-term financing, but you should also estimate the interest rates to be charged and repayment terms. Both interest rates and repayment terms are integral parts of your pro forma projections.

Acquisition Financing

If you plan to acquire a going business, it's necessary to make estimates about financing the purchase. Will the acquisition be financed totally by leveraging long-term loans? Will additional equity investors be sought? Will venture capital be used? Regardless of how the acquisition is eventually financed, you should make an effort to at least estimate in broad terms how it will happen and explain the possible variations from your estimates.

That finishes the preparation of business plans. This chapter has covered mainly the narrative part. Be sure to read the other chapters in this book dealing with financial statement analysis, forecasting, and raising capital from outside sources.

Chapter 10

Strategic Planning

Strategic planning may be one of the most overworked, misused terms in modern-day business. Every type of business plan has at one time or another been mislabeled a strategic plan. Pro forma financial forecasts, cost-center budgets, capital budgets, financing plans, acquisition business plans, and sales forecasts have all, at one time or another, been called strategic plans. The only reason that comes to mind is that the phrase *strategic planning* has a mystique; there is something magical about it that somehow makes it seem more important than other planning activities.

Without question, strategic plans include part or all of these other types of plans. However, true strategic plans encompass much more. To clarify this point, perhaps some definitions are in order:

- A strategy is a plan of action based on one or more measures intended to accomplish a specific, long-term goal.
- A plan is a method or program in accordance with which something is to be done or accomplished.
- A strategic plan is such a program based on a series of anticipated decisions aimed at enhancing the growth of a company's sales and/or profits over the long term.

Another way of looking at it is that strategic plans are, by definition, long-term plans that provide a road map for the route a company must travel if it hopes to reach its ultimate objective. The flexibility to make abrupt tactical changes in market penetration and product configurations when dictated by cyclical or long-term variations in customer demand and competition underlies all effective long-term strategies. You have to be able to see the opening of new markets and move quickly to capture a major share. In other words, you have to plan for the implementation of strategies long before they have to be implemented. And that's where strategic planning comes in.

A well-conceived strategic plan enables a company to test growth assumptions as occasions warrant and then move quickly to capture new markets, discard low-margin product lines, and develop operating policies to exploit virtually any situation. With sufficient flexibility in people, products, facilities, and capital, companies can *create* opportunities rather than *react* to those that others have already recognized.

The process of testing alternative strategies can best be accomplished with a forecasting model. This model must be based on the cost/sales/asset functional relationships that a company currently experiences. It should be so constructed that the various levels of sales, costs, and assets associated with a series of what-if scenarios can be tested against one another. Sales, profits, and return on investment resulting from each strategy can then be compared to determine the strategies that result in the best overall company performance. Although this type of forecasting is equally adaptable to manual and computer-based computations, the complexity and number of what-if alternatives encourage the use of computer-based spreadsheet programs. Chapter 4 describes in detail a convenient computer-based model that is easily adaptable to long-term strategic forecasting.

Company Mission

The starting point for any strategic plan is the determination of a realistic company mission. The importance of defining an achievable mission can most easily be seen by comparing two examples that first appeared in my book *Entrepreneurial Growth Strategies*, which is part of this Adams Business Advisor series.

Assume that the owner of Movies-for-Rent, Inc., became impatient with stagnant revenues and decided to diversify by offering new product lines of movie projectors, camcorders, and TV and stereo furniture, and by presenting movie-editing seminars. Competing stores that specialized in each of these product lines had lower overhead and hence were able to price their products below Movies-for-Rent's full cost. Although total revenues increased 10 percent the first year, low competitive prices, coupled with the company's expanded debt service obligations, kept margins on each of the new lines well below those earned from movie rentals, thereby driving down total company profits.

In contrast, assume that Hollywood Tonite kept to its original mission, renting movies. As revenues stagnated, the temptation to diversify led the owner to prepare a long-term strategic plan. He saw at a glance that while Hollywood Tonite had the lion's share of the video rental market, several nearby stores had already captured major market shares for each of the new product lines that Movies-for-Rent was introducing. Seeing this, Hollywood Tonite's owner increased advertising for movie rentals and initiated a bonus rental program. Although revenues did not increase as fast as they did for Movies-for-Rent, profits soared far above those of this diversified competitor.

Without question, diversification is called for under certain circumstances. When it is consistent with your company's original mission, diversification should add to total profits. However, when diversification into new products or markets is at variance with the original mission, more often than not, profit and return on investment suffer.

Your company's mission may be anything you desire. In a university study of private companies in the Philadelphia area, business owners were asked to define a mission statement that best described their businesses. In order of popularity, the responses were to

1. Maximize cash draws for the business owner.
2. Provide the best service (or product) at the least cost.
3. Sustain a steady growth rate commensurate with available resources.
4. Provide steady employment for long-term employees.
5. Maximize estate assets for the owner.
6. Maintain a socially responsible position relative to employees, the community, and the environment.
7. Meet the needs of employees and the community while maximizing profits and return on investment.
8. Gain and sustain a commanding market share.
9. Provide a constant challenge and mental stimulation for the owner and key managers.
10. Be recognized as the leader in a given market/industry.

Mission statements may be broad or narrow. In some cases, product or market diversification is necessary. For instance, if a company's mission is to maximize return on investment, it may be necessary to purge unprofitable product lines, or to initiate a high-margin export program, or to do a leveraged buyout of a competitor, or to source components offshore.

In other cases, a company's mission might involve narrow business choices. For instance, to gain and sustain a commanding market share might mean directing all available resources to advertising and promotion programs, or expanding current facilities for higher production volumes, or initiating labor training programs in the community.

Regardless of the specifics, effective long-term growth strategies call for a finite statement of company mission, followed by a strategic plan to achieve it.

Growth Objectives

In addition to a wide diversity of missions, businesses may have different growth objectives. In a dynamic business environment, companies will, over time, experience either increases or decreases in sales and profits. Remaining at the current level is not an option. Also, since it seems unlikely that a company would intentionally choose to decrease profits, one can assume that growth of one type or another is a prime objective. In that case, it is necessary to precisely define the nature of that growth objective.

Although there are many variations, the four most common growth objectives relate to market share, sales, return on investment, and diversification (to insulate against business cycles). Improving market share is probably the most far-reaching of the four. Markets may be defined by

- Geographic boundaries, confined by region, state, city, or neighborhood
- Product superiority or uniqueness
- Technological advances
- Marketing and distribution originality
- Customer service supremacy

In all cases, market dominance gives you the ability to control pricing, and hence profit margins, unfettered by competitive interference.

For companies that dominate markets, the ultimate consumer, not competitors' advertising, giveaways, or price-cutting discounts, is the sole determinant of pricing strategies.

The sustainability of extraordinarily high prices for Mercedes-Benz automobiles sold in the United States, in bad times as well as good, is an excellent example of dominance by one company in the top-of-the-line luxury car market. The consistently high prices for Sears Craftsman brand power tools is another example of market dominance. In cutthroat home appliance markets, General Electric sustains its market dominance (and prices) by providing twenty-four-hour, seven-day, do-it-yourself repair service consultation.

Many companies regard steadily improving sales volume as their primary growth objective. Although in the long term, strategies aimed at increasing sales at the expense of profit margins can be dangerous, companies with a high fixed-cost-to-sales ratio—such as hotels—may find this a reasonable trade-off, at least for interim periods.

Sales strategies run the gamut from cutting prices to increasing advertising to improving customer service to speeding up deliveries. More than one retailer has increased sales by offering free delivery service (e.g., Domino's Pizza) when competitors either charge for the service or do not deliver at all. After-sale service, free or low-cost customer training, no-questions-asked return policies, and two-for-one sales promotions have proven to be successful sales strategies in specific industries. Hard-sell tactics that pinpoint locales or products have also proven to be effective strategies, as in lawn-care businesses.

By focusing on sales objectives, you may be able to increase market share and, in so doing, achieve market dominance. The main idea is to pick one or more specific marketing ploys to increase sales in identifiable markets without eroding long-term profit margins.

Companies that focus on return-on-investment objectives usually find it more difficult to develop strategies that can be quickly implemented. In many cases, three to five years is considered normal. The efficient use of assets as reflected in *assets employed* and *asset turnover* ratios is the key to improving return on investment. Although rising profit margins also help, without steady improvement in asset turnover, it's virtually impossible to reap significant increases in return on investment.

Strategic plans that call for the acquisition of new product lines or businesses have, in many cases, been the most successful in reaching return-on-investment objectives. However, it's important to recognize that such acquisitions must be selected for their contribution to overall returns, not necessarily to meet diversification or sales objectives.

Companies that suffer wide business-cycle swings in sales and profitability frequently try to mitigate the effect of seasonal, short-term, or even long-term dips and spurts in market demand. Those businesses that are affected mostly by national economic swings might find that market diversification in offshore locations offers the best alternative. Carefully chosen foreign markets with counteracting economic cycles can go a long way toward mitigating the effects of wide swings in domestic demand.

Similarly, scarce materials or energy, high labor wage rates, or erratic sources of supply for parts or components frequently lead companies to diversify both their supply lines and production or assembly operations to offshore facilities. Diversification objectives might also take the form of joint ventures with companies having complementary, but cyclically offsetting, product lines.

In addition to clearly defining a company's mission and its growth objectives, the strategic planning process should earmark specific market niches to exploit or to abandon.

Market Niches

In contrast to large companies with abundant resources, wide product offerings, and diverse marketing organizations, private businesses usually look to one or a limited number of market niches for growth opportunities. The broad-brush, something-for-everybody approach to product offerings or markets proves to be too costly and unwieldy.

As previously pointed out, markets, and hence market niches, may be defined by geography, products, customer base, technology, or distribution channels. In any case, to develop a strategic plan, it's necessary to define as precisely as possible those market niches that are the focus of a company's current sales efforts. Nearly all companies offer more than one or two services or products, or sell to more than one or two classes of customers. The greater the number of either, the higher the probability that one or more is draining cash and other resources without producing acceptable profit margins. These are the products or customers to dump, leaving more resources available for those market niches that produce the highest margins.

During the strategic planning process, you will probably identify one or more market niches that are not currently being exploited. Tapping these markets may require modification of products or distribution systems, or it could involve a restructuring of customer mix.

For instance, assume that a baseball bat manufacturer sells exclusively to retail chains such as Kmart, Sears, and J.C. Penney. While exploring alternative markets as part of the strategic planning process, the sales manager learns that Little League teams, secondary schools, and universities buy their disposable athletic equipment (such as baseball bats and balls) in volume through national distributors. Although unit margins are less than on retail sales, this could probably be offset by production efficiencies realized by large-volume orders. Furthermore, assume that only one major bat manufacturer sells to this market. If major sales and delivery efforts are redirected toward national distributors, advertising expenses should be less and customer returns completely eliminated. Such a redirection of marketing efforts could increase the growth rate of both sales and total profits.

Four criteria should be used to analyze market niches:

- Market size and growth potential
- Major competitors
- Ease of entry
- Resource requirements

Market Size and Growth Potential

The whole concept of focused marketing is based on gaining major market shares while expending minimum resources. A market's size and growth potential depend on the current and projected demand for a given product. Both the current status of a market and its future potential should be recognized as basic criteria for continuing or expanding market penetration.

When exploring the possibilities for entering a new market, more than one business owner or sales manager has made the common mistake of equating customer demand with customer need. This is always a serious error because seldom, if ever, are the two equal. It may be logically argued that customers *need* a new product or service, but if they are unwilling to buy it, their need for it is irrelevant.

An excellent example has been the overwhelming need to eliminate nonbiodegradable plastic from consumer packaging. Environmental studies clearly indicate the need to stop flooding landfills with plastic containers and packaging. Current technology could easily replace plastic packaging with biodegradable material. But manufacturers have been hesitant to incur the added costs of converting packaging machinery, deferring the development of alternative products. And federal and state legislatures have been unwilling to meet the need with regulations that ban plastic packaging. Despite market need, the absence of consumer demand for biodegradable packaging is the main reason we continue to stuff landfills with ecologically damaging plastic.

Clearly, customer need is not sufficient reason to enter a new market. There must also be substantial customer demand. In and of itself, however, even strong market demand isn't enough. The strategic planning process must also reveal the nature and extent of competition.

Competition

If the objective of entering a new market niche is to gain a controlling share, picking a niche that already has a market leader could be a very expensive proposition. The odds of capturing new customers are much higher in markets where many small companies compete but none has a major share. Such a tack is also far less expensive than unseating an entrenched market leader. However, there are opportunities to gain control of niche markets within broad markets controlled by a few major companies, such as woodworking power hand tools.

For years, major brands such as Craftsman, Black & Decker, and Skil have controlled the lion's share of the national power hand tool market, with product offerings ranging from circular saws and saber saws to routers, drills, and sanders. Complaints from do-it-yourself customers and professional carpenters about the awkwardness of using extension cords have fallen on deaf ears. Recently, Skil came out with a rechargeable battery power pack for its line of miniature circular saws used for finishing work and model building. The first company that can extend this concept to full-size tools at an economical price will certainly capture a niche, fulfilling not only customer need but market demand.

A similar case evolved in the small battery market for flashlights, portable stereo equipment, and toys. By being the first to enter, GE effectively controlled the price and distribution of the rechargeable small battery market, still a minor niche in a broad national market. However, the first company to develop rechargeable batteries that are priced competitively with traditional small batteries should have a clear shot at capturing a significant market share from GE.

The idea behind searching out new niche markets with little, if any, serious competition is to gain pricing and probably distribution control (thereby increasing margins) at minimum cost and in the shortest time period. A strategic focus along these lines will inevitably result in faster growth than pursuing highly competitive markets.

Ease of Entry

As a corollary to competitive saturation, ease of market entry determines to a large extent how long a company can remain in control of a niche market. Low-cost, low-technology, high-volume markets are naturals for new entrants. Unless the manufacturing process or distribution system requires extensive capital investment, many large and small companies will be attracted to such a market.

The tax return preparation business is a prime example. Literally thousands of micro businesses and hundreds of large firms continually enter and leave this industry. Market demand is always high, capital investment is nonexistent (except perhaps for a personal computer and a tax library), certification is not required, and the technical ability to prepare individual tax returns is easily learned (to wit, the many H & R Block offices).

It would make little sense to include this market in a strategic plan unless a sales gimmick could be developed. One such gimmick was the filing of tax returns electronically. Another gimmick initiated by H & R Block was instant refunds. Although short-lived advantages were certainly achieved in both cases, other competitors soon jumped in with the same offers.

Conversely, attacking a niche market that by its nature has stringent entrance barriers could be a highly desirable strategy. Barriers might be (1) technological, as with laser-optical gun sights or night-vision goggles; (2) regulatory, as with state licensing or FDA approvals; (3) cost, as with capital-intensive products; (4) financing, as with hotels, office complexes, shopping centers, and other real estate–based development projects; or (5) craft, as with mural design, fiberglass layup, or teaching (such as Berlitz language schools).

The major drawback to strategies aimed at capturing barrier-prone markets is that not infrequently, they require substantial capital and dedicated personnel. To the extent that capital and qualified personnel are available or can be obtained with little cost or time, low-entry markets generally offer disproportionately high profit margins and the chance to capture significant if not controlling shares.

Resource Requirements

Of the four major criteria, the resources required to capture new market niches can often be the most difficult to achieve. Few companies have large amounts of excess cash available to promote their entrance. Even fewer have technical or managerial personnel capable of adding new assignments to their current responsibilities. And hardly any companies enjoy excess facilities that may be used for new production, storage, or office functions. A shortage of resources more than any other element blocks market entrance. This is why flexibility is so important. Companies that have restructured to achieve flexibility in their capital reserves, personnel skills, product mix, operating procedures, and marketing organization will inevitably be in the best position to draw on current resources for new, fast-growth opportunities as needed.

Moreover, by developing a comprehensive forecasting model based on cost/sales/asset functional relationships, companies are in a good position to determine with a high degree of certainty those resources that must be obtained and when they must come on line to meet strategic plans. Without the ability to predict the need for new capital, personnel, and facilities well in advance of moving to new markets, fast growth is nearly impossible.

Comparative Analysis

Athletes who compete in races keep one eye on the finish line and one eye on other athletes in the race. Original strategies for positioning and pace must be altered during the race as competitors surge ahead or fall behind. The same analogy holds in the business world. The specific tactics for achieving your long-term growth strategies that you originally planned must be altered as competitive forces ebb and flow. And to know which tactics to change and when to change them, you must know how your competitors are doing. Blindly following your original plan without considering how your company's market position and pace stack up against competitors and industry standards can lead to missed opportunities and lost markets.

One of the best ways to judge the merits of tactical decisions is to compare your company's key financial ratios with those of other companies of comparable size, producing similar products, or selling to similar market niches. (See Chapter 3 for a full discussion of financial ratios.) To make such comparisons with publicly held companies is relatively simple. Annual reports, SEC filings, and a stream of reports from securities analysts reveal just how well or poorly a publicly held company is doing. It isn't quite as simple to make comparisons with closely held companies, although with a little digging and creative analysis it can be done.

Four steps are involved in deciding which companies to use as comparison standards:

1. Compile a list of all known companies in your industry.
2. Cull this list down to companies that compete in your niche markets—product niches, location niches, distribution niches, and so on.
3. Separate publicly traded companies from those that are closely held.
4. Dig out as many financial ratios and as much raw data as possible about those companies that seem to be the closest match.

The first selection should be made from sources that supply data on publicly traded companies in your industry. This is relatively simple once you define the applicable Standard Industrial Classification (SIC) codes. Many companies serve more than one class of customer, however, or sell more than one product line or service. In those cases, it's necessary to choose the appropriate SIC code for each industry—whether market-oriented or product-oriented. As a general rule, it pays to make the industry definition as broad as possible, thereby keeping the number of SIC codes to a minimum.

All SIC codes are listed and defined in the federal government's *Standard Industrial Classification Manual*, down to the lowest sub-headings. These codes are structured to permit the collection of data for all business-oriented statistics published by the government and therefore must be kept up-to-date and complete.

The easiest and fastest way to begin is at a public library. Most libraries have many reference works containing data on national, regional, and local companies, both public and privately held. In fact, libraries are the only practical source of data, short of spending a small fortune on reference-oriented computer databases.

Once the appropriate SIC code has been determined, it's possible to trace companies from other reference works. The following describes several readily available sources that are easy to tap:

1. *Standard & Poor's Register of Corporations, Directors, and Executives* and *Standard & Poor's Corporation Records*. These directories probably provide the most complete listing of companies found anywhere. The only problem is that they do not distinguish between public and privately held firms. To make such a distinction, use the National Quotation Bureau's *National Monthly Stock Summary* in conjunction with the S & P volumes. This publication can be invaluable for determining whether small, unknown companies are public or private. It lists all companies whose stock has been quoted within the past month on the *pink sheets*. The pink sheets list the bid and ask prices of unlisted stocks as compiled by the National Daily Quotation Service. Of the 13,000-plus small companies that have issued public stock, only about 4,500 find their way into NASDAQ markets. The rest remain relatively unnoticed, with most trades conducted between brokers from pink-sheet advertisements.

   Between the S & P volumes and the *National Monthly Stock Summary*, you can get information about company history, list-ings of subsidiaries, location of principal plants and other properties, business and products, officers and directors, com-parative income statements, balance sheet statistics, financial ratios, and a description of outstanding securities. If your library doesn't carry these publications, they can be obtained from Standard & Poor's Corporation, Inc., 25 Broadway, New York, NY 10004, and National Quotation Bureau, Inc., Plaza Three, Harborside Financial Center, Jersey City, NJ 07302.

2. *Moody's Manuals.* In many respects, Moody's five manuals, *Bank & Finance*, *OTC Industrials*, *OTC Unlisted*, *Public Utilities,* and *Transportation*, give a more comprehensive description of companies than the *S&P Register.* These manuals list both large and small companies whose stock is traded in public markets. Of the five, the *OTC Industrials Manual* and the *OTC Unlisted Manual* are the most helpful. Both provide a range of information about smaller public companies; the first covers those listed in the NASDAQ market, and the second covers "pink-sheet" companies. The range of data includes company history and background, mergers and acquisitions, subsidiaries, business and products, location of principal plants and other properties, names and titles of officers and directors, financial statements, and a description of capitalization, including financial and operating ratios. Any of the Moody's manuals can be found in libraries or from Moody's Investors Services, 99 Church Street, New York, NY 10007.

3. *DIALOG information services.* DIALOG is one of the country's biggest computer database companies and is reachable on-line through CompuServe and other telecommunications systems. An array of services can be purchased, depending on the specific information being sought. One of the most popular is "DISCLOSURE II," which is also available from several other on-line database suppliers. In addition to other data, "DISCLO-SURE II" provides access to the Value Line Surveys database. Subscribers to on-line database services can download public company annual reports and SEC 10-K filings directly to their computers.

The major drawback in using on-line database services is

that they cost money—and fairly large sums for comprehensive coverage. Except in rare cases, a relatively good selection of potential comparisons can be drawn from the hard copy S&P and Moody's references. If you want to hook up with DIALOG, CompuServe's address is CompuServe Information Services, 5000 Arlington Center Boulevard, Columbus, OH 43220.

4. *Value Line Investment Survey*. This is one of the reference services most widely used by both individual investors and stockbrokers. In tracking the financial and business performance of 1,700 publicly owned companies, it presents a one-page summary, updated periodically, for each company, including historical trends, historical and current stock prices, description of the business and product lines, beta, and a wealth of profit, sales, and asset information. It also has a unique evaluation system that rates the timeliness and safety of investing in each company's stock, based on historical trends and regression analysis. Value Line volumes can be found in the reference section of libraries. To subscribe, contact Value Line, Inc., 711 Third Avenue, New York, NY 10017.

5. *Dun & Bradstreet's Key Business Ratios*. This publication contains fourteen significant financial ratios for more than 800 different lines of business, listed by SIC code. Current ratios, quick ratios, debt-to-equity ratios, and net-income-to-sales ratios are representative of those included. Although this service doesn't pinpoint specific companies, ratios by SIC code can help establish comparative standards. The major drawback is that the ratios are drawn from relatively large, public companies.

With a workable list of companies to compare against, the next steps aren't too time-consuming, unless, of course, you happen to be looking at an obscure or highly specialized market. Begin by phoning or faxing each company and asking for sales literature, product descriptions, published quarterly and annual reports, statistical compilations, names of board members and officers, and facility locations. It's truly amazing how much information companies are willing to disclose for the asking.

Most active trade associations compile annual or quarterly statistics from member firms. Normally, data relating to specific member companies are merged into industry averages, which can then be used for comparison purposes. However, some associations do release a modest amount of specific membership data of a qualitative nature. If available, qualitative comparisons can be nearly as valuable as numerical statistics. Some of the key elements to look for include

- Credit status (easily obtained from Dun & Bradstreet or other credit agencies if trade associations won't provide it)
- Depth and experience of management (based on technical certification and tenure with the company)
- Competitive position and intensity of competition (derived from market size and number of member firms)
- Tenure of the business (not usually available)

Valuable statistics may also be available. Here are the main ones to ask for:

- Employee turnover
- Number of employees
- Average sales
- Gross profit and operating profit as a percent of sales
- Annual capital expenditures
- Annual R&D expenditures
- Inventory turns
- Receivables days' sales

Although such data will probably be incomplete and will not reveal performance results from the highest- or the lowest-rated members, they should be enough to permit at least gross comparisons.

Government bureaus can also help. The Department of Commerce (supported by the Department of Labor) collects reams of monthly, quarterly, and annual reports from practically every company doing business in the United States—both public and private. These data are sorted by various levels and sublevels of SIC codes. They can be especially valuable when trade associations either do not publish compilation reports or are hesitant to release data to nonmembers.

The categories of government-compiled statistics are almost identical to those gathered by larger and more active trade associations. In addition to sales, employee turnover, and other traditional information, however, the Commerce Department compiles a virtually unlimited number of statistics in special areas. Here is a sampling that tends to be universally applicable to large and small companies:

- Sales volume compared to inventory purchases
- Number of new employees hired compared to employees terminated
- Square feet of floor space used in production
- Building permits and building starts (for construction industries)
- Various employee benefit statistics
- Employee accident statistics
- Bad debt ratios

The Department of Commerce staffs offices and libraries in many major cities. They are open to the public, and for the asking you can peruse vast files of data for the current year and for many prior years. Some offices have progressed to computer databases that are also available for public use.

Economic/Business Cycle Indicators

The final leg in the strategic planning process—an analysis of pertinent economic indicators—needs to be completed before you create pro forma forecasts. Such a macro analysis gives the framework within which a company must operate. Like it or not, we are all subject to the vagaries of recession, inflation, federal monetary and fiscal policies, and currency exchange rates. The first step in any planning cycle must be an analysis of the economic and business conditions that are expected to occur during the plan period. And the most important assumptions underlying such analyses have to do with national economic cycles and industry business cycles.

In fact, without a thorough understanding of your company's current position relative to both cycles, it's impossible to forecast sales with reasonable accuracy. Although marketing programs, selling techniques, and market demand affect sales levels, very few businesses are immune from cyclical trends. It goes without saying that it's necessary to choose only those indicators that apply to your company. It does little good to worry about national unemployment rates if you employ two people. Or to be concerned with building permit trends if you manufacture motorcycles. Or to crank in aerospace industry statistics for ladies' garment stores. However, certain conditions affect all businesses—interest rates, inflation rates, consumer spending, and perhaps business investment, to mention a few.

For those readers who are not familiar with the major economic indicators, a brief review might be in order. The federal government regularly prepares indicators that make up an analytic system for assessing current and future national economic trends, particularly cyclical expansions and recessions. These indicators are grouped into leading, coincident, and lagging indexes, according to their tendency to change direction before, during, or after the general economy turns the corner—either from recession to expansion, or from expansion to recession. The leading indicators reflect business commitments and expectations, the coincident indicators indicate the current stage of the economy, and the lagging indicators identify business cost trends.

The Bureau of Economic Analysis in the U.S. Department of Commerce releases monthly synopses of each set of indicators in press releases and in the bureau's monthly magazines, *Business Conditions Digest* and *Survey of Current Business*. The concept behind economic indicators is that profits are the prime mover in a private-enterprise economy and that recurring business cycles are caused by changes in the outlook for future profits. Such an outlook is reflected in the leading indicators and in the ratio of the coincident index to the lagging index (which is itself a leading indicator). The components of each index are:

Index of Leading Indicators
- Average weekly hours of manufacturing production workers (average weekly hours)
- Average weekly initial claims for unemployment compensation
- Manufacturers' new orders for consumer goods and materials industries in 1982 dollars (manufacturers' orders)
- Vendor performance (percent of companies receiving slower deliveries)
- Contracts and orders for plant and equipment in 1982 dollars
- New private housing building permits (housing starts)

- Manufacturers' unfilled orders for durable goods industries in 1982 dollars (manufacturers' orders for durable goods)
- Prices of crude and intermediate materials, monthly change (producer price index)
- Stock prices of 500 common stocks (stock market price index and dividends yield)
- Money supply (M-2) in 1982 dollars (money supply)
- Index of consumer expectations (consumer confidence index and consumer statement index)

Index of Coincident Indicators
- Employees on nonagricultural payrolls (employment)
- Personal income less transfer payments in constant dollars (personal income)
- Industrial production index
- Manufacturing and trade sales in constant dollars

Index of Lagging Indicators
- Average duration of unemployment (unemployment)
- Inventory-to-sales ratio for manufacturing and trade in constant dollars (inventory/sales ratio)
- Labor cost per unit of output in manufacturing, monthly change (unit labor costs)
- Commercial installment credit outstanding to personal income ratio
- Average prime rate charged by banks (interest rates)
- Consumer price index for services, monthly change (consumer price index)

Since World War II, when the government began compiling these indexes, the index of leading indicators has consistently declined for nine months and the coincident/lagging ratio for thirteen months before the onset of a recession. Also, the index of leading indicators predicts an expansion in the economy four months before it begins, and the coincident/lagging ratio predicts such expansion two months before the official turn. Although these indexes are only a rough guide to the direction of the economy, they can be useful in preparing pro forma forecasts and developing strategic plans.

Global economic conditions also affect an increasing number of companies. Those that import materials from abroad, that export products and services, or that have foreign subsidiaries or branches are affected by exchange rates, international financial markets, and economic cycles.

Stock market, commodity market, and currency market trends might also be relevant to the future growth of your company. To the extent that consumer or industrial buying habits are influenced by capital market trends, statistics relating to these markets must be analyzed.

The number of sources of national and international economic, financial, and trade data boggles the mind. By far the biggest collector of such data is the federal government. The *Federal Reserve Bulletin*, the *Statistical Abstract of the United States*, the *Survey of Current Business*, and the *Economic Report of the President* are popular sources. Eximbank puts out a wealth of data relating to international trade. The U.S. Department of Commerce has offices in all major cities that are chock full of data, reports, government booklets, and a plethora of other information.

Many states and a few major cities also provide more localized economic and business data. California, New York, Texas, and Illinois all do excellent jobs, as do New York City, Los Angeles, and Chicago.

Major investment banks publish financial market statistics by the carload. Standard & Poor's, Moody's, Value Line Surveys, and Dun & Bradstreet compile valuable statistical tabulations. Money-center banks like Citibank and Chase routinely circulate current economic trend information. The sources go on and on.

On the industry side, trade associations and trade magazines are invaluable sources of current data and statistical trends. The *U.S. Industrial Outlook* and Standard & Poor's *Industry Surveys* include data on most industries. And major securities houses like Merrill Lynch, Bear, Stearns, and so on, publish data on a wide range of industries. Once you start looking, you'll find an endless number of data sources. Just be certain to use only those indicators that relate to your company or your markets.

Part IV
Financing

Chapter 11

Venture Capital

Venture capital, also known as *risk capital*, is the primary source of financing for start-up businesses, R&D ventures, and companies bringing out new product lines. Selling equity shares directly to venture investors avoids the costly exercise of using underwriters when making a public stock offering. It also gets cash into your company much faster than the convoluted process of going through an initial public offering (IPO). However, not all firms can attract risk capital. Venture investors expect to make high returns on their investment, and this can happen only through an initial public offering in the future—usually within five to seven years.

The underlying assumption made by venture capital investors is that as a company's products are accepted in the marketplace, sufficient investor interest will be generated to make an IPO feasible. The resultant trading market should then enable the original investors to cash in their chips and realize a substantial appreciation on their investment. In the right situation, they may hang around for a while to see whether the market will drive the share price up, but only when the spread between the offering price and the expected gain is fairly wide.

In most cases, venture capital investors want to monitor their investment by taking seats on your board of directors. In other cases, fearing the potential liability that goes with board membership, they will choose to be *board advisers*. Either way, they usually, but not always, insist on the controlling vote. At the same time, most venture investors recognize that, if and when a company needs additional financing down the road for expansion or development programs, they must stand ready to provide it. No investor with a sizable equity stake will let a company die for lack of financing.

Companies use venture capital—both equity and debt—for three broad purposes:

1. As *seed capital* to cover initial market research, testing equipment, facility rent, basic operating supplies, experimental materials, perhaps the payroll for a few employees, and, at least partially, the entrepreneur's living expenses. Such expenditures occur during the setting up, development, and testing stages of a new product, process, or business.
2. As *working capital* during the finalization of the development stage when the product or process nears market potential. This additional first-stage financing pays for the materials, labor, overhead, and selling expenses required to produce and sell the products in quantities that meet market demand.
3. As *acquisition capital* to fund the purchase of a going business by an established company or group of entrepreneurial investors.

Companies in the process of developing new technologies or products are the main recipients of venture capital. Under certain conditions, however, service businesses trying to enter new markets (such as trading companies) or offering variations on existing markets (such as desktop publishing advertising) may also be attractive to venture investors. Banks and other mainstream financial institutions regard these embryonic ventures as too risky for loans, and this makes venture capital about the only feasible source of funds.

Although other criteria enter the equation, the basic requirement of venture investors is that companies generate a five to ten times return on investment in less than seven years. This is in addition to dividends or interest during that period. Since cash flow during the start-up period generally isn't sufficient to pay such high returns each year, most, if not all, of the cumulative gain must come from an IPO. This becomes a decisive factor in the timing and pricing of the IPO. (See Chapters 12 and 13 for descriptions of both public and private stock offerings.)

Investment Instruments

As your business grows and additional financing becomes necessary, venture capital investors might come up with additional equity capital, although fresh loans are more likely. By making loans, the original investors avoid diluting their equity interests. The idea is to continue lending sufficient capital to see the start-up company through to an IPO, and then to settle the obligation with proceeds from a public stock issue. Two types of loans are commonly used:

- Term loans secured by all hard assets of the start-up business and the personal assets of the entrepreneur/business owner, backed by personal guarantees. Typical interest rates run two to three percentage points above prime.
- Mezzanine loans to bridge the gap between the sum of the original equity contributions and secured term loans, and the amount of capital needed to bring the business to a public offering. Mezzanine loans are usually unsecured, although a pledge of common shares may be necessary. Because of the risk, mezzanine interest rates run very high—usually double-digit. Interest is payable monthly or quarterly, with principal payments deferred until the IPO.

More often than not, term loans, and in some cases mezzanine loans, carry warrants convertible into common shares upon default or when the business goes public.

At this stage, the business has not developed sufficiently to go public but probably needs new capital for equipment purchases, further overhead expansion, or perhaps an expanded facility for production quantities. If the original investors put additional equity into the company, perhaps that will attract new private investors. However, most venture capitalists prefer to solicit new investors to spread the risk over a broader base.

The case of PVN Pharmaceuticals is an excellent example of how a small company funded by venture capital attracted new equity investors. PVN had developed new vaccines for treating previously fatal bovine diseases. MultiCapital LP financed the initial development, but when the product caught the market's eye, PVN needed additional production and test equipment. MultiCapital, which held a controlling interest, solicited outside investors. As an incentive, investors who would put up a minimum of $50,000 for noncumulative, 9 percent preferred shares with warrants received a board seat plus annual director's fees of $20,000.

Three investors took the bait. When the company went public three years later, each new investor received $182,000 for his shares.

When to Use Venture Capital

Venture capital is clearly the most expensive way to finance a business—not in terms of interest rates, but with respect to returns to equity shareholders. An annual return of 30 to 45 percent, even if paid out of a future public offering, is a luxury that not many companies can afford. If you go this route, you will probably have to give up significant authority over your company's policies and relinquish a significant share of your company.

Raising capital through venture funds should never be seriously considered unless all other reasonable means have been exhausted. While there can be little question that some firms have benefited greatly by the addition of investor expertise and financial contacts, the cost is more than most companies can manage.

However, venture capital does fill a market niche. Therefore, it should at least be considered along with other sources for seed money, first-stage financing, and business acquisitions. In the case of business start-ups, the product should already be designed, a prototype built, and most of the market research completed. For first-stage financing, three conditions must be met:

1. Further market testing must substantiate a growing market with both domestic and international potential.
2. Key management personnel should have already been hired.
3. An advertising and promotion program should be in place and functioning.

If you use venture capital firms for business acquisitions, they should be treated as *financing packagers* when commercial banks and other traditional financial institutions normally won't fund the deal on their own.

Venture Capital Markets

Many years ago, venture capital investors were interested only in high-tech start-up businesses with rapid growth potential, such as companies engaged in developing health care diagnosis and treatment products, housing and transport services for the elderly, top-of-the-line travel and leisure activities, advanced telecommunications, and alternative fuel sources. This type of company has never had much difficulty attracting first-stage short-term financing. Risk-oriented, high-return venture investors are constantly in search of such opportunities.

The success of high-tech venture capital investments—primarily the enormous success of advanced computer technology companies—encouraged venture funds to look at other industries as equally high-potential targets. Throughout the 1970s and 1980s small venture capital firms became large investment conglomerates. Their funds multiplied geometrically. The euphoric explosion on Wall Street encouraged even greater risk taking in first-stage, rapid-growth businesses. Although the late 1980s saw a slackening in the number of venture opportunities, by the mid-1990s venture capital had made a comeback.

Venture Capital for Small Business

There are venture capital funds interested in financing small-business growth in nearly every state in the country. These firms range from one-person operations to divisions of large commercial banks. Venture capital funds are normally grouped into four categories, in addition to Small Business Investment Corporations (SBICs):

1. *Investment banks.* Several reputable investment banks have separate divisions or departments that finance small-business R&D ventures. They are attracted to businesses that have very rapid growth potential and are managed by entrepreneurs who come highly recommended.

2. *Divisions of large corporations.* Many *Fortune* 500 corporations have venture capital divisions or subsidiaries with a mission to search out new small-business technology. This gives them a much wider choice of new products at a much lower price than they could get through their own R&D departments.

3. *Family funds.* Many very wealthy families (Rockefeller, Mellon, Coors, Cudahy, and so on) have traditionally funneled some of their wealth into small, high-potential start-up companies with state-of-the-art product development ideas. Their main interest is in products and companies that will have a positive social effect.

4. *Private investment firms.* These are limited partnerships and corporations that have the financial backing of insurance companies, pension trusts, and other large blocks of capital. Some are small ($2 million in funds); some are much larger (over $100 million).

With the surge in mergers and acquisitions during the 1980s, venture capital funds also expanded into fields other than new technology development, such as investment banking, asset-based lending, mineral exploration, and even international development projects. However, the venture funds that offer the greatest possibility for new financing continue to concentrate on high-growth or stable but expanding companies. They are also still heavily involved in small-business acquisitions.

Finding Venture Capital

Despite the availability of vast pools of venture capital, many funds have become more conservative in their assessment of first-stage risk. Still, small businesses in high-growth markets that need first-stage working capital can attract small venture funds, provided they can demonstrate a high probability of very substantial investment appreciation.

The best sources of first-stage venture capital are well-established national firms such as Hambrecht & Quist (San Francisco), Golder, Thoma & Co. (Chicago), or Sprout Group (affiliated with Donaldson, Lufkin & Jenrette, New York). *Pratt's Guide to Venture Capital Sources* is a comprehensive directory that lists the addresses and phone numbers of these and other firms.

The National Venture Capital Association is another good source. Its membership directory may be obtained by contacting the organization at 1655 North Fort Myer Drive, Suite 700, Arlington, VA 22209; (703) 528-4370.

Finally, the *Directory of Venture Capital Clubs* can be helpful in locating private investment clubs formed specifically to invest in first-stage ventures. It is available directly from the International Venture Capital Institute, Inc., P.O. Box 1333, Stamford, CT 06904.

It should be noted, however, that small venture capital firms come and go like ocean tides. The few big firms are permanent fixtures in the industry; the numerous small ones are not. In addition, since the small ones do not have the breadth of management talent that well-established firms do, they cannot provide valuable free assistance in technical or management matters. Their size also limits their access to further financing. If at all possible, it pays to stick with the big firms. They have a reputation to sustain, have extensive contacts in financial markets, and, more often than not, can provide capable management assistance.

Stable Industry, Growing Local Market

The cooling-off period in the late 1980s and early 1990s forced venture funds to broaden their horizons beyond high-tech start-ups. They began looking at investments in companies serving stable industries but capable of penetrating small, usually local or regional niche markets.

The financial services industry represents one example. As banking regulations loosened controls over intra- and interstate bank expansion, a merger wave eliminated many banks from neighborhoods and small towns. Evaluating this vacuum as a potentially high-growth niche market, investors formed new small banks to serve small businesses and individuals in local areas.

Waste management is another example of a growing local niche market in some parts of the country. Environmental pressures forced the development of technologies to convert liquid and solid waste to socially beneficial products. New technologies were developed and new facilities built to convert trash to alternative energy sources or to other salable products such as composted fertilizer.

Venture capital provided much of the first-stage financing for companies involved in these opportunistic local markets. Many funds began as limited partnerships, soliciting investments from high-net-worth individuals and local corporations. Others branched out from original venture funds in an effort to diversify their holdings.

Although venture funds still favor research and development projects, they are also a good source of capital for stable, local-market businesses. However, as with national venture funds, expect to give up an ownership share, perhaps a controlling interest, and plan to take your company public in five to seven years.

Forming Your Own Venture Capital Club

Many small venture funds are structured as limited partnerships made up of doctors, lawyers, public accountants, and other high-income individual investors. In a sense, these funds are merely the high-risk version of investment clubs. Typically these groups are structured as limited partnerships, although limited partnerships can no longer be considered effective tax shelters.

If you have good local business contacts, you might consider forming your own venture capital club. You may be able to raise capital for your own company and have enough left over to invest in other businesses. You could retain jurisdiction over management decisions by becoming the general partner. Limited partners could supply investment capital in exchange for a share of the profits and the opportunity for capital gains if and when the company goes public.

If you are interested in forming your own venture capital club, here is how you could structure the arrangement to retain the greatest flexibility for yourself and the most protection for investors:

1. *General partner.* The business owner(s) form(s) an S corporation to be the general partner.
2. *Limited partners.* Limited partners may be people affiliated with financial institutions, lawyers, professional accountants, consultants, physicians, or other professionals or business-people. As passive investors, they contribute the major share of investment capital and have no say in the running of the operating business. All limited partners must be individually indemnified against liabilities arising from the business.
3. *Allocation of profits and losses.* The partnership agreement allocates all profits, capital gains, and capital losses from the

business investment to the limited partners and all operating losses to the general partner.

4. *Management fees.* As general partner, you charge the start-up business management fees as compensation for time and expertise contributed to the business. These fees can then be offset by the general partner against operating losses for tax purposes.

5. *Additional limited partners.* The partnership agreement provides for the admission of additional limited partners and specifies the new allocation of profits, capital gains, and capital losses, based on either contributed capital or other yardsticks.

6. *Dissolution.* The partnership agreement provides for a definite life for the partnership. It also stipulates that at the dissolution date, a majority vote by all partners can reset the date to a later period. Of course, getting-out positions for each member must be defined.

7. *Conversion to equity.* The partnership agreement specifies that when the operating business goes public, limited partnership units can be exchanged for common shares at a predetermined conversion rate. Typically, the general partner and limited partners share proportionately in the conversion, although the agreement may be written to permit either general or limited partners a greater amount.

In addition to the basic limited partnership agreement, provisions must be made for raising additional capital as the business grows—either additional equity contributions or debt. Ideally, further equity investments will be equally spread among all partners. In practice, however, one or more limited partners have the responsibility for generating new equity as needed. Regardless of the source, as new equity comes in, ownership percentages and profit/loss allocations must be revised.

It's important to choose limited partners who not only have sufficiently deep pockets or good contacts with financial institutions to see the venture through, but also bring specialized expertise and personal contacts in financial markets, legal disciplines, and accounting techniques.

To compensate for the high risk incurred by limited partners, be prepared to pay substantial returns as previously described.

Business Acquisitions

Although we usually think of venture capital in relation to small-business start-ups or expansions into new product lines, it can also serve as a viable source of capital for business acquisitions, provided the acquisition price is at least $10 million. Venture capital clubs will occasionally invest in smaller acquisitions, but such funds are becoming increasingly difficult to ferret out (unless you already know someone who owns or participates in one). Also, banks and secured lenders tend to monopolize the very small acquisition finance market. If you're going for a bigger deal, however, venture capital could easily be the best way to raise capital.

All the big investment banks are involved in venture capital in one form or another. Goldman Sachs, Merrill Lynch Capital Markets, Bear, Stearns, and so on, are excellent sources of capital for acquiring a fairly large business—but again, they are not interested in small deals. Typically, an investment bank acts as a *financing packager*. By that I mean that the venture fund serves as the primary or lead source of capital and brings in other financial institutions or individuals to spread the risk: perhaps a commercial bank for a credit line and a secured lender for term loans secured by equipment and machinery. The venture fund itself makes mezzanine loans and equity contributions for the balance of the purchase price.

In exchange for an equity contribution, venture funds receive from 15 to 75 percent ownership interest. However, equity interests in excess of 50 percent are required only for very special deals. Most venture investors do not want the responsibility that goes with owning a controlling interest in a company.

Many small venture funds, or *boutique* houses, specialize in specific industries or special products and can be invaluable as a source of management or technical assistance as well as capital. For business buyers with less than $100 million in sales or an acquisition deal of less than $50 million, boutique funds are usually the way to go. In addition, smaller houses are able to give the deal personal attention, and such hands-on participation often makes the difference between closing a deal and losing it.

It's important to select the right size venture fund to match the size and type of acquisition. Going after a large firm for a small deal or a small fund for a large deal only wastes time, money, and effort.

Selecting the Right Venture Fund

If you try to attract capital from sources that don't match the criteria of the deal, you will only become frustrated and waste a lot of time. A venture capital firm may seem to meet your objectives but still not be interested in financing the deal because its portfolio is already full. Without exploring the market, it's impossible to tell what may be available. Still, the following criteria can help to point you in the right direction:

1. *The size of the deal.* The size of the venture fund should be matched with the size of the acquisition deal. The break points for closely held acquisitions are deal sizes of
   a. Up to $1 million
   b. $1 to $10 million
   c. $10 to $20 million
   d. $20 to $50 million
   e. Over $50 million
2. *The size of the acquiring company.* Although the target company may be larger than the parent buyer, venture capital firms prefer the size relationship to be reversed. It's much easier to finance the deal if the acquiring company has sales of, for example, $10 million and the target is in the $5 to $7 million range.
3. *The financial history of both the acquiring and acquired companies.* Unless both companies are on a growth curve for sales and profits, don't aim at venture capital financing. Some venture funds will consider a modest growth curve; most will not. It's necessary to find one that likes the growth curve you are on.
4. *Type of industry.* Although in recent years low-tech or stable industries have been attractive to an increasing number of venture capital firms, it's still more difficult to interest one in this type of market than in a high-tech, environmental, or other visibly rapid growth industry. Moreover, venture funds do not like to finance acquisitions of companies in the government contracting business. You will probably get the best results if you use a venture fund that specializes in your industry.
5. *The personality match of venture fund principals and acquiring company management.* The relationship with venture fund managers over a five- to seven-year period can get

very touchy. It always works best when personalities don't clash.

6. *Geographic proximity*. Larger companies can afford to fly around the country for meetings. Smaller ones cannot. It's better to choose a venture fund near your company or the one you are buying.

Case Study: DoRight Engineering, Inc.

In my book *The Complete Book of Raising Capital*, I related a true case history that was a perfect example of a small company using venture capital in an acquisition. I repeat it here to demonstrate how a deal might be structured to benefit all parties.

DoRight Engineering, Inc., (DRE) designed and assembled electric and electronic control and measuring devices. It was a closely held company with annual sales approaching $30 million. DRE had always been profitable, and over the past five years it had doubled its sales volume. Competition was getting keener, however, and the owners saw that to continue the growth pattern, new product lines and management talent had to be added. They decided that the fastest way to obtain these resources was through an acquisition.

After an intensive search, the company located an ideal candidate, Heavy Metals, Inc. (HMI), which had sales of more than $18 million. DRE negotiated a purchase price of $12.3 million, cash at closing. To finance the deal, the DRE president contacted a midsize venture fund, Venture Dynamics Corp. The following deal was structured.

For a placement fee of $250,000, Venture Dynamics agreed to package the financing. They brought in a commercial bank, a secured lender, an insurance company, and a small venture capital limited partnership. The initial plan called for a private placement of convertible debentures to take out the Venture Dynamics mezzanine loan in approximately nine months after the acquisition closed. As the deal progressed, however, these plans changed. The following financing package was put together:

		(million)
1.	Equity contribution from DRE	$1.2

2. Long-term loan from asset-based lender, with interest at two points over prime, interest and principal payable quarterly based on a seven-year amortization schedule with a balloon payment due at the end of the fifth year, secured by a first position on the machinery and equipment and a second position on the real estate of HMI

5.6

3. Long-term mortgage loan from an insurance company, with interest at 8.5 percent, for thirty years, interest and principal payable monthly, secured by a first position on the real estate of HMI

2.7

4. Preferred stock issue to a secondary investment bank, assigned for administrative purposes to Venture Dynamics, with a dividend rate of 5 percent, cumulative and callable at face value plus accrued dividends, carrying warrants convertible to common shares after the fourth year at a ratio of ten shares of preferred to one common share

1.0

5. Mezzanine loan from Venture Dynamics with interest at 10 percent, payable on demand, secured by a promissory note from DRE

0.8

6. Equity contribution from Venture Dynamics, with warrants to purchase additional common shares within seven years at a price equal to the lesser of market value or DRE book value

<u>1.0</u>

Total acquisition price   <u>$12.3</u>
Short-term operating line from a commercial bank, with interestat 1.5 points over prime, secured by receivables and a demand note

<u>$3.0</u>

Debentures were never floated because the market for such issues dried up. The mezzanine loan was eventually converted to long-term debt with a second position on the machinery and equipment. Four years after the acquisition, DRE went public with a $15 million stock issue representing 40 percent of its common shares. Eventually, both venture funds cashed in their warrants, and everyone came out a winner.

Two conditions must be present to interest a venture fund in financing a business acquisition:

- The combined entity—parent and acquisition target—or the acquisition target alone must be in an industry and have product lines that, at some future date, will have the potential to attract investors to a public offering.
- The deal must be large enough to warrant the risk. The smaller the deal, the greater the perceived risk. The DRE deal for $12.3 million is an attractive size for small venture funds. Anything less than $5 million is much harder to place.

The following guidelines should be used to determine whether your particular acquisition transaction fits venture capital criteria:

Your Company Should
1. Have a profitable history and a recent upward trend in sales, profits, and cash flow.
2. Have a sound business reason for making the specific acquisition.
3. Have a strong management team.
4. Be willing to take the company public within five years.
5. Demonstrate the ability to integrate the acquired company with existing marketing, engineering, production, and management activities.
6. Be willing to give up an equity share.
7. Be willing to accept operating recommendations from the investment bank.
8. Be unable or unwilling to finance the deal with the company's own equity contribution.

The Company You Are Buying Should
1. Be able to demonstrate the ability to generate enough cash flow after the acquisition to make required debt service payments.
2. Be on the same growth curve as the acquiring company, or better.
3. Be in an industry that is compatible with the acquiring company.
4. Have a strong management team.
5. Have a good reputation in the industry, the marketplace, and the community.

The Combined Companies Should

1. Be able to demonstrate the cash flow to return 30 to 40 percent per year to the investment bank.
2. Be able to demonstrate that combining the two companies will result in cost savings, additional growth potential, management efficiencies, and other benefits not attainable by the two companies separately.

Small Business Investment Companies

Small Business Investment Companies (SBICs) are venture capital firms that specialize in first-stage financing for businesses in fragmented, local markets that cannot attract private venture funds. Changes in tax laws and innovative financing schemes over the years have resulted in the popularity of SBICs fluctuating widely.

From their 1958 inception as a new financing source for small businesses, to their relegation as an also-ran, SBICs have survived the test of time. In the 1990s, SBICs still provide an easily accessible source of funds, not only for small-business start-ups, but for R&D projects and expansion.

Originally, SBICs were conceived as offshoots of the Small Business Administration, with a charter to help finance small start-up businesses that were unable to raise capital through normal commercial bank channels. That is still their primary objective, accomplished with loans and equity capital from a pool of public and private money. SBIC equity contributions normally run to 15 percent ownership. Loans are normally repaid over three to five years.

SBIC Ownership

Although they are licensed by the Small Business Administration, SBICs are privately organized, owned, and managed. They set their own policies and make their own investment decisions. Many remain under private ownership; however, an even larger number operate as divisions or subsidiaries of large commercial banks. Because of this diversity in ownership, each SBIC has different loan and equity investment criteria. Some may favor debt over equity; others, just the reverse. The amount of financing available varies, as does the industry specialization. Because of these licensing requirements, SBICs must follow federal regulations governing the types of financing they can and can't engage in.

SBICs concentrate on first-stage financing, although they also participate in smaller second-stage loans. The dollar amounts vary, but are generally under $100,000. SBICs that are divisions of commercial banks also have the ability to package deals with bank participation.

For years it was relatively easy to set up an SBIC. Federal regulations required a modest capital investment on the part of the owner and then matched this equity with federal funds. Consequently, many entrepreneurs formed their own SBICs, not to go into the banking business, but as their own private source of government money. Now, however, the rules have changed. Today, most SBICs are owned by commercial banks and larger venture capital firms, with a much smaller number in the hands of private investors.

Types of SBIC Financing

SBIC term loans for the purchase equipment and machinery normally extend three to five years, occasionally longer. Interest rates run three to five percentage points over prime—higher than bank loans, but less than the interest charged by secured lenders. Some SBICs also charge placement fees of up to $10,000.

SBICs do not require hard-asset collateral other than the equipment being purchased. On the other hand, they nearly always require personal guarantees. The outstanding exception relates to companies already doing business with the SBIC's parent commercial bank.

Instead of extra collateral, many SBICs get extra security by insisting that restrictive covenants be embedded in the loan agreement. These covenants, just like those demanded by commercial banks, enable the SBIC to monitor a borrower's business and provide another mechanism for controlling the company.

Furthermore, larger loans commonly include provisions that give the SBIC an equity interest in the company, either upon default or within a specified time period if the loan has not been fully liquidated. However, barring default, most SBICs seldom want to hold more than 15 percent of a company's outstanding shares.

Just like private venture capital firms, SBICs participate in working capital financing as well as hard-asset term loans. In fact, many prefer to operate in both spheres. Obviously, this makes it easier to get the financing you need. However, it also reduces competition among financial institutions, making it more difficult to get new financing at the lowest cost and best terms when and if it is needed later on.

Advantages of SBIC Financing

The biggest advantage of SBICs over typical venture capital firms is that SBICs are not after outrageously high returns. Most will settle for 15 to 20 percent per year, in contrast to 35 to 45 percent for venture capital firms.

In addition, SBIC participation encourages other financial institutions to look favorably on loan requests. If you can get an equity contribution or a loan from an SBIC, other financial institutions are usually more interested in considering additional financing at the appropriate time. Both commercial banks and secured lenders feel more comfortable knowing that an SBIC will monitor its financial commitment, thereby relieving them of a very big variable. Such a commitment gives credence to the viability of the business.

Furthermore, to receive a license from the SBA, SBIC managers must furnish evidence that they have a wide range of management talent outside the banking industry. If you can get an SBIC officer to sit on your board, other lenders will have greater confidence that their loan repayment schedules will be met.

A listing of SBICs in your area may be obtained from the National Association of Small Business Investment Companies, 1156 15th Street, NW, Suite 1101, Washington, DC 20005, (202) 833-8230.

Applying for Financing

Preparation is the key to getting venture capital from either an SBIC or a venture capital fund. And the most important step is to construct a detailed financing plan founded on well-conceived business plans and strategic plans. Whereas banks place the greatest emphasis on historical financial performance and asset collateral, and secured lenders are mostly concerned with asset liquidation value, venture capital firms look to the future. Clearly, past performance and collateral are important. However, without a clear, concise pro forma forecast, no venture capital fund will consider investing.

Moreover, since venture capitalists are primarily business-oriented managers rather than bankers, they want to see a thorough description of the business—product lines, customer base, competition, market size and share, and so on, with about the same amount of non-financial detail as in a business plan. They also want a complete profile of the background and credentials of the management team. Without a detailed pro forma forecast, however, all the rest is meaningless.

When searching out R&D venture capital, both the impact of the development effort and the benefits derived once the products are marketable should be highlighted in the pro forma projections and within the body of the plan. Detailed descriptions of the new product should be accented:

- Why is it unique?
- What is the market demand for it?
- Why does the market need and want such a product?
- How will products be priced and distributed?
- What competitive products are already in the market?
- Are there any substitute products available?

The financing plan takes on a slightly different character for new ventures without a prior history. This is a far riskier investment, and many larger firms won't touch start-ups. SBICs are also reluctant to get involved, unless you can furnish additional, nonbusiness collateral.

Convincing investors that you are not just blowing hot air and working out a dream is the hardest job in attracting venture capital. This makes it all the more important to build the financing plan on well-documented and carefully researched market facts. Competitive products must be compared with your company's product lines in terms of quality, price, delivery, and technological pros and cons.

Pro forma forecasts should be conservative, yet positive. An excellent way to cope with investor skepticism is to include pro forma financial statements at three different volume and profit levels: minimum, most likely, and maximum. Of course, this involves a thorough analysis of the factors that will influence the attainment of each level, such as market forces, economic factors, cost overruns, product failures, and so on.

It is nearly impossible to attract venture capital to start-up situations without rock-solid evidence that

1. You and your key managers are experts in the field and have outstanding technical and managerial abilities to develop the product and bring it to market. Reference letters that prove achievements in prior endeavors are excellent credentials, as are technical certifications. Ideally, reference letters should come from persons or companies well known to the venture capital firm. Bankers, key management personnel of well-known companies, and technical authorities serve the purpose well.

2. You and other principal shareholders are willing to risk a substantial portion of your personal assets on the venture, either as collateral for loans or as equity contributions. Investment portfolios, real estate, pension proceeds, stockholdings in the new venture, and even personal residences may have to be pledged for a personal guarantee.

3. Venture investors can realize significant gains in the future through additional ownership interests if and when the start-up is successful. Equity interests should be offered right up front, including warrants to acquire additional interests if the product is successfully marketed. Pro forma financial statements should extrapolate the timing and proceeds of an initial public stock offering.

Chapter 12

Public Stock Issues

For many companies, and perhaps yours, selling stock to the public may be a foolish exercise. Stock issues are very costly. They absorb a great deal of your time and that of your key managers. To a large extent, the proper timing of a stock issue to coordinate it with favorable financial market and economic conditions determines its success or failure. After the stock is sold, many complex reports must be regularly filed with federal and state regulatory agencies. Financial analysts must be kept abreast of your company's progress and its plans. And, in most cases, stockholders must be rewarded with dividend checks.

On the other hand, issuing public stock is a great way to raise significant amounts of equity capital. In fact, if your company is already highly leveraged, or if it doesn't have the type of assets banks want as loan collateral, a public stock issue might be the only way to raise sufficient capital to expand your business. And as long as institutional and private investors retain their seemingly insatiable appetite for equity appreciation, the market for new stock issues will continue to be strong.

Before we get into the mechanics of *going public*, it might be helpful to review a few basic definitions:

- Public stock issues may be sold in two distinctly different ways: (1) to the public at large, which of course is a *public* issue, and (2) to a select group of buyers, in which case it is referred to as a *private placement*.
- Both public issues and private placements may be sold nationally (interstate) or limited to one state (intrastate).
- Public issues can also be divided into segments, or *tranches*, with one tranche sold in U.S. markets and another sold internationally.

- The first time a company sells stock to the public, the issue is called an *initial public offering (IPO)*.
- Once a company's stock begins trading in public markets, if the company comes out with additional new stock issues, they are called *secondary issues*.

The significance of these distinctions is related to regulatory requirements, cost, stock appreciation potential, flexibility, and market acceptance. Prior to developing specific plans to sell common stock, you need to weigh each of these factors in light of your company's capital needs, its previous profitability, and the capabilities of your management team. You also must decide how your company will use the new capital. And—what is probably the most important decision—you must decide how much of your company's ownership you are willing to give up.

Uses of New Equity Capital

Except in very rare circumstances, it doesn't make sense to issue public shares if you plan to buy them back in a few years. Although it is certainly possible to reverse a public stock issue—that is, to take a public company private—this is expensive and should not be done indiscriminately. Therefore, the only time you should consider going public is when you cannot raise the capital you need through alternative means.

Some business owners look at an IPO as a convenient way to finance short-term working capital needs or to pay themselves dividends. These are the wrong reasons for going public and will almost certainly hurt the company. When long-term capital (i.e., equity capital) is used for short-term purposes, it cannot generate the new assets needed in the future to compensate investors.

But there are some very legitimate reasons for going public. Here are the most common:

- To repay current debt obligations
- To make a major expansion involving the acquisition of facilities and machinery
- To acquire a going business
- To build or acquire an offshore facility

- To establish a company's market value for purposes of selling the entire company
- To increase the value of management-held shares
- To spin off a division or subsidiary

Of these reasons, the first—to pay off current debts—seems to be far and away the main reason smaller companies go public.

Should You Refinance?

As your company matures, you will probably find that the bank loans and equity arrangements that filled the bill in earlier years no longer meet your needs. Sales volumes increase. Equipment must be replaced. New product lines require additional space. Venture capitalists must be paid off. Market rates drop below high fixed interest charges. More balance sheet flexibility is needed. Any number of reasons could make refinancing with new equity capital a viable choice.

Yet, for a variety of reasons, companies shy away from going public. Inertia sets in, even though evidence clearly indicates the need for action. It's too easy to justify the postponement of refinancing decisions. Comfortable relationships with current lenders and investors make necessary decisions more difficult. Meeting loan covenants without much effort tends to lead to complacency. Trade payables may be stretched, but cash flow remains sufficient to keep the company afloat and bonuses paid.

Time and again I have seen companies survive and grow if they have the foresight to maximize liquidity and hence flexibility by restructuring (and refinancing if necessary) before tough times hit. Complacent owners, more often than not, end up selling their company at less than market value and looking for jobs.

The smaller the company, the more reasons for refinancing. By paying off current debt, you can increase the amount of cash available to withdraw from the business. Additional cash may be needed to expand into global markets. Very often small companies find that refinancing improves their tax position. You may want to liquidate as much debt as possible to improve your company's book value prior to retiring. And companies on the skids quickly learn that refinancing may be the only way to save the business. Use the following checklist to determine whether you should consider refinancing with a public issue:

It's Time to Consider Refinancing When

1. The monthly sales trend is declining, has leveled off, or is not accelerating as rapidly as planned.
2. More than 2 percent of receivables have slipped beyond sixty days.
3. Trade payables are stretched longer than receivables.
4. Inventory is increasing faster than sales.
5. Personnel are not fully occupied with productive work.
6. Bank relationships have deteriorated beyond repair.
7. Published financial statements show your company's profits and ratios deteriorating.
8. The company's debt-to-equity ratio exceeds 3 to 1.
9. The value of collateralized assets has increased.
10. Lease payments are higher than debt service would be; or the reverse.
11. Expansion requires additional capital, but all assets are already pledged.
12. Additional capital is needed to develop a new product and bring it to market.
13. The acquisition of another business makes strategic sense.
14. A management incentive program needs major improvements.
15. The present owners want to sell the company or retire.
16. Either debt service or dividend payments are draining too much cash.
17. Your bank is about to call its short- or long-term loan.

Chapter 15 offers creative ways to refinance and restructure your company without tapping public stock markets.

Timing the Issue

When a public stock issue looks like the way to go, the financial market may not be ripe. The country may be in the throes of a recession. Your industry may be under siege from government regulators or foreign competition. Stock market averages may be plummeting. Time and again companies have spent thousands of dollars getting ready for an IPO, only to find that investors do not want their stock, or will buy shares only at a very low price. Here are the main events that tend to dissuade the market from accepting IPOs:

- A national event of major proportions creating gross uncertainties, such as a war, a presidential election, or a financial market crisis
- Stock market jitters, causing averages to trend downward
- Stock market collapse (e.g., October 1987)
- An industry in rapid decline (e.g., machine tools and semiconductors in the 1970s)
- Out-of-control inflation, causing rapidly rising prices, interest rates, and unemployment
- The country or your region in a hard recession—but only if economic indicators continue to trend downward

Of course, many other factors may affect the timing of a stock issue, but these are the types of circumstances under which it becomes increasingly difficult and costly to raise large amounts of capital through public issues. Capital may be available, but the cost will be higher than necessary, and it usually makes sense to wait until conditions improve.

The High Cost of Going Public

Public stock offerings are very expensive and usually cannot be justified for amounts of less than $5 million. To make an IPO cost-effective, a company should be generating annual sales of at least $10 million, although this figure decreases for very high-growth industries. Issues of less than $7.5 million (defined as *small issues* by the Securities and Exchange Commission [SEC]) will be less expensive than larger issues. However, even a small issue could cost you from $250,000 to $500,000.

Once the issue is sold, ongoing administrative costs add a significant amount of overhead. Costs to produce periodic SEC reports and proxy statements, printing and mailing expenses, and annual fees for accountants, lawyers, registrars, and transfer agents add up in a hurry. New shareholders also look for dividends on their investment. Since dividends are not deductible for tax purposes, after-tax dollar payments increase operating costs even more.

Other than cost, three potential problems must be dealt with. First, before the stock can be sold, you must get approval from the SEC for interstate issues or from a state securities commission for intrastate issues. Because market timing is such a crucial element, the actual issue date requires careful planning. More than one issue has flopped because the SEC or a state commission took too long to grant approval and the market window closed before the offering was ready. The decision to proceed in spite of such a delay is likely to result in a share price substantially lower than anticipated.

After the stock is sold, there is no assurance that active trading will follow. This could nullify incentive programs structured to reward management employees with noncash stock options and make it difficult to use stock for business acquisitions.

A third problem relates to managing your company. It doesn't take long to realize that the trading price of a company's shares is directly related to its earnings trend. It's very easy for key management personnel to spend more time worrying about increasing earnings per share than about running the company efficiently. Short-term decisions that favorably affect earnings for this quarter or this year may in the long run do more damage than good.

Probably the most aggravating condition is the loss of privacy. SEC regulations require complete disclosure of the most intimate and proprietary matters, such as officers' compensation, personal histories, incentive programs, forecasts of future earnings, planned new product developments, and strategic operating plans. Not only must this information be revealed in the offering, it must also be continually updated in quarterly and annual reports—all of which are open to the public.

Both issue costs and continuing compliance expenses must be considered when evaluating the desirability of going public. Theoretically, the up-front costs should be covered by the proceeds of the issue, just like a real estate agent's commission for the sale of a house. But what if the market buys only part of the offering? Or, worse still, what if the issue fails completely? Either way, the costs of preparing the issue could have a major impact on your company's cash flow and profits.

The following examples indicate the types of up-front costs that must be incurred, although the amounts vary depending on the company's circumstances and market timing:

1. *Legal and filing fees.* Lawyers perform three functions. They assist in the writing of the prospectus, coordinate the preparation of the registration statement, and issue legal opinions in

compliance with SEC regulations. Larger law firms charge more, smaller ones less. The range of legal fees runs from a minimum of $75,000 to a maximum of $150,000 for a small issue. Large issues command fees in excess of $250,000. Filing fees with the SEC add another $50,000 to $100,000. States also want their share and assess filing fees of another $40,000 to $60,000.

2. *Public accounting fees.* A stock registration statement requires audited financial statements: two years for a small registration, three for a standard one. Audits by major accounting firms easily cost from $30,000 to $150,000 per year, depending on the complexity of the audit. These firms charge additional fees of the same magnitude for assisting in the preparation of the registration statement, the compilation of pro forma forecasts, and the calculation of various statistical tables required by the SEC. On an hourly basis, fees of $150 to $250 per hour for special IPO work are not uncommon. Smaller CPA firms charge less, but not much.

3. *Printing registration statements and other documents.* Once everything is prepared, the registration statement, proxies, offering prospectus, and official notices must be printed and bound. Printing costs vary significantly in different regions of the country, but an average of $40,000 to $100,000 for typesetting, printing, collating, and other clerical preparation costs is not unreasonable.

4. *Underwriting fees and commissions.* You can't make an IPO without using an underwriter, at least with any assurance that it will be a success. Underwriters assist in the preparation of the prospectus and registration statement. They also coordinate with lawyers, accountants, and the SEC. An underwriter's primary tasks are to sell the stock issue and then to provide a market for the shares. An underwriter is the key to a successful IPO. A good one can make things happen. Without an underwriter's constant attention and dedicated efforts, issues very often fail. The accounting and legal firms that help with the registration continue to be the best source for locating a competent underwriter. These professionals know which firm will do the best job for your company.

Initial underwriting fees run 1 to 2 percent of the issue

value. On top of that, underwriters get a commission of 7 to 10 percent of the actual value of the stock sold. It doesn't take long for these costs to add up. Smaller public issues typically cost up to $500,000; larger issues much more.

Moreover, after the issue is on the street, an assortment of administrative duties (with associated costs) must be performed on an ongoing basis. Quarterly and annual SEC reports must be prepared. Annual certified audits must be performed. Proxy statements must be prepared and distributed to shareholders. Quarterly financial reports and annual reports must be prepared, printed, and distributed. Shareholders' meetings must be announced and held. If you list your company's shares on a stock exchange, special reports must be filed periodically. Dividend notices, checks, and tax reports must be handled. Most companies find that they must hire additional financial personnel to manage these compliance requirements.

Given the high cost of a public issue and the inevitable aggravation that market trading brings, going public may not seem like such a great idea. However, despite high costs and aggravating regulations, public stock offerings remain the best way to raise large amounts of equity capital. But it's important to take the step for the right reasons. Also, it makes sense to prepare for an offering well in advance and then to time the offering with market conditions.

The following criteria should help reduce the variables in reaching the decision about going public:

Company Structure
1. The company must already be incorporated.
2. If an S corporation election has been made, and the new shareholders will total more than thirty-five, the company must convert back to a C corporation.
3. The company must be large enough to have professional management, such as a controller, sales manager, chief engineer, and so on.
4. At least some of the products or services offered by the company should have high growth potential over the next five years.
5. This potential growth must be demonstrable, not a reflection of your hopes and dreams for success.

6. A commanding market share or unique market niche is highly desirable.
7. The company must have three years of progressively improving profitability (two years for a small IPO under $7.5 million).
8. Projections for the next five years should show continued improvement.
9. The prior three years' financial statements (two years' for a small issue) must be audited by a reputable CPA firm.
10. You must get a clean certificate from your audit for each of the years.

The Economic Picture

1. Stock exchange averages should be rising.
2. Average price/earnings ratios should be running above ten times.
3. General optimism should prevail in the national economy.
4. Regional economic indicators should be at least stable, and preferably rising.
5. Interest rates, national unemployment statistics, and inflation projections should be at modest levels.
6. Industry trade statistics should indicate favorable growth projections for the next three years.
7. Federal international trade policies should not be detrimental to the company's product lines.

Preparing to Go Public

Going public is not a decision to be made on the spur of the moment. A successful IPO requires extensive planning long before the actual issue. Most companies that have successfully launched an IPO began preparations up to three years in advance. Obviously, if you don't have annual audits, you must begin at least that far in advance to meet the requirement for a two- or three-year certified audit. Here are some tips for getting a company ready for a public issue:

1. For companies serving low-tech, unglamorous, and perhaps declining markets, try to develop a complementary product line that hits rising markets.

2. Fill all key management positions and replace managers who cannot meet performance standards.
3. Clean up all contingent liabilities: lawsuits, insurance claims, tax audits, pension liabilities, and so on.
4. Implement a five-year strategic plan.
5. Get a hot new product through the initial development stage (nothing attracts investors like a chance to get in on the ground floor with a snappy new product introduction).
6. Embark on a well-conceived public relations campaign.
7. Develop a reputation for aggressive marketing and new product introductions, including promotions that will get the company's name known in its local community, its industry, and the financial community.
8. Try to get a well-known personality to join your board of directors (anyone from the financial community is a big plus).
9. Accumulate market and competitive trend statistics.
10. Watch the share price movements of competitors or companies in similar or complementary industries.

Whenever I mention IPOs to small-business clients, the one question I get asked more than any other is: "If we go public, will I lose control of my company?" The answer is no. That's one thing you don't have to worry about. Other than losing the total privacy of your business and being restricted by certain rules and regulations previously discussed, you will not lose control of your company—unless you want to.

A company may issue as many shares as it wishes, assuming that underwriters can sell them. Few small-company IPOs ever exceed a 25 percent interest, however. The most successful offerings for smaller companies tend to be under 20 percent. Bear in mind that underwriters prefer the initial issue to be for a small minority interest rather than a controlling interest, mainly because when an issue gets into the 30 to 40 percent range, it becomes increasingly difficult to sell. When trading picks up, secondary offerings can always be used to raise additional capital if desired.

Pros and Cons of Going Public

Obviously, every company has its own prerequisites and constraints when issuing stock to the public. What works for one company won't work for another. Nevertheless, certain benefits and risks tend to be universal (some of which have already been discussed). Without attempting to be inclusive, the following represents the opinions of many financial executives of companies large and small that have issued common stock to the public for the first time. The consensus seems to be that the major advantages are

- *Financial stability.* A public stock issue may be the only way to raise enough growth capital for third-stage internal expansion or business acquisitions. Most companies reach a point where additional growth cannot be financed internally and debt is too expensive.
- *Amount of capital available.* Greater amounts of capital can be raised than with debt financing. Strategic plans may call for the outlay of substantial sums for such activities as implementing major R&D programs, expanding market coverage, establishing offshore facilities, or buying a going business, which require more cash than is available internally. Concurrently, credit constraints or high interest rates may preclude using debt.
- *Flexible payouts.* Equity capital does not require a fixed cash outlay on a predetermined schedule, like interest and principal payments. This can be extremely important when developing new products or markets that may require several years to generate income. Although shareholders will expect dividend returns, the timing and amount of payments are unilaterally determined by the company.
- *Ownership control.* Initial issues are better received by the market in small segments. Owners of privately held companies can raise a substantial amount of equity capital without losing control. Secondary offerings that disperse ownership interest among hundreds or even thousands of shareholders can be structured to leave previous owners in effective control with less than 51 percent stock ownership.

- *Ready exit.* Disposing of shares in a privately held company when it's time to retire or otherwise get out can be a sticky problem. With an established trading market, insiders (original owners, managers, and other early shareholders) have a ready means of disposing of their interests, subject, of course, to insider trading rules. Also, the market value of shares can be readily established for estate valuations.

- *Employee incentives.* Stock options can provide a valuable incentive for key employees. Not only do options make employees feel a part of the company and therefore, hopefully, stimulate better performance, they also offer employees the potential of earning substantially more than with cash bonuses.

- *Improved borrowing capacity.* Banks and other financial institutions view additional equity infusions favorably, since cash balances are increased and at the same time debt-to-equity ratios improve. Not infrequently, banks are willing to offer extended lines of credit once a company has accomplished an IPO. Moreover, a substantial reduction in the debt-to-equity ratio leaves the door open for a potential public bond offering.

- *Improved company image.* Most privately held companies have a difficult time establishing a profile in industries dominated by large public firms. The publicity that goes with a public offering can easily change that, increasing public visibility and thereby stimulating sales and attracting higher-quality personnel.

- *Increased personal net worth.* Nothing boosts personal net worth faster than establishing a market value for an owner's stockholdings. A good many millionaires have made the jump with an IPO.

Although these advantages appear overwhelming, IPOs also create several headaches. In addition to the initial cost of going public, here are the main drawbacks:

- *Ongoing expense.* The ongoing expense after the stock begins trading can be a significant burden for smaller companies. A variety of reports must be regularly filed, including 10-Ks, 8-Ks, and 10-Qs. You must also issue what, at times, seems like a constant barrage of news releases. Costs must be incurred for annual certified audits, added legal fees, printing expenses, and public relations programs that privately held companies can do without. And employees must now spend time complying with SEC and exchange regulations. It is not uncommon to see these ongoing costs add up to $60,000 to $100,000 a year for a small company.

- *Closing out venture capital.* Typically, venture capital firms finance privately held companies with the understanding that at a future date the company will go public. An IPO now closes this door. Although this is not an important consideration for larger companies, it could eliminate a valuable source of capital for those incurring heavy R&D expenditures.

- *Loss of management flexibility.* Once a company has gone public, its management personnel lose flexibility in making decisions and developing strategic plans. Abiding by SEC disclosure regulations can easily compromise valuable competitive secrecy. Furthermore, some corporate strategies require shareholder approval, such as mergers, business acquisitions, new stock issues, and so on, preventing management personnel from making these decisions on their own.

- *Liability.* Officers and directors of public companies remain fully liable for any violations of SEC or exchange regulations. This can become an extremely burdensome feature. Devising procedures for protection against such liability steals valuable time that could otherwise be put to developing growth policies.

- *Potential loss of control.* Depending on the percentage of ownership in public hands, the loss of control of the board of directors can be an onerous possibility. Many adversarial proxy fights have resulted in the dismissal of a company's original owners.

- *Unveiling of company skeletons.* Once a company issues public stock, its past, present, and future affairs become public knowledge. Bankruptcies, criminal records, lawsuits, and other potentially damaging events involving officers and directors must be disclosed in prospectuses and registrations.

- *Wrong market timing.* A company might expend a substantial amount of cash getting ready to go public, only to learn that the market timing is off.

The Public Offering Team

As we have seen time and again, an IPO is a major undertaking for any company—and the smaller the company, the more difficult it seems to be to keep focused on the myriad matters that need to get accomplished. The only proven way to manage an IPO is with the team approach. The team's responsibility will be to manage the entire offering from start to finish, marshaling those resources necessary to get the job done. To a very large extent, the caliber of the members of this team determines the success of the offering.

The IPO team should be made up of a company executive, corporate counsel, securities counsel (probably from the same law firm), auditor, underwriter, financial printer, and, for good measure, a representative from a financial public relations firm. The responsibilities of each are as follows:

- *Company executive.* The first step is to prepare a comprehensive strategic plan covering the next five years. The plan should provide a complete description of new product line introductions; personnel requirements; new equipment and facilities (if needed); competition, market trends, and advertising/promotion plans; and, of course, pro forma balance sheets, statements of income, and cash flow schedules.

    The second step involves pulling together all the information needed for a registration statement, including data needed for the prospectus. Scheduling charts should be prepared, with time budgets and assigned responsibilities for each segment. Preparation for the road show and the coordination of all participants comes next. And finally, after the offering is completed, the company executive assumes responsibility for meeting the regulatory and financial markets' reporting requirements.

- *Legal counsel.* Corporate counsel may or may not have securities experience. If not, such expertise must be brought on board. The primary functions of securities counsel are to (1) make sure that all state and federal regulations are complied with, including the determination of the appropriate filing vehicle, and (2) coordinate the preparation and filing of the registration statement. This involves performing all the preoffering planning, including the review of all contracts, corporate bylaws, and articles of incorporation (updating where appropriate); the coordination of the scheduling of the offering; and the appropriate due diligence investigations to meet full disclosure requirements.

- *Auditor.* The auditing firm can make or break a securities registration. Most smaller firms do not have SEC experience, so be sure to hire one that does. A major international firm will do the best job, although these firms' fees are high. Since two to three years' audited financial statements are required, the earlier a firm with securities experience comes on board, the more smoothly the registration will go. The auditor's main duties are to:

1. Advise the company about the financial implications of going public.
2. Verify that adequate internal financial controls are in place and functioning.
3. Advise the company about alternative tax ramifications.
4. Prepare the disclosure portion of the registration statement.
5. Provide the underwriter with *cold comfort* letters.
6. Provide ongoing audits and financial advice to meet SEC requirements.

- *Financial printer.* Financial printers are highly specialized in the art of printing SEC registration statements and all other required notices, mailings, and documents. Most are quite large and have years of experience. A qualified printer knows the current SEC printing regulations, can provide tight security, and has sufficient staff and facilities to ensure the timely and accurate printing and delivery of filings.
- *Financial public relations.* In an effort to reduce costs, it's easy to ignore the importance of financial public relations; but that can be a big mistake. A competent public relations firm can increase the likelihood of a full subscription by developing your company's image; preparing and distributing news releases; preparing high-powered road show materials, such as videos, slides, and pamphlets; helping to distribute offering materials to the media; preparing scripts and assisting

management in speaker training; and assisting in company promotions, distributions, presentations, and other postoffering requirements.

- *Underwriter*. Underwriters serve as brokers, consultants, buyers, and hand-holders before, during, and after the offering. The underwriting activity begins with a review of the company's strategic plan and an assessment of the probability of the offering's success. Underwriters set the price of the shares and the total amount of the offering based on market conditions. They also coordinate with other underwriters to support the issue.

  Underwriters file the registration statement, make arrangements to comply with SEC and stock exchange regulations, and distribute securities. They determine how much of the offering should be withheld for the selling group of underwriters and institutional sales (typically 25 percent of the issue). And they collect the sales proceeds for the company. Without a highly qualified, active, and energetic underwriter, IPOs nearly always fail to meet expectations.

IPO shares may be sold on a *best efforts* basis, through a *firm commitment underwriting*, or on a *standby* arrangement. A best efforts sale means that the underwriter has the option to buy stock and the authority to sell stock, and pledges to do the best it can to sell the offering shares. With a firm commitment underwriting, the underwriter buys all the offering shares and then resells them to the public. From an issuing company's perspective, this is clearly the best way to go. Standby agreements are normally used in rights offerings.

Preparing the Offering Prospectus

Once the decision has been made to proceed with an IPO, and appropriate professional advisers have been selected, a rather complicated offering prospectus and registration statement must be prepared. The offering prospectus serves two purposes: It is a primary source of disclosure within the SEC registration statement and it is the primary selling tool that the underwriter uses to market the issue.

The prospectus gives potential investors a clear, concise picture of the company, its management, its financial history, and the intended application of funds raised through the issue. It also gives management's estimate of the company's financial results for five years into the future (pro forma financial statements). SEC regulations specify that the offering prospectus and the registration statement must represent a conservative picture of the company, and clearly identify investment risks in buying the stock. There must be a full disclosure of pending lawsuits, claims, or other contingent liabilities, and a detailed explanation of how the proceeds of the issue will be used.

SEC regulations specify exactly what items must be included in the prospectus and even how financial statistics must be displayed. It is essential to engage qualified attorneys and public accountants to oversee the writing of each section of the prospectus and registration statement.

The elements to be included are much more extensive than those required in other financing plans. Plans presented to banks, the SBA, venture capitalists, and other lenders or investors should be optimistic and emphasize the company's strong points, its expansion plans for the future, and its management. Conversely, an offering prospectus and the accompanying registration statement must emphasize the risks to potential investors. Optimism is kept to a minimum. Descriptions and forecasts continually highlight how investors might lose their entire investment. The following describes the major topics to be included:

1. Name of registrant, the title and amount of securities being offered, and the date.
2. Statement of whether any securities being registered are from current stockholders. Later in the prospectus, disclosure must be made of the names of these security holders, their relationship with the company, and the number of shares owned before and after the offering.
3. A cross-reference of material risks in connection with the purchase of the securities.
4. An estimate of the minimum/maximum range of offering price and number of shares.
5. The share price to the public, underwriting discounts and commissions, and proceeds to the issuer or other persons.
6. Notices about stabilization of the offering price.
7. Summary of the information contained in the prospectus, complete address and telephone number of the company's

principal executive offices, risk factors (those factors that make the issue speculative or of high risk), and the ratio of earnings to fixed charges.

8. Use of proceeds, including the following:
   - Listing of uses of proceeds by priority
   - Debt to be retired, including amount, maturity, and interest rate
   - Contingencies that could cause a change in the application of the proceeds

9. Determination of offering price as follows:
   - Description of the various factors considered in determining the offering price
   - Description of the various factors involved in determining the exercise price or conversion price of warrants, rights, or convertible securities

10. Dilution of shareholders' interests, as follows:
    - A comparison between the public offering price and the effective cash cost to officers, directors, promoters, and affiliated persons (but only if there is a substantial difference)
    - Net tangible book value per share before and after distribution
    - The amount of increase in book value attributable to the cash payment of investors in the offering
    - The amount of immediate dilution from the public offering price absorbed by such purchasers

11. The company's dividend policy, including its dividend history, policies currently followed, restrictions on dividend payments (if any), and a statement of whether future earnings are to be reinvested in the company rather than paid out in dividends.

12. A description of the company's debt and equity position (its capitalization) before and after the offering.

13. A management discussion and analysis section that provides enough information to allow investors to analyze the company's cash flow position. It must be complete, factual, and conservative. It must include three subsections:
    - A thorough explanation of the company's balance sheet and statement of income for the past three years, including any interim periods since the last annual statement
    - Long- and short-term purchase commitments or other non-balance sheet obligations, future plans for growing the

company, and expected future sources of capital to fuel this growth

- A thorough discussion of all significant events affecting the current and future operations of the company, such as a threatened labor strike or the loss/gain of major new order contracts

14. A business description section that discloses everything an investor needs to know to make an informed judgment about investing in the shares. Although the specific topics vary by type of business, the general items to be included in this sec tion are

- Company history over the past five years
- Primary products/services sold
- Principal markets
- Methods of distribution
- Patents, trademarks, or licenses held
- Sources and availability of materials, parts, or components to produce the finished products
- Identification of any single sources of critical materials, parts, or components and whether the company is dependent on a single customer or a very small number of customers
- Firm customer order backlog
- Expenditures on research and development
- New products under development
- Legal proceedings against the company or for the company

15. A properties section that identifies the location of all company-owned or leased properties and gives a description of them.

16. Under legal proceedings, identification of any pending or ongoing legal actions involving the company.

17. A management and certain security holder section that is dedicated to disclosing all pertinent information about directors, officers, and key employees. The following must be included:

- Names, ages, and business experience
- Compensation, including stock options and other indirect fees for directors and executive officers
- Loans to these individuals or their family members
- Certain transactions with directors, major shareholders, and members of management
- *Golden parachute* clauses in employment contracts

- Stock ownership of all officers, directors, and shareholders owning more than 5 percent of the stock
- For companies that have been in business less than five years, the names of promoters and transactions with the company by the promoters

18. The plan of distribution, including everything about the underwriters and how the stock will be distributed:
    - The name of each underwriter and the underwriters' obligations
    - Distributions other than those made through underwriters (i.e., dividend or interest reinvestment plans and securities for mergers or acquisitions)
    - Exchanges on which the shares will be listed, if any
    - Underwriters' compensation—commissions, discounts, warrants, etc., as set out by the National Association of Security Dealers
    - Arrangement for a representative of the underwriter to be elected to the board of directors
    - Indemnification of underwriters, if any
    - Identification of and amounts paid to finders or other intermediaries and their relationship to registrant or its officers, directors, principal stockholders, or underwriters

19. The identification of any interest in the registrant by parties acting as counsel or experts.

20. A listing of all expenses relating to the issuance and distribution of the securities.

21. A list of all required exhibits.

22. Company financial statements and the related auditors' opinion certificate. These must include
    - Audited balance sheets for each of the past two fiscal years
    - Audited statements of income, changes in financial position, and shareholders' equity for each of the past three years
    - Unaudited interim statements, along with those of a comparable period during the prior year, if the effective date of the offering is more than 134 days after the last fiscal year-end

If the registration is for less than $7.5 million, use a Form S-18 for the filing. With this simplified version, the differences from the standard S-1 registration are

- An audited balance sheet for one year rather than two
- Income statements and statements of changes in financial condition for the past two years instead of three
- No management discussion or analysis of financial condition and no selected financial data section

Listing Shares

Theoretically, when an IPO is properly priced, a steady rise of 10 to 15 percent in the market price of the shares should occur over the first month or two; however, this seldom happens. Initial investors may be quick to capture profits by selling at the first rise. They may dump shares when prices decrease. If unchecked, the aftermarket price of IPOs is likely to undergo a fairly wide fluctuation once the shares begin trading.

To prevent large fluctuations, the SEC has granted underwriters the authority to enter into stabilization activities—buying shares in a weak market, selling shares when the market price escalates too fast. When an underwriter undertakes such stabilization, it must inform the SEC immediately.

During the early stages of the offering process, a decision must be made about listing the stock on one of three financial markets: the New York Stock Exchange (NYSE), the American Stock Exchange (AMEX), or the over-the-counter market. Two choices are available for over-the-counter listings: (1) the National Market System (otherwise known as NASDAQ), and (2) the *pink sheets* (broker sheets listing company shares available for sale that are not listed on the NASDAQ).

New York Stock Exchange

Only larger companies can be listed on the New York Stock Exchange (NYSE). The minimum requirements are

- At least 1,000,000 publicly held shares
- Market value of $16 million for those shares
- Annual pretax net income of $2.5 million
- A minimum of 2,000 shareholders
- Net assets of $18 million

Quarterly and annual reporting requirements are the strictest of any exchange. And the company must engage a registrar and a transfer agent in New York City. Delisting is complicated and can occur in only two ways: (1) at the request of the NYSE with approval from the SEC, or (2) at the request of the company. A company request must be supported by a vote of two-thirds of the shareholders; furthermore, less than 10 percent of individual investors can vote no. The exchange can request delisting if the company fails to meet reporting requirements, the security trading is inactive, or the company no longer meets initial listing requirements.

American Stock Exchange

Requirements for listing on the American Stock Exchange (AMEX) are more lenient, making this smaller exchange more attractive to smaller companies. The minimum listing requirements are

- At least 300,000 publicly held shares
- Market value of $2.5 million for those shares
- Annual pretax net income of $750,000
- A minimum of 900 shareholders, of which 600 must own 100 shares or more
- Net assets of $4 million

Delisting procedures on the AMEX follow those of the New York Stock Exchange.

NASDAQ

NASDAQ is the acronym for the National Association of Securities Dealers Automated Quotation system. Prices of stocks traded on the NASDAQ are quoted simultaneously on the NYSE and all regional exchanges, providing both buyers and sellers the best possible price at all times. The system provides a wealth of information about a stock, including its trading history, daily trading volume, dividends paid, daily high and low price, the high and low price of the last fifty-two weeks, daily closing price, and the price change from the previous day's close. Minimum listing requirements for the NASDAQ are

- At least 100,000 publicly held shares
- A minimum of 300 shareholders
- Net assets of $2 million
- Net worth of $1 million
- Two or more market makers
- Annual fee of $2,500 or $0.0005 per share

Of the estimated 48,000 stocks traded on the over-the-counter market, fewer than 5,000 are listed on the NASDAQ; the rest are included in the pink sheets.

That finishes the review of public stock offerings. The next chapter takes a look at selling stock through private placements.

Chapter 13

Private Placements and Special Topics

Once you decide to go public, you must choose among (1) a full registration filed on Form S-1, (2) a simplified registration filed under S-18 regulations, or (3) a private placement (an exempt offering). Your choice will affect up-front costs, ongoing expenses, reporting requirements, and the market value of the stock. It will also affect the degree of control that the SEC and the financial markets have over your company's strategic plans. S-1 filings carry the most constraints, exempt offerings the least. The greatest difference between the three filings is in the amount and type of disclosure.

Unfortunately, you don't always have a free hand in choosing which one to use. Your choice will depend on the following:

- Type of business and industry your company is involved in
- Availability and amount of information already in public hands
- Type of security you wish to sell
- Class of security buyers you hope to sell shares to

Although the S-1 filing is used by the majority of midsize and larger companies, it is the most complex and requires the most extensive disclosure. (See Chapter 12 for a full description of S-1 filings.) Such a filing also requires three years of audited financial statements. It must be used, however, if your company does not qualify under one of the other two options.

Simplified Registration on Form S-18

A Form S-18 filing requires two years of audited financial statements. Except for investment companies and certain insurance companies, an S-18 filing can be used by any U.S. or Canadian company not subject to continuous reporting requirements of its respective country. The amount of the offering is limited, however, and cannot exceed $7.5 million in any twelve-month period.

As an alternative to S-18 filings, small companies may file under Regulation A of the Securities Act of 1933. Regulation A offerings are limited to $5 million, and the rules for qualification are very complex. For the record, the major features of Regulation A offerings are

- The company files a *notification*, not a registration statement.
- Notification is filed with a regional SEC office, not with Washington.
- An offering circular, not a full prospectus, is required, with the amount of disclosure similar to that required under an S-18.
- Uncertified financial statements may be used.
- Regulation A cannot be used by a company if affiliated persons or the underwriters have been convicted of securities violations or postal fraud.

Private Placement Rules

A *private placement* is an exempt offering. This means that a company does not have to file a registration statement, obviously saving substantial time and cost. It should be noted that *exempt* means that you do not have to comply with the Securities Act of 1933 (a federal law). It does not mean that your offering will necessarily be exempt from the securities laws of all fifty states. However, states that do require formal registrations are generally more lenient than the SEC.

Private placements are used to raise a limited amount of equity capital in a relatively short period of time at the least cost. Because private placements are exempt offerings, up-front and ongoing costs are substantially less than those for public offerings. Although federal antifraud securities regulations must still be complied with, you do not have to file a formal registration statement. However, several reasons other than cost influence the decision to go with a private placement, the most common being the following:

- The economic or market timing for an effective public offering may be way off.
- A company might not have two or three years of steadily increasing earnings (normally a prerequisite for a successful S-1 or S-18 offering).
- More lenient public disclosure requirements can keep many company skeletons buried.

Who Buys Private Placement Shares

A private placement involves a limited number of investors. They can be relatives, friends, business associates, or strangers. If you have enough personal contacts with ready cash to invest, then sell the stock yourself. Otherwise, use a securities broker.

Typically, you can expect investors to come from the following:

1. Customers, suppliers, commissioned sales personnel, employees, and other individuals and companies with whom the company does business
2. Professional investors who specialize in getting in on the ground floor of a potentially high-flying company
3. Private investors looking for opportunities in small companies that can be taken public within a reasonable time frame
4. Venture capital funds expecting a public issue in the future

Competent securities brokers in any major city who specialize in private placements know where to find investors in each of the last three categories. You might have some ideas for the first.

Different Types of Private Placements

Regulation D was adopted in 1982 in an attempt to establish uniform private placement requirements for the SEC and the states. Most states allow Regulation D filings; a few do not. The designations of private placement rules relate to the section of the securities regulations to which they apply. They are

- Rule 504 for offerings of up to $500,000
- Rule 505 for offerings of up to $5 million
- Rule 506 for offerings of above $5 million

In addition to these specific rules, Regulation D stipulates three other rules—501, 502, and 503—that apply to all three classifications. The major provision is that security sales may be made only to *accredited* investors, who, by definition, fall into the following categories:

- An individual with an annual income of at least $200,000 in each of the two most recent years
- An individual investor (along with his or her spouse) with a net worth of at least $1 million
- An individual purchasing up to $150,000 of the security as long as the investment does not exceed 20 percent of the investor's net worth
- Insiders of the issuing company, who are defined as directors, executive officers, and general partners
- Institutional investors (e.g., banks and insurance companies)
- Plans established by state governments and/or their subdivisions for the benefit of their employees that have assets in excess of $5 million, such as state employee pension funds
- Nonprofit organizations with assets exceeding $5 million
- Private business development companies defined by the Investment Advisors Act of 1940

Moreover, the issuing company must provide proof that each investor meets one of these requirements. Such proof must be in writing and attested to by the investor. Other general provisions of Rules 501, 502, and 503 that apply across the board include the following:

1. The number of investors is restricted under Rules 505 and 506. The method for calculating this number is set out in Rule 501.
2. There cannot be any general solicitations, such as newspaper advertisements or articles, during the offering period.
3. Investors must buy the shares for investment purposes only, with no consideration given to the distribution of the security to other parties.
4. To ensure compliance with this provision, stock certificates must bear a legend across their face stating this restriction against resale.

5. The issuer must use Form D to file with the SEC within fifteen days after the first sale and no more than thirty days after the completion of the offering.
6. No other offer or sale of securities may take place within six months prior to or six months following the offering.

Rule 504

Of the three private placement categories, Rule 504 includes the fewest restrictions. Rule 504 filings may be used by corporations, partnerships, trusts, or other entities that are not otherwise *reporting companies* or *investment companies*. As long as the issuing company does not make a general solicitation, it may sell shares to an unlimited number of investors.

Although investors must be made aware of any adverse impact on the business that would influence the decision to invest, no special disclosure rules apply. As with any exempt or nonexempt offering, however, omissions or misstatements that amount to fraud are expressly forbidden.

An important aspect of the 504 exemption is that it does not mention the level of sophistication of the investor. This opens the door to relatives, friends, business associates, and others who do not hold other investments or would be considered *unsophisticated* investors.

Rule 505

Rule 505 allows a stock issue of up to $5 million by any organization other than an investment company. The number of investors is limited to thirty-five, however, unless they fall into the *accredited investor* category. In that case, there is no limit. Accredited investors are not only those defined under Regulation D, but also entities in which all the owners are accredited investors.

Rule 506

Rule 506 applies to any issuer. There isn't any maximum amount for the offering. It includes the same provisions as Rule 505, plus one additional provision for the thirty-five nonaccredited investors. These investors must meet a definition of *financial and business expertise*. This requires a statement that the investor is capable of evaluating the merits and risks of the investment.

The following conditions also apply under both Rule 505 and Rule 506:

1. Disclosures must be provided on SEC Form 1-A for issues of up to $2 million. Offerings from $2 to $7.5 million must use Form S-18. Those over $7.5 million are considered public offerings and must comply with full SEC disclosure requirements as if the securities were registered.
2. Disclosures may require two years' financial statements, one of which must be audited. If this cannot be reasonably done, only a balance sheet need be audited.

Section 4(6)

This exemption applies to issuing companies that sell stock only to accredited investors. A maximum limit of $5 million applies. No public solicitation is permitted. This exemption closely resembles the Rule 505 exemption, except that

1. Section 4(6) is available to investment companies as well as to all other issuers.
2. Previous violators of securities regulations are not prohibited.
3. The $5 million cap does not include other offerings within the previous twelve months unless they are part of the same issue.

Rule 147—Intrastate Offering

To qualify for an intrastate offering exemption, all securities must be offered and sold to persons residing within the state in which the issuing company is incorporated, and in which it does a significant part of its business. These securities, once issued, must remain in the state. There are no instructions that say how these provisions should be monitored; the rule says only that issuers are held responsible.

Rule 147 does not impose any maximum amount on the offering or on the number of investors. The nonsolicitation rules of Regulation D do not apply, either. It should be noted that Rule 147 is a federal regulation and relates only to federal offering requirements. This does not mean that intrastate offerings are exempt from state regulations. Nearly every state has its own set of disclosure and other requirements that must be met. Although some have adopted common regulations, most remain unique. If a private placement seems like a viable alternative, a securities attorney can fill you in on your state's requirements.

To meet the federal compliance requirements under Rule 147, the issuing company must

1. Be a resident of the state or territory in which the private placement is made.
2. Do business in the state in which all offering solicitations and sales are made. *Doing business* is defined as follows: (1) At least 80 percent of gross revenues are received from sales within the state, (2) at least 80 percent of the issuing company's assets are located within the state, and (3) at least 80 percent of the proceeds of the offering must be used within the state.
3. All investors to whom securities have been offered or sold must be residents of the state.
4. Resale of securities is restricted to residents of the state, and this restriction is noted on the face of the stock certificate.
5. No sales of securities can be made within six months before or after the offering.

Clearly, the range of public stock offerings can be intimidating. This is precisely why the previous chapter stressed the need to assemble a team of experts early in the process. This team will guide the choice of registration format and appropriate timing for the issue. To reiterate, the choice of an S-1, S-18, or private placement, together with the choice of exchange listings, is predicated on three factors:

1. The nature of the company and its business
2. The amount of capital needed
3. The type of investors desired

Once the offering vehicle has been selected, you can develop an intelligent assessment of the market timing and begin putting the offering together. The rest of this chapter reviews several innovations that might affect your approach to a first-time public stock issue.

Emerging Company Marketplace

In March 1992, the American Stock Exchange initiated a new market for small-company stocks, called the Emerging Company Marketplace (ECM). Companies listed on this new *incubator* market do not have to meet the usual financial standards imposed on bigger companies. Of course, AMEX officials hope that ECM companies will eventually grow and become listed on the regular market. Initially, shares of construction firms, technology concerns, medical-instrument makers, and a few others were listed. Looking ahead, AMEX officials expect to capture several of the listings currently traded on the NASDAQ.

In the beginning, the ECM sparked fears that the AMEX would become a dumping ground for ill-fated penny stocks. To prevent this from happening, regulations were issued requiring companies applying for listing to get approval from each state in which the shares were sold. Of course, shares listed on other exchanges are exempt from state regulations.

As discussed previously in this chapter and in Chapter 12, one of the main reasons for going public (other than raising new equity capital) is to establish a market for company stock. The shares can then be used both for management stock options and to value the business. Over the long term, you stand a better chance of having a trading market established for shares on the AMEX than you do by leaving the shares on the pink sheets. Although the ECM was well received in the marketplace, small companies did not initially flock to this new innovation. As the ECM gained momentum, however, companies learned that small-company stocks benefited from open trading to approximately the same degree as those from large companies.

Securities and Exchange Commission Innovations

During 1992, in an effort to stimulate a stagnant economy and sluggish financial markets, the Securities and Exchange Commission adopted several new rules. One of the most important was an easing of regulatory red tape for the nation's 20 million small businesses. The commission's objective was to encourage small companies to go public for their expansion capital. As bank credit had practically dried up, this had some merit, although state regulators had a fit.

The North American Securities Administrators Association, a group of state securities regulators, warned the SEC that such an easing would "put investors at extreme and unnecessary risk." The same concerns about phony penny-stock fraud voiced when the AMEX opened its ECM were heard this time as well. The SEC stuck to its guns; however, to appease state regulators, it decided to bar *blank-check offerings* from using the easier disclosure rules. Blank-check offerings permit promoters to make an IPO without specific projects in mind. During the last decade, blank-check offerings were subject to many abuses, and several penny-stock brokers were convicted of fraud. The most important features of the new SEC rules are

- The ceiling for Rule 505 exemptions was raised from $5 million to $25 million.
- The definition of companies that could use the simpler filings under Regulation A was expanded.
- The maximum offering under Regulation A was increased from $1.5 million to $5 million.
- A provision was enacted to allow companies to test the waters for their securities before committing their resources to registration fees (previously, companies could not begin soliciting potential investors until their registrations were approved by the SEC).

In addition, the SEC has opened the door for pension plans and insurance companies to invest in unregistered private placement stocks and bonds. This little-advertised provision should eventually prove a boon to small-company private placements. The commission also broadened the investor base for small companies by relaxing regulations that govern investment by mutual funds in small-company stocks. On the surface this seems to be aimed at investors more than at small companies; however, by permitting mutual funds to invest in less widely traded small-company stocks, the SEC has, in effect, created a new trading market that enhances the desirability of going public for small companies.

Spinout IPOs

Beyond SEC and stock exchange innovations, other creative financing devices are constantly being tried, many with great success. One such device is the spinout IPO. This can be especially attractive to companies planning to restructure by disposing of part or all of a division, product line, or subsidiary, particularly when the price of the parent company's stock is depressed. Reverse leveraging (returning the equity of prior-year LBOs to the public markets) and privatizations (the selloff of government-owned businesses to the private sector) also contribute to the spinout IPO craze. This is how a spinout works.

Assume that a company has several diversified manufacturing divisions, one of which makes power tools. The parent company, Diversified Corp., has suffered several years of declining earnings, and its stock trades on the NASDAQ at $3.50, eight times earnings in a market that averages a multiple of twenty.

As part of its restructuring plan, Diversified Corp. forms a new corporation, DriveHard Corp., and sells its power tool division to DriveHard for stock. It then takes DriveHard public with an IPO. Initial shares totaling a 70 percent interest in DriveHard sell for twenty dollars.

The market views the investment potential of DriveHard based on its performance and projections. It separates DriveHard from Diversified Corp., since after the IPO, the parent company will own a mere 30 percent of the outstanding shares. Coincidentally, it's entirely possible that when Diversified finishes restructuring, market enthusiasm for the spinout will boost the price of Diversified's shares too. Everyone wins!

Spinouts may be worth a try under three conditions:

1. *When a subsidiary/division and a parent company are competing for cash.* If the parent raises capital, it will be spread throughout the entire organization, reducing the benefit to any single operating unit. Conversely, the rest of the corporation may be doing fine, but the cash-hungry unit is draining the corporation's coffers. Spinning the unit out makes it more independently responsible for its own cash.
2. *When the parent company is in trouble.* If the earnings record, dividend record, or (for bond issues) credit rating of a parent

corporation is tainted, spinning out a subsidiary/division removes the taint from that entity.

3. *As a management incentive when the stock of the parent organization isn't performing.* The manager of a spinout entity will see direct results from efforts to improve the unit's performance in the form of rising stock prices. Stock options in this case mean a lot more than options in the parent company.

One of the big drawbacks of spinouts is that they can be very costly. All the accounting, registration, and legal costs described in the previous sections of this chapter and the previous chapter apply to a spinout IPO. If your company's cash position isn't very good, you probably should not consider spinout IPOs. Furthermore, a spinout forces a more arm's-length relationship with the parent, especially when pricing goods and services between entities. This takes extra administrative and accounting effort, and managers tend to become absorbed in these administrative details rather than in managing the business.

Nevertheless, spinout IPOs can be a clever way to solve several problems while simultaneously raising new capital. And companies of any size with separate divisions, product lines, or subsidiaries can use the technique effectively.

International Tranches

The globalization of financial markets has encouraged a number of innovative approaches in equity issues. One of the most interesting innovations is the increasingly popular international tranche, dubbed the *eurotranche* simply because most are done by American companies selling shares in European markets.

The first international tranche for a U.S. stock offering was created by First Boston in 1984. Today they have become a favorite way to play European and U.S. markets off against each other. A good example of the popularity of eurotranches involved one of my clients in the early 1990s, prior to the advent of the European single market in 1993. This is what happened.

My client (who was a small but very astute investor) was especially bullish on opportunities in the London markets. The Danes hadn't voted down Maastricht yet, but it seemed obvious that it was only a matter of time before France, Ireland, Denmark, the Mediterranean countries, or even Britain would throw a monkey wrench into the planned European Monetary Union. However, the advent of a European single market in 1993 looked certain.

Britain, and much of Europe, were deep in recession; market conversions in Eastern Europe were threatened by political splits; Middle East financial markets were still shattered from the Persian Gulf war; and American investors were buying stocks at multiples of twenty to thirty.

Something had to give, and my client guessed that within a year or two, small American companies in unique niche markets would find the European welcome mat out. Attracted to small caps, preferably IPOs, the client located a tiny electronic-toy manufacturer preparing to go public with a $6 million stock issue that included a 35 percent cross-border tranche. He jumped at the London offering price of $9.10. While the American tranche went up 20 percent in 12 months, the London share price tripled!

Cross-border tranches have not always been good for smaller companies. Many of the early ones were done exclusively to promote the names of American underwriters in international markets, with little effort devoted to selling shares. Smaller-company stocks went begging. Then conditions changed and lesser-known companies got into the act.

From two surveys, one conducted by Sharon Kane of *Global Finance* magazine and one by investment adviser Jim Cloaker, here are a few of the smaller companies that have successfully used cross-border tranches:

- A tiny, unknown company, Deprenyl Animal Health, included 34 percent of its $5.4 million offering as a eurotranche.
- Dillard Department Stores allocated 11 percent of an offering to a eurotranche.
- Small Visions Forever floated $7 million with 34 percent in a eurotranche.
- Dell Computer sold 20 percent of its issue overseas.
- Horsam Productions offered 12 percent of a $10 million issue to overseas buyers.
- Virtually unknown Maverick Tube included 20 percent of an offering for international markets.

There can be little doubt that overseas markets are playing an increasingly greater role in U.S. equity issues from companies of all sizes. European investors are especially hungry for equities of smaller U.S. companies that have the potential for tapping European Union markets or that plan to make direct investments in Eastern Europe or the ex-Soviet Union republics. Most financial markets have already discounted the role of U.S. multinationals in megamarkets and megaprojects, but niche roles for smaller U.S. firms remain fertile ground.

Small-company IPOs have been the rage in U.S. markets for several years. Now eurotranches from smaller U.S. growth companies are also catching the fancy of European investors. It may seem far-fetched to issue stock on a foreign exchange, but that is the wave of the future. The use of eurotranches gives small and midsize companies a chance to learn the ropes with a minimum of risk.

Chapter 14

Leasing

Tax laws change with dizzying speed. Accounting regulations shift like the rolling sands. Innovative financing tools pop in and out of favor like jumping beans. But leasing stays the course as tenaciously as a bull terrier. Perhaps the main reason for leasing's popularity is that, in contrast to other financing methods, its flexibility and versatility are virtually unlimited. Many companies are attracted to leasing because it requires very little or no down payment. Moreover, in contrast to the inhibiting constraints of bank loan documentation, leases can be customized to meet any company's needs. In fact, rental payments can often be stretched over a much longer period than most banks will accept for loan payments.

At the beginning of this decade, the U.S. Department of Commerce released statistics showing approximately $130 billion in outstanding equipment leases alone. The leasing industry estimates that new leases in excess of $1 billion are written every year and that that number is likely to triple in the foreseeable future.

The form of a lease depends on a company's needs and the assets being acquired. Certain leases are really lease-purchase agreements, wherein the lessee records the equipment or property as an asset and the lease obligation as a liability. For leases that do not meet this criterion, no asset or liability is recorded and rental payments are written off when paid, just like any other operating expense.

The Internal Revenue Code also affects lease structures. The deductibility of rental payments, lease-related expenditures, and tax credits obviously plays a major role in a company's cash flow. Don't be misled, however. The tax benefits of leasing may be greater or less than those of purchasing an asset.

Although repayment terms, tax considerations, and balance sheet conventions make leasing a good choice in many situations, its high cost remains a major obstacle. Leasing has other negatives as well, and the decision to lease or buy is not always straightforward. The disadvantages of leasing include the following:

- Complex, frequently changing tax laws affect not only the availability of leases but their cost and structure.
- Rental payments usually exceed term-loan interest expense for comparable financing, thereby diminishing a company's income.
- Legal fees for drafting complex lease agreements can run high.
- You lose a potentially valuable addition to your balance sheet when the asset appreciates in value (as with real property).

Before getting into comparisons and analyses of leasing options, it might be helpful to review basic lease terminology, fundamental leasing principles, and the various structures of leases currently in vogue.

Leasing Terminology

Finance Lease

All leases are either finance leases or operating leases. Finance leases normally extend over a long time period, with the total of monthly, quarterly, or annual payments approximating the purchase price of the asset plus finance charges. Large pieces of production equipment, heavy-duty trucks, store fixtures, and production facilities are examples of assets typically falling under a finance lease.

Finance leases represent long-term financial commitments by both lessor and lessee. They usually run for the entire useful life of the asset. From the lessor's perspective, rents must be sufficient to cover the original equity investment in the asset, any debt service payments for financing the asset purchase, administrative costs, and a profit.

The projected cash flow from the asset is also a factor in setting monthly rentals. Cash flow to a lessor is the sum of (1) the actual rent charged, (2) the tax benefits of the lease, and (3) the residual value of the asset after the lease expires. Projected tax savings and the estimated market value of the asset at the end of the lease term increase the lessor's cash flow and reduce the rent charged.

Because a finance lease involves a long-term commitment and the lessor relies on the entire lease period to recover costs and earn a profit, the lease agreement typically includes severe prepayment provisions to discourage a lessee from breaking the lease. At a minimum, such penalties include the recovery of the lessor's investment, the lessor's total costs, and the lessor's profit to the date of cancellation.

Most finance leases are *net* leases. That means that the lessee remains responsible for the maintenance of the asset, property and other taxes, and insurance premiums. The lessor's role is strictly that of a financier whose responsibility extends to financing the asset purchase but stops short of any liability arising from its use.

With a finance lease, the lessee also absorbs any risk related to equipment obsolescence. Theoretically, and under the best of conditions, rental payments over the term of the lease should yield a residual value of zero. Lessors don't care if the equipment becomes obsolete during the period because they recoup their entire investment, plus profit, through rental payments. Pragmatically, however, to keep rents competitive, lessors do calculate a small residual value and therefore assume some responsibility for obsolescence.

The biggest risks to a lessor are default by the lessee and the destruction of the asset through a casualty occurrence, such as a fire, flood, or explosion. Lease agreements include provisions to protect against both conditions. They also include requirements for insuring the asset. In most cases the lessee pays the insurance premium and names the lessor as first-party beneficiary.

In leasing jargon, a *hell or high water provision* can be included to protect the lessor against lessee default. This provision stipulates that the lessee must pay the lease in full, "come hell or high water." The lessee may not offset any claims against the lessor, regardless of the reason for the claim.

Operating Lease

Equipment and property leases that are not classified as finance leases must be operating leases. Operating leases involve shorter-term financial commitments. The lease term may or may not approximate the life of the asset. It could be measured in hours, days, or months. The sum of the rental payments is always less than the purchase price of the asset. Leases for automobiles, computer equipment, and office furniture are typically operating leases.

Rapid obsolescence of this type of asset can be a major problem for lessors. With the lease period so short, the lessor bears the brunt of product usage or design obsolescence. To compensate for this risk, rental payments run substantially higher than those under finance leases.

Furthermore, because of the short rental periods, lessors cannot expect to recover their investment and profit over the term of a lease, as with finance leases. Therefore, they place heavy reliance on selling or re-leasing the asset at the end of the lease period to recover a large part of their investment. The costs and risks of this are included in the calculation of rental charges.

Even though operating leases require higher rental payments, they serve an important market niche. If you need equipment that carries rapid technological obsolescence, such as computers, short-term leases can be a good alternative to keeping the equipment for ten or more years, even with higher rental payments. Also, with automobiles, if you need the car for only a short period of time—a day, week, or month— the higher rent is still less expensive than buying the car outright.

Both finance and operating leases can be structured as leveraged leases, nonleveraged leases, or service leases.

Leveraged Lease

A leveraged lease is exactly what the term implies: a lease covering an asset purchased by the lessor with borrowed money. In other words, the lessor *leverages* its acquisition. The distinction is important to lessees because rental payments are always calculated to return the original cost of the asset, cover administrative expense, and make a profit for the lessor.

With a leveraged deal, lessors earn 100 percent of the return on their money but invest only 20 to 40 percent of the price of the asset. Therefore, rentals under leveraged leases should be significantly lower than those for nonleveraged leases. Nearly all net finance leases are leveraged, making this form of long-term financing competitive to some extent with term loans.

Long-term loans used to acquire leased assets are nearly always nonrecourse. This means that the lender, in this case a bank or other financial institution, has no recourse against the lessor in the event of default. The lender must look for recovery to the stream of rental income, the lessee, and the leased asset. However, recourse against a third party can be very difficult to collect. To compensate, lessors assign their rights in the lease to the lender, giving the lender direct recourse to the lessee. As an alternative, a lessor might subordinate lease rights to the lender's first position.

Nonleveraged Lease

A nonleveraged lease covers equipment or property whose purchase was financed entirely by the lessor, without resorting to borrowed funds. Agreements covering nonleveraged leases are always much simpler than those for leveraged leases. This saves time in negotiating the transaction and a significant amount of legal fees for both the lessor and the lessee. Nothing is free, however. Legal fees may be lower, but rental charges under nonleveraged leases run substantially higher.

Service Lease

Under a service lease, the lessor retains responsibility for the expenses associated with operating the equipment or building. The lessor maintains the asset, pays for insurance coverage, and remains liable for all property, sales, and use taxes. Service leases are all relatively short term. And, of course, rental payments must be very high to cover the extra expenses incurred by the lessor.

Different Types of Leases

Over the years, the simple idea of charging rent to use an asset under contract has undergone enormous changes. Although each change has added complexity to contracts, a corollary benefit has been additional flexibility in structuring leases. Such flexibility helps both leasing parties.

Traditional Lease Structure

Traditional lease structures have been around for generations. Typically used for real property (e.g., land, buildings, office space, farmland), traditionally structured leases can also be used for equipment with a long useful life. The major characteristics of traditional leases are

1. The lessee has a legal obligation to pay rent for a specific period of time and may use the asset for any purpose that does not violate the lease agreement. The lessor cannot deprive the lessee of such use. This is known as the *principle of quiet enjoyment*.
2. The lessor owns the property and retains responsibility for its upkeep. This may include repairs and maintenance, insurance coverage, and property taxes. With net leases, typically used as finance leases for equipment, the lessor charges the lessee for part or all of these expenses.
3. The lessor benefits from any appreciation in the value of the asset over the course of the lease, and likewise suffers any depreciation in value.
4. Tax benefits associated with the asset—deductions for depreciation, interest, and property tax, as well as any tax credits currently available—flow to the lessor.

Traditional leases offer the lessee three primary advantages:

1. The risk of unusual loss of asset value rests with the lessor.
2. Leases are simple, straightforward agreements. Lessors cannot vary the standard terms with peculiar restrictions or covenants. Most leases are simple enough to execute without a lawyer.
3. Traditional leases are executory contracts. This means that neither the asset nor the lease liability needs to be recorded by the lessee.

Although traditional leases are far and away the easiest to execute and understand, they are seldom used anymore except for certain long-term real property. Nowadays, lessors seem to want either special restrictions or covenants included in the lease document or unusual terms applied to rental payments. These complications turn a traditional lease into a more complicated document frequently referred to as a *capital lease*.

Capital Lease Structure
Although it is not practical to list all the possible modifications that can be incorporated, the following represent the more common provisions in capital leases.

- The life of the lease is indeterminate. You may rent the asset for as long as you wish.
- The lessee pays for maintenance, insurance, and taxes on the asset.
- A purchase option can be added, allowing the lessee to purchase the asset at the end of the lease or during the lease period. The price can be set at fair market value, a stipulated value, or a nominal value, such as one dollar.
- Terms may include mandatory purchase of the asset at the end of the lease for a flat amount, fair market value, or other amount.
- Rental payments can be variable. They can be based on a percentage of operating results—sales, profits, production levels—or they can be geared to interest-rate fluctuations.
- Leases may cover groups of assets. Rent is then based on a percentage of the value of the total asset group. This allows additions or deletions of assets without rewriting lease agreements.

Capital leases may be called leases but they are really loans collateralized by the equipment. The lessor finances the acquisition of the equipment. The lessee pays back the loan through rental payments corresponding to principal and interest on a loan plus the lessor's profit. Currently, most capital leases carry an implicit interest rate of four to six percentage points over prime. The two major advantages of using capital leases rather than borrowing money directly to purchase assets are that the lessor retains the risk of ownership and that capital leases require little or no down payment.

The ownership risk of certain assets can be substantial. For example, assume that computer equipment leased under a five-year operating lease has a calculated residual value of 20 percent of its original cost. If new technology makes it practically worthless after three years, the lessor suffers this loss, not the lessee.

Many operating leases give the lessee the option of rolling the lease over with new equipment. Trading in the old computer for a new one in three years provides an operating company with state-of-the-art equipment without rewriting the lease, or, alternatively, buying a new computer.

Capital leases can also be written to change the rules of owner-ship. Provisions can be included to treat the operating company as the owner of the assets rather than the lessor. In addition, the residual value of the asset at the end of the lease may revert to the lessor, or it may revert to the lessee, or the lessee may be required to purchase the asset for residual value or a portion thereof.

Venture Leases

Venture leases are a fairly recent innovation. They were invented to encourage lessors to participate in the growth of start-up or first-stage companies. A venture lease is nothing more than a capital lease with provisions giving the lessor the right to acquire an equity interest in the lessee company.

Venture leases usually require very low rental payments in the first year or two to reduce the cash outflow for the new operating entity. In exchange for this concession, the lessor is granted warrants or stock options for the acquisition of an equity interest in the lessee company within a specified time. In the same manner as with venture capital funding, the venture lessor wins if the company grows rapidly and eventually goes public. Conversely, it loses along with other investors if the company fails.

Tax Consequences

Acceptable methods for recording leases and reporting rental payments frequently influence how to structure a lease for a given asset acquisi-tion. The optimum agreement, of course, balances benefits between lessor and lessee, recognizing both accounting and tax regulations.

Acceptable accounting treatment of lease obligations can materi-ally affect both the earnings and the balance sheet ratios of publicly held corporations, either enhancing or detracting from a firm's ability to attract additional public capital. On the other hand, for privately held companies, tax implications far outweigh accounting concerns.

The complex tax considerations involved in various lease structures could fill an entire book. However, because tax savings or penalties are so crucial when making lease-or-buy decisions, a brief review of current regulations might prove helpful. Be aware, however, that the following summary is far from complete, and that because of constantly changing regulations, the only safe bet is to turn tax questions over to your tax adviser.

When Is a Lease a Lease?

Both the IRS and the accounting fraternity worry about whether a specific lease is really a lease or a camouflaged purchase. Although accounting definitions affect balance sheet ratios, and therefore future borrowing power, IRS treatment affects immediate cash flow.

As previously mentioned, a lease that is defined as a purchase in disguise must be recorded on the lessee's books as both an asset and a liability. Depreciation deductions can then be taken over the useful life of the equipment. Rental payments must be divided between theoretical interest expense, which is written off as an expense, and principal payments, which reduce lease liabilities.

Conversely, if the IRS rules that a lease is really a lease and not a purchase, neither asset nor liability is recorded and the full rental payment can be deducted as a business expense. The IRS has established four tests to make this determination. If the transaction passes all four, it is a lease. Otherwise it will be classified as a purchase. These four tests involve the following:

- Minimum investment standards
- Purchase and sale rights
- Lessee participation through equity investments, loans, or guarantees
- Profit requirements

Minimum Investment

Throughout the period of the lease, the lessor must demonstrate that it holds at least a 20 percent equity interest in the asset. Lessors can fulfill this requirement with a leveraged lease by establishing the reasonableness of estimating a residual asset value at the end of the lease period equal to either 20 percent of its original useful life or one remaining year of usefulness. Under a nonleveraged lease, the lessor retains a declining equity interest in the asset for the lease period, at which time the 20 percent rule kicks in.

Purchase and Sale Rights

At the end of the lease period, or at any time during the period, the lessee cannot buy the asset for a price less than the asset's fair market value at the time of transfer. Neither can the lease agreement stipulate that such a right exists, even though it may never be exercised.

Lessee Investment, Loan, or Guarantee

The lessee is prohibited from financing any part of the purchase of the asset or any improvements made to it. This financing prohibition includes equity investments, loans, or guarantees to or on behalf of the lessor.

Profit Requirement

The lessor must present demonstrable proof that a profit will be made on the lease transaction. Such a profit may not include tax savings resulting from the transaction.

Making a Lease-or-Buy Decision

Financial analysts and academicians struggle with complex formulas for comparing the benefits of leasing versus buying an asset. From a business perspective, however, the decision to lease or buy can be reduced to a relatively simple process. Seven factors should be considered:

1. Availability of capital
2. Asset characteristics (obsolescence, length of time asset is needed)
3. Cost (interest rate)
4. Cash requirements (down payment)
5. Tax implications
6. Effect on financial statements
7. Collateral requirements

Availability of Capital

Financially strong companies seldom need to worry about being able to get loans whenever they are needed. Even during recessions, when credit is tight, most banks lean over backwards to lend money to companies with strong balance sheets and substantial cash flows. In such cases, the lease-or-buy decision rests primarily on cost comparisons and the impact on balance sheet ratios.

Most companies, however, are not so fortunate. Leasing has gained favor over the years not because it was less costly or offered tax advantages, but because it was the only source of capital for buying hard assets that many companies could attract. Why? Because lessors weigh the value of the specific asset being purchased and the lessee's ability to meet rent payments more heavily than balance sheet ratios or prior profit performance.

For this reason, companies with weak balance sheets or nonqualifying cash flow projections can negotiate lease financing when they cannot get bank loans.

Asset Characteristics

Probably the biggest advantage of leasing over buying occurs with assets that have a high obsolescence factor or that are needed for only a short time. Computer hardware is a prime example of a high-obsolescence asset. Rapidly changing computer technology brings faster, bigger, more complete hardware on the market long before current equipment wears out. While open-end leases enable companies to turn in old computers for state-of-the-art equipment as it becomes available, if they owned the equipment they would probably have to sell it before buying new models.

Special equipment such as inventory scales, storage trailers or warehouse space, and automobiles for business travel are examples of assets with the second characteristic, that is, assets that are needed for only a short time. It makes little sense to buy assets that are needed for a day, a week, or a month. Leasing fills the void, even though the per-day cost is exorbitant compared with purchasing the asset.

Cost

The cost of leasing relates directly to the cost of the lease to the lessor. Lessors view investing in a lease the same way that lenders evaluate loans, or investors judge investments. They must weigh the cost to acquire the asset against the gain derived from the lease. To the extent that the actual cash received over the lease period covers a lessor's cash outlay for acquiring the asset and all associated costs, and still yields a satisfactory profit, the asset has been a good investment.

Rent is a function of the lessor's investment risk and costs, including the cost of capital. The cost of capital includes both debt and equity funds. A lessor's costs remain beyond the control of a lessee, but risk assumptions do not. The level of risk in projected cash flow over the lease period represents the key variable that a lessee must negotiate.

From the lessor's perspective, two types of risk enter the formula: (1) credit risk and (2) residual-value risk. Credit risk relates to leases exactly as it does to loans. If a lessee fails to meet lease payments, the lessor must stand ready to reclaim the leased asset. The more evidence a lessee can present to prove a good credit history, the better the chances of negotiating a lower credit risk factor. Such evidence is derived from credit reports, bank reference letters, character verifications, and so on.

Residual-value risk is a different story. No step in evaluating bank risk compares to evaluating a lessor's residual-value risk. Residual value is the market value of an asset at the culmination of a lease period. To the extent that a lessor captures a higher amount upon selling the asset, extra profit accrues; if the market value ends up being less than estimated, the lessor loses. Residual-value risk is the risk that the lessor will guess either correctly or on the low side when initiating the lease.

A lessor mitigates residual-value risk in two ways. The most straightforward way is to insist that lessees guarantee a specific residual value at the end of the lease. If the asset doesn't bring such a price, the lessee must make up the difference. In assessing this type of risk, the same procedures are followed as in determining credit risk. If a lessee has a good credit history and meets obligations when they are due, the probability of recovering any shortage in residual value increases. A poor credit history results in the reverse, and rental payments will probably be increased accordingly.

The second risk-evaluation method relates to shorter-term leases or to leases covering equipment with a limited technological or useful life. In these cases, lessors must rely heavily on cash flow generated from the sale of the asset after the lease ends to recover investment principal and profit. This means higher rental payments. The type of asset leased, its marketability as a used asset, alternative uses for the property, the cost of refurbishing or repairing the asset, costs involved in relocating the asset, and the historical and current market price movements of similar assets all affect the residual-value decision.

Historically, lessors of real property estimated high residual values because the market prices of commercial real estate continued to climb. This enabled a lessor to settle for less rent. The residual value of automobiles is well documented in *blue book* catalogs and used car auctions. This makes rental payments for cars less negotiable.

Conversely, office equipment, specialized production equipment, and customized office facilities carry high residual-value risk. These assets are nearly always rented at a premium. Renting specialized equipment or high-tech equipment directly from a manufacturer or dealer usually results in lower payments than structuring a deal with an independent leasing company.

Cash Requirements

Although requirements vary with general economic conditions, the state of the banking industry, and the borrower's credit history, in most cases banks restrict their lending to not more than 75 percent of the asset cost. That means at least a 25 percent down payment. Most large equipment leases also require a down payment, but the amount is generally 5 to 15 percent rather than the higher bank standard.

It may also be possible to stretch larger leases beyond the typical repayment schedule banks require. Leases for large pieces of machinery or equipment normally run up to ten years. Real property leases may extend fifteen to twenty-five years, perhaps with built-in five-year options. Generally, these periods are significantly longer than those granted by banks.

Tax Implications

It's difficult to identify how the misconception got started that leasing permits bigger tax deductions than buying assets, but leasing companies do nothing to discredit it. Potential lessees should be aware, however, that the same IRS *legitimate business purpose test* applies to leased assets as to those that are purchased.

Assuming that that test is met, rental payments against a true lease, as opposed to a camouflaged installment purchase, are deductible in full. For purchased assets, interest expense on loans is deductible, as is depreciation of the original asset cost. Theoretically, the tax implications of leasing versus buying should result in a wash. This rarely occurs in practice, however, mainly because total lease payments reflect the lessor's built-in overhead and profit.

Consequently, in most cases total lease payments exceed the original price of the asset plus interest on borrowed funds, resulting in greater tax deductions. Concurrently, however, leasing also increases the total cost of the asset.

Effect on Financial Statements

Leases that are considered purchases have the same impact on balance sheet ratios as assets that are purchased with borrowed funds. In both cases the asset is recorded at original cost and depreciated according to standard depreciation guidelines. In most cases, however, that portion of the total lease obligation that represents noninterest payments increases the original cost of a leased asset beyond that of one purchased directly.

Concurrently, the total capitalized lease obligation that must be recorded as a liability is generally greater than a corresponding loan for a direct purchase. Both asset cost and capitalized lease obligations are higher because the noninterest portion of total lease payments reflects the cost of the asset purchased by the lessor, plus the lessor's overhead and profit add-ons.

Collateral Requirements

Since leases relate to specific assets—a specific building or section of land, or identifiable pieces of machinery, equipment, or vehicles—the related asset should serve as sufficient collateral for the lease. Upon default, the lessor merely reclaims the asset. Occasionally, when a company has a very poor credit history and the down payment is negligible or zero, a lessor may insist on external collateral—other business assets or personal guarantees. Generally, however the leased assets themselves are sufficient collateral.

Banks, on the other hand, nearly always insist that extra assets be pledged. It is not unusual for banks to require the pledge of all business assets and, for privately owned businesses, the owner's personal guarantee. Obviously, this makes default risk substantially more than with a lease.

Lease Contracts

Although clauses in lease contracts vary all over the lot, certain commonalities do exist. Depending on the size of a lease and the length of time it covers, a lease contract may be either very short and simple (as in a standard automobile lease) or long and extremely complex (as in leases covering real property, a group of large pieces of machinery, or a multicomputer installation). However, the common elements in most leases, whether simple or complex, include the following:

- Definitions of terms
- Rental payment terms
- Location of asset
- Termination rights
- Obligations of lessee
- Indemnifications of lessor
- Lessor inspection rights
- Lessor warranty disclaimer
- Events of default and remedies
- Fair market value of asset
- Assignment rights
- Return of asset at conclusion of lease

The following summary outlines the type of information included under each heading.

1. *Definitions of terms* clearly describes each term used in the contract that might be misinterpreted or confusing.
2. *Rental payment terms* specifies
   - How much rent is payable and when it is payable
   - Grace period (if applicable)
   - In what form payments will be transmitted to lessor and to what address
   - Percentage of lease payments considered as interest (if applicable)
   - The term of the lease
   - The purchase price of the asset at the end of the lease (if applicable)
3. *Location of asset* identifies the exact location/address where the asset will be used, stored, maintained, and otherwise situated.
4. *Termination rights* lay out
   - The conditions under which either lessor or lessee may terminate the lease

- How the termination notice will be transmitted
- The disposition of the asset upon termination
- Responsibilities of both parties for settling open commitments upon termination

5. *Obligations of lessee* spells out in detail all obligations of the lessee:
   - Timely rental payments
   - Asset maintenance standards
   - Asset security
   - Insurance coverage
   - Payment of property taxes
   - Replacement of damaged parts or replacement of the entire asset if it is destroyed

6. *Indemnifications of lessor* sets out *hold harmless* clauses by which the lessee indemnifies the lessor for a variety of potential liabilities arising from the lessee's use of the asset or claims against the asset:
   - Income tax claims
   - Property and use tax claims
   - Product failure suits
   - Any other liabilities that may arise as a result of actions taken by the lessee relating to manufacture, purchase, acceptance, rejection, return, lease, ownership, possession, use, condition, operation, or sale of products or services created in, by, or with the asset under lease

7. *Lessor inspection rights* identifies under what conditions the lessor may inspect the leased asset to ascertain its existence and well-being.

8. *Lessor warranty disclaimer* is used only when the lessor is not the manufacturer of the asset. It specifically states that the lessor does not warrant or represent, either implied or express, the design or condition of the asset, or the quality of its material, equipment, or workmanship, and makes no warranty of the fitness of the asset for any particular purpose.

9. *Events of default and remedies* sets out
   - Definitions of default
   - Time periods under which default may be remedied by the lessee

- Taking possession of the asset by the lessor
- Financial and other remedies the lessor may impose on the lessee
- Applicable state and/or country laws

10. *Fair market value of asset* outlines the formulas, appraisal procedures, and other techniques for establishing the fair market value of the asset for purposes of calculating additional rents due upon lease termination or to determine the purchase price at the end of the lease.

11. *Assignment rights* specifies the rights and conditions under which either the lessor or the lessee may assign the lease to third parties.

12. *Return of asset at conclusion of lease* is a clause that specifically outlines

- The procedure for evaluating the condition of the asset returned to the lessor upon the termination of the lease
- Remedies against the lessee for damages
- How the asset will be shipped to the lessor
- Any grace period allowed

Negotiating a Lease Contract

With the exception of very simple, small, short-term leases, all lease contracts are negotiable. Success in getting favorable language or clauses to override boilerplate terms depends directly on two factors: the lessee's clout, and the competition between leasing companies for the particular type of asset being leased.

Larger and financially stronger companies can always achieve better terms than small or financially weak ones. On the other hand, small companies generally have more flexibility in granting concessions to obtain better terms. You might grant tax concessions to the lessor, for example. Deductions for depreciation might be more valuable to a lessor than to your company. In that case, structuring the lease to permit the lessor to take the deduction could result in reduced rental payments or, at a minimum, more favorable indemnification conditions. Of course, not all lessors need or want tax benefits.

On the other hand, many lessors reduce rental charges in exchange for tax benefits and then turn around and sell the lease. A solid secondary market exists in the leasing industry, especially for leases covering large commercial or industrial property.

The following checklist should help you identify the details that should be included in a lease. Nearly all items are subject to negotiation, so don't buy boilerplate contracts without an attempt to get better language or terms.

1. Lease form
   Finance lease?
   Capital lease?
2. Residual value
   Appraised?
   Compared to similar assets?
   Upward rental adjustments for depreciated asset?
   Downward rental adjustments for appreciated asset?
3. Credit verification
   Personal reference letters?
   Bank references?
   Prior leases?
4. Termination
   Timing of termination notification?
   Hold harmless clauses for lessor termination?
   Liability for cost of returning asset?
5. External collateral
   Other business assets?
   Cross-collateralized assets from other businesses?
   Personal guarantees?
   Personal assets?
6. Default provisions
   Grace period?
   Notification of repossession action?
   Financial penalties?
   Cross-indemnification from lessor?
7. Tax matters
   Ownership of asset?
   Which party gets depreciation, investment tax credit, or other tax benefits that may arise from changes in the tax code?

Interest rate used in establishing rental payments?

8. Miscellaneous contract clauses

Insurance coverage?

Maintenance standards?

Lessor inspection updates?

Determination of condition of asset at end of lease?

Asset purchase terms when lease ends?

Assignment rights?

Secondary guarantees on assignment?

Security of asset?

Challenging Leasing Myths

After the key elements have been negotiated, but before signing a lease, it's always a good idea to take a last look at the true cost of leasing versus buying the asset. Previous sections dispelled the myth of major tax advantages to leasing. Another common misconception is that leasing is less expensive than borrowing funds to purchase an asset outright. Or, to put it another way, that the sum of the rental payments over the life of a lease will be less than the original purchase price of the asset.

Occasionally this may be true, but in most cases it is not. The cost to the lessor *plus the lessor's profit* is the cost to the lessee. A lessor's cost is measured by the price paid for the asset, plus administrative costs, less the residual value of the asset. If the lessee were to sell the asset itself, it should get the same residual-value recovery as the lessor.

Perhaps a lessor can borrow money at a lower interest rate, and for a leveraged lease, this of course means lower cost. On the other hand, instead of paying a lessor for administrative costs and profit, you may be better off buying the asset outright with borrowed funds, even at a slightly higher interest rate.

Another assumption that needs to be challenged is that leasing conserves operating cash. This argument assumes that the sum of the lease payments will be less than the combined principal and interest payments on a term loan. If the residual value is very high relative to the original cost, this may have some merit. The lessor takes less rent but plans to sell the asset to recoup the investment and make a profit.

Nothing prevents your company from doing the same thing. If you don't need the asset anymore, why not sell it? If a lessor can get market price, a lessee should also be able to. Considering residual value on both sides, it is hard to see how lease payments that include a lessor's costs and profit can be less than principal and interest on a term loan.

It doesn't take an elaborate calculation to determine that leasing costs more and results in more cash outflow than buying an asset. The lease-versus-buy decision must be based on factors other than cost. In fact, there are several noncost advantages to leasing, although in some instances, cost and cash flow do enter the equation.

As with so many other business decisions, there is no pat answer to the question, Should we buy or lease? If a definitive answer were forthcoming, either leasing companies would be out of business or banks would no longer make hard-asset loans. The facts obviously tell a different story.

As a financing tool, leasing makes sense for some companies but not for others. With all the variations of lease agreements, the number of factors influencing a lease-or-buy decision may very well be limitless. Nevertheless, certain circumstances seem to favor a lease decision whereas others quite clearly point to buying. Here are the main features that tend to favor leasing, followed by some that point to buying.

Circumstances favoring leasing rather than buying are

1. When a company does not have the capital to make a down payment
2. When the asset will probably become obsolete before the end of its useful life
3. When a company has a poor credit rating and financial institutions insist on very high interest rates (this is not always a good reason, however, because a lessor takes this into consideration when evaluating credit risk for establishing rental payments)
4. If implicit interest rates are close to market rates, but a loan could involve other costs or restrictions, such as commitment or application fees, compensating balances, nonbusiness collateral, or personal guarantees
5. If the equipment has unusual service problems that would be costly, or even impossible, to handle internally

6. If the equipment or building will probably be difficult to dispose of or has a very low resale value when it is no longer needed
7. When assets are needed for only a short period of time
8. When a company wants to use its collateral and borrowing power for other financing
9. When a comparison of tax advantages clearly favors leasing

The biggest disadvantages to leasing occur

1. When the sum of the lease payments exceeds the cost of buying (the purchase price, of course, must be reduced by the asset's resale value)
2. When a company gains an advantage from owning the asset free and clear after the loan gets repaid
3. When tax benefits clearly point to buying
4. When a possibility exists for selling a privately held company before the expiration of a lease period (many sellers find that their company brings a significantly lower sale price with leased assets and that these frequently preclude a leveraged buyout)
5. When the property is likely to appreciate in value

Sale/Leaseback as a Financing Tool

Selling currently owned assets to a leasing company for cash and then leasing them back over a period of time (commonly referred to as a *sale/leaseback transaction*) has become an increasingly popular method for raising immediate capital. Sale/leasebacks are especially useful when you have poor relations with your bank and cannot arrange additional credit or when your company owns assets that are not obligated, or at least not fully obligated, to secure existing debt obligations.

Sale/leasebacks allow you to raise capital against your company's assets while still maintaining control over these assets. When bank loans are scarce or interest rates and fees are exorbitant, this can be an excellent way to bring cash into the company.

Manufacturing businesses with equipment securely in place find sale/leasebacks calculated with zero residual value a bit expensive. On the other hand, when cash is scarce, paying a high rental may be preferable to many other forms of survival financing. When a zero residual value results in rental payments that are too high to meet, a company can arrange a purchase option in the lease to buy back the equipment at the end of the lease period. Hopefully, by that time your company will be on its feet again and be able to raise capital elsewhere.

The biggest disadvantage of equipment sale/leaseback arrangements (other than losing the value of owned assets for future collateral) is the very high rental payments required by lessors. Since many companies going this route have poor credit ratings and a sale/leaseback is their last chance to raise capital, lessors price the leases accordingly.

Sale/leasebacks are also popular for real property. Because real property tends to appreciate rather than depreciate over time, very often the lease value of a building far exceeds its existing mortgage (which is why financial institutions favor mortgage loans).

With commercial and industrial buildings, the sale/leaseback technique is not restricted to companies with poor credit ratings or those that cannot raise capital elsewhere. For example, assume that a company took out a twenty-year mortgage for 80 percent of a building's value. It has made mortgage payments for ten years, and the mortgage balance has decreased 30 percent.

If the property has risen in value 3 percent per year, its market value today is 38 percent higher than when the mortgage was placed. The combination of a 30 percent decrease in the mortgage loan and a 38 percent increase in the asset's market value results in an equity increase of over 300 percent. For a property originally worth $100,000, a sale/leaseback would result in a cash infusion of $82,000!

Since leasing companies also recognize that real property values tend to appreciate, many welcome the opportunity to compete for a sale/leaseback arrangement. This competition keeps rental rates much lower than for equipment deals. In many cases, monthly rentals will be no more than payments on the old mortgage. If mortgage rates have been dropping, rents could even be less.

Sale/leasebacks are seldom used for raising capital by relatively new companies, however, since these companies usually don't have sufficient equipment or real property to make a sale/leaseback viable.

Where to Locate Leasing Companies

The leasing industry has undergone many changes over the last twenty years. As in the banking industry, a wide assortment of businesses and financial institutions have entered the leasing arena. They range from independent leasing companies to divisions of large corporations, departments of commercial banks, subsidiaries of secured lenders, affiliates of franchisers, branches of mortgage banks, and subsidiaries of commercial real estate agents. Even the investment banking and venture capital industries have representation in both equipment and real property leasing.

LeaseAmerica Corp., Cedar Rapids, Iowa, and GE Capital Corporation (with offices in all major cities) are two of the most active equipment leasing companies. All commercial real estate agents with national affiliations maintain direct contacts with lessors handling real property.

Specialized Leasing Companies

Independent and affiliated leasing companies have recently sprung up to serve specific industries. The automobile, hotel, restaurant, aircraft, boat, and machine tool industries are all served by specialized leasing companies, although many are very new. Any reputable trade association knows which leasing companies serve its specific industry. Also, most leasing companies advertise in trade journals.

Venture Leasing Companies

Private limited partnerships are rapidly becoming a major factor in the leasing of specially designed equipment and custom-built commercial property. Venture leases for equipment used in industries such as health care diagnostics, laser sensing and penetrating, advanced telecommunications, space technology, electronic guidance systems, and so on, are frequently placed through limited partnerships. Most of this high-tech equipment has limited applications and experiences rapid technological obsolescence. It is extremely expensive, and buying it is out of reach for most small companies.

These highly specialized limited partnerships raise capital by soliciting funds from wealthy U.S. and foreign private individuals, large corporations interested in technology development, venture capital funds specializing in these industries, and a few foreign securities houses. They do not advertise. If this source appears to be a viable choice, consult one of the reputable brokerage houses that maintain large investment banking capabilities. They won't handle a deal directly, but they should point the way to venture firms that will.

One caution about going this route: Venture firms nearly always insist on an equity share in exchange for providing leases—or any financing, for that matter.

A multitude of leasing sources exist, both in the United States and overseas. Commercial banks, secured lenders, venture capital partnerships, and independent leasing companies all offer leases for both equipment and real property. However, equipment leasing is not as competitive as real estate leasing, and therefore the cost is significantly higher.

Chapter 15

Restructuring and Refinancing

With increasing frequency, many companies—especially small businesses, which are often more susceptible to changes in market demand and credit constrictions—find their current loan payments too much to handle. One of the best solutions to this dilemma is to restructure outstanding loans to reduce monthly or quarterly payments. Unfortunately, this isn't always possible. When a company has become so mired in excess costs and dropping market demand that there isn't time to restructure, the logical solution is the bankruptcy court. However, that involves another whole set of strategies that will not be covered in this book. If you're interested in developing strategies to tackle a bankruptcy filing, I suggest my book *The Complete Book of Raising Capital* (McGraw-Hill).

This chapter is devoted entirely to methods for restructuring loans (otherwise known as *recapitalizing*) and refinancing a small company. If you're not in a cash bind, if your debt obligations are not depriving you of needed cash to expand your business, or if conditions are such that you can delegate the responsibility for handling these matters to another person, then skip this chapter. It will be of no interest to you. But if you are in a cash bind now because of overburdening loan payments, or you think you might be in the foreseeable future, then this chapter should give you a good background in proven techniques for managing the situation.

You have probably already tried everything you can think of to free up cash. Your cash management program is in place. You have a working cost-reduction program. You've tried your bank for additional loans. You've looked at the possibility of a sale/leaseback of your hard assets. Nothing seems to work. None of the traditional cash management techniques help, and conventional recapitalization methods don't make sense. Obviously, more stringent measures must be taken. This is probably the time to consider restructuring current loans to reduce interest and/or principal payments and to try to raise money from non-bank sources to retire existing debt.

Loan payments may be restructured in four ways:

1. Eliminate short-term debt (e.g., revolvers, lines of credit, credit card debt).
2. Convert short-term loans to long-term obligations.
3. Defer monthly loan payments until cash flow improves.
4. Convert outstanding loans to equity shares in the company.

Eliminate Short-Term Debt

Short-term debt is any loans that must be repaid within one year. It may include bank revolvers, open lines of credit, promissory notes payable on demand, current payments against mortgages or other long-term loans, credit card balances, amounts due to suppliers, income taxes, or any combination of these obligations. Companies use a number of different tactics to defer payments due to suppliers and the federal government. These are valid alternatives that you may have to consider when the going really gets tough. But for now, we'll concentrate on the more traditional forms of debt from banks and other financial institutions.

Short-term bank loans (revolvers) are usually the most difficult of all debt obligations to reduce or eliminate completely. The worst are loans against specific receivables and identifiable groups of inventory that keep revolving on a continuing basis. Perhaps a review of the concept of revolvers as outlined in Chapter 5 is in order.

Companies increase short-term cash inflows by borrowing 80 to 85 percent of customer invoices rather than waiting for collections to come in. As payments are received, the loan balance plus interest is repaid. The same principle holds for loans against inventory. Pragmatically, however, banks don't make a new loan against every receivable account or inventory purchase. Each day, week, or month, banks make one loan at the agreed-upon percentage of new invoices (normally 80 or 85 percent), called the *borrowing base*. This system works fine as long as sales increase, just as any leveraging scheme does. When sales decrease, however, revolvers live up to their name and can be deadly. In that case, payments against revolvers always exceed loans against new invoices, creating cash shortages.

During a business downturn, open lines of credit can be nearly as devastating as revolvers. In this case, however, instead of matching paybacks against invoices, principal and interest payments are due on demand notes—usually every thirty days. As with revolvers, as long as sales keep increasing, ever-greater collections can be used to pay off loans taken at lower collateral levels. As sales drop, however, collections and new loans become unbalanced, and debt service absorbs an ever-increasing share of cash.

One of the best ways to get out of short-term debt is to use cash generated by cost reductions or the disposal of product lines to pay off loan balances. Once outstanding loans fall significantly below the borrowing base, a good portion of the cash generated from new sales can be used for operating needs rather than for the payment of loans.

The implementation of tighter collection procedures also hastens cash inflows that can be used to reduce short-term debt. The faster a revolver or line of credit can be repaid, the less impact high debt service payments have in a downturn, and the more new credit is available in an upturn.

Another alternative is to use the cash received from selling business assets to pay down short-term debt. This reduces monthly payments, and, even though it uses up some or all of the new capital, it saves cash that would otherwise be needed for debt service.

Convert Short-Term to Long-Term Debt

Over the long term, you will always pay more for long-term than for short-term loans. From a lender's viewpoint, the reason is obvious: The bank's money is tied up for a much longer period of time (thereby increasing the risk of its not being repaid), and therefore higher interest rates must be charged. Despite the higher cost, however, many times it makes sense to increase cash balances now by converting to long-term debt that can be paid off in the future. Every dollar kept in the business now gives you more flexibility to do the things you have to do to get the business growing again.

If such a conversion sounds appealing, first try to negotiate a deal to convert part or all of your revolving loans and credit lines into a term loan, with payments over two, three, or four years. Because of the normal bank preoccupation with repayment rather than income, this doesn't always work, but it's worth a try. If you can't interest a commercial bank, you might try a *secured lender*. This type of financial institution is the modern-day version of a finance company. More often than not, secured lenders will finance your working capital needs when commercial banks won't. Picking up an extra point or two in interest looks more attractive than liquidating the loan. Even at a greater cost, conserving short-term cash might be as good a trade-off as a sale/leaseback.

Another method that is more palatable to commercial banks is to offer additional loan collateral in exchange for extended payment dates. Banks like this type of arrangement because extra collateral increases the security of the loan, keeps bank examiners happy, and permits additional loans to more creditworthy customers. Additional collateral might include

1. A second mortgage on a company-owned building
2. Production machinery and equipment that isn't already used as collateral
3. Company-owned automobiles
4. On-road and off-road vehicles, such as trucks and forklifts
5. Office equipment
6. Furniture and fixtures
7. Operative patents or copyrights that pay royalties

Most banks will take any asset of value that is free of liens, whether it is owned by the company, shareholders, or third parties. Given the right circumstances, they will also take a second position on assets already securing loans to other lenders.

Personal Collateral
When all business assets already secure outstanding debt, you might try offering personal assets. Be aware, however, that this could lead to trouble for you and your family. Unless your company has a

high probability of recovering quickly, permitting business assets to be substituted for your personal assets, you could easily lose everything. Examples of personal assets that banks love to have as security include

- A second mortgage on your home
- Personal automobiles
- Certificates of deposit and other cash-equivalent bank instruments
- Life insurance policies
- Mutual fund investments
- Listed stocks and bonds
- Pension entitlements
- Valuable collector's items—antiques, gold, paintings, etc.

Even if you do not have sufficient personal assets to satisfy lenders, personal guarantees usually work. Obviously personal guarantees make you liable for business debts if and when your company can't pay. If you have to go this route, by all means don't let your spouse, relatives, or friends cosign the guarantee. That makes them as liable as you.

A New Bank

When all else fails, try shopping for a new bank that might be willing to make the conversion. Although in smaller communities banks are very close-knit and one will generally not compete directly with another, the same is not true in larger cities. In any metropolitan area, there are usually one or two banks that are hungry enough to take your business, especially relatively new, small banks trying to establish a market niche.

Shopping for a new bank requires the same type of preparation recommended in Chapter 6. To briefly review, here are the rules:

1. *Prepare a financing plan.* Never approach a bank for a loan without a well-conceived financing plan. It should be typed, be neatly packaged, and include sufficient market and product information about the business so that the bank can quickly form a judgment. It should also include a recap of the personal backgrounds of all managers, and financial projections for the business.

2. *Submit a list of collateral.* The list should include all business assets that can be pledged after existing short-term debt is liquidated. Each asset should carry an estimate of its market value.

3. *Bring a personal financial statement.* This should list all personal assets and outstanding loans against each.

4. *Make an appointment with a senior loan officer.* Applicants frequently get shuffled down the ladder when submitting the actual loan application, but it helps to set the stage by starting at the top.

5. *Carry a reference letter* from the lender currently holding company loans. This may not be feasible. If it is, rest assured that the new bank will take the loan application more seriously. When it isn't possible, carry reference letters from friends or associates in other financial institutions.

6. *Keep shopping.* The first bank may reject the application, but it's important to keep trying.

Foreign Banks

During the last six or seven years, a great many large foreign banks have set up shop in the United States, especially in the metropolitan areas of New York, Washington, Chicago, Los Angeles, Miami, Dallas, and Atlanta. Many have already expanded to midsize cities around the country. It is not unusual to find a foreign bank that is more receptive to granting long-term loans than American banks. Moreover, foreign banks tend to be more competitive than their U.S. counterparts. Branches are generally eager to get new accounts—even small-business accounts. And foreign banks tend to be more creative in structuring loans. If you are short of collateral, this might be the answer to your prayers.

Secured Lenders

Another possibility, provided your business has a significant amount of hard assets—land, buildings, machinery, and equipment—is to refinance with a secured lender. These financial institutions specialize in long-term loans secured by hard assets. Their interest rates are higher than those of commercial banks, often more than eight points over the prime rate, but amortization schedules can be as long as five to seven years. There can be no question that this is an expensive way to go. But, as with other short-term tactics, converting to long-term debt with a secured lender conserves cash now when it is most needed.

As a rule, loan officers who work for secured lenders are fairly good businesspeople and in most cases will at least make an effort to understand your business before granting a loan. On the other hand, they are also tough to deal with when cash is tight and you have to miss a payment. Commercial banks seldom foreclose; they just don't have the personnel (some would say the guts!) with the qualifications to handle a foreclosure. Secured lenders do. In fact, they are experts at it.

Defer Debt Payments

If converting short-term loans into long-term obligations isn't feasible, you might try negotiating deferred payments with your bank. Since most commercial banks, especially the smaller ones, are not equipped to auction off foreclosed business assets and would much rather have the loan repaid than foreclose, they tend to be amenable to almost any reasonable solution, provided you can't meet your loan payments.

Obviously, this situation can work to your advantage. Clearly, bankers recognize that the risk of never getting repaid is less if they help you over a short-term cash shortage. Except in rare instances, banks reason that if they get you through bad times, conditions will eventually improve. Then, not only will the old loan be repaid, but new loans will probably be needed.

For example, assume that a company's revolving line of credit has fully absorbed its receivables borrowing base. Business slacks off temporarily, and new shipments generate less cash than collections, which must be used to pay back the revolver. By deferring payments on the revolver for six months, the lender in effect grants an extra loan by allowing its customer to use collections for buying materials, meeting payrolls, and covering other operating expenses. Such a cash infusion could be just enough to get the company back on track.

Assuming that you have built up a solid working relationship with your bank and that you can prove that the current cash shortage is temporary, you should be able to negotiate deferred payments. In most cases, banks understand that the granting of deferred payments is the least-risk action (although at times they have to be nudged in the right direction to admit it).

If your bank is amenable to deferred payments, chances are good that you will have to continue making monthly interest payments. However, the deferral of principal payments should relieve cash flow shortfalls at least somewhat. Here's an example of how one company benefited by such a deferral.

Slugger Bat Company manufactured aluminum baseball bats, gloves, and several accessories primarily for Little Leagues, but also sold through Kmart and other discount retailers. Over the previous few years, Slugger had found competition increasing. The CEO decided to offer a dating program to large accounts but faced a financing problem. Until that time, the company had managed well with a straight bank line of credit, secured by inventory and receivables. However, the new dating program meant that receivables wouldn't be collected for up to 180 days—much too long to sustain a normal line of credit.

Slugger's CEO approached the bank with a proposition to defer loan payments until six months after the dated receivables came in— actually twelve months from that time. This would allow the company to catch up on payments against its supplier accounts and provide a partial cushion against the next dating program. The bank agreed. Furthermore, the bank agreed to an additional demand loan for 150 days to tide this good customer over.

Obviously, Slugger was in a very fortunate position. Most banks aren't that generous. However, if you have maintained good relationships and your company has a profitable track record, you should be able to negotiate a deferral of some type.

Nonbank Sources of Capital

When you can't refinance through a bank or other financial institution, and you can't convert short-term loans to long-term obligations, you might try to raise additional equity capital or nonbank loans to take out the bank entirely. And, with a little ingenuity and some digging, you should be able to locate such investors. Among the most likely choices are

1. Large customers—equity contributions, advances, or loans
2. Suppliers—equity contributions or loans
3. Employees—equity contributions or loans

Some would add friends and relatives to the list, and in certain situations this may be a desirable way to go. Under the right circumstances, you may entice friends or relatives to kick in with either loans or equity contributions. More than one business owner has called in long-forgotten IOUs to raise at least modest amounts.

As a general rule, however, asking friends or relatives for money is not a good idea and can lead to more problems than you've bargained for. My experience has been that friends and especially relatives love to give advice and verbal support, but as soon as you ask for money, friends are no longer friendly, and relatives get greedy. You'll probably do better going with other investors.

Customer Assistance

Many small manufacturing companies have at least one or two large corporations as customers. The larger the customer or the more important your company is as a critical source of supply, the greater the potential for getting financial assistance. Even service companies can tap this source if their services are unique, have a high value, and are sold on contract (such as annual maintenance contracts). In some cases, customer financing may be the only reasonable source of funds when contracting for large jobs or projects.

For example, the automobile and aerospace industries are characterized by a handful of large manufacturers or prime contractors, supported by thousands of small firms that design and manufacture components and assemblies for these giants. This is also true for virtually the entire defense industry, the shipbuilding industry, segments of the oil industry, and major industrial and commercial construction projects. In each case, a large number of small suppliers provide products and services for a few major customers. Financing from these customers typically takes the form of advances, progress payments, loans, equity contributions, or a combination of these.

Advances

Advances are used most frequently when suppliers must incur substantial costs before the product is made or the service rendered, such as those for large purchases of raw materials, the addition of a sizable labor force, or a significant labor training period. Banks are loath to lend against future performance contracts or customer orders, and you may not have any other source of working capital.

In virtually any circumstances, customer advances are preferable to bank loans. Customers usually do not charge interest on advances, and, because payment is received prior to the sale, customers do not have to show the receivable on their balance sheets. Assuming a continuous customer/supplier relationship (as opposed to a one-time sale), regular advances can provide enough working capital so that you will never have to apply for bank loans.

Progress Payments

Progress payments are very popular in industries where long production cycles are the norm. The construction industry also relies heavily on progress payments for working capital, especially when contracts extend over several months or years. It is common practice for subcontractors as well as prime contractors to go this route instead of using bank loans. As a contractor reaches each milestone in the project, progress payments fund the next period.

Nearly all government orders can be structured with progress payments, except for very small, retail-type products. Since many government payments are based on the actual cost of materials purchased and labor hours, it's possible to structure a contract so that you receive progress payments well in advance of actual material and labor expenditures.

Loans

Under certain circumstances, large customers will lend small suppliers short-term funds when the supplier has difficulty getting help from a commercial bank. From the customer's perspective, this makes sense. Many profitable companies have excess cash to invest in marketable securities, Treasury paper, or other secure, short-term holdings.

A good working relationship with important suppliers makes loans to them as secure as other alternatives.

The biggest danger in this type of arrangement is that customers may insist on exorbitant interest rates. Even at that, when you can't get bank loans, you can't be choosy. Also, borrowing from a customer can be both easier and quicker than borrowing from a bank. And committing a customer to future purchases is an indirect benefit, but in some cases the greatest benefit. Not all customers will lend money to suppliers, but enough do to make it worth the effort.

Equity Contributions

Getting a customer to buy shares in your company may seem far-fetched; however, given the right circumstances, this may be the best alternative of any for raising immediate cash. Not infrequently, customers would rather invest in a supplier's shares to lock in a technology or manufacturing process than make loans.

A good example occurred with a small company that had developed a sophisticated optical sensor used for detecting objects moving at high speeds, such as jet aircraft. The company ran short of cash and was fully leveraged with a local bank. Its traditional business dropped off, and the company faced potential bankruptcy. An Australian customer was particularly interested in the new optical sensor technology and bailed out the supplier with a $200,000 equity infusion in return for 25 percent of the company. The reasoning was that if the new technology proved marketable, the Australian company would have the right of first refusal to buy a controlling interest in the supplier.

You certainly don't have to be large to get customers to invest equity capital. In fact, the smaller the business, the more attractive an investment opportunity it may be. One of two conditions must be present, however: Your product or service must be unique and valuable in and of itself, or it must be critical to the customer's supply line.

A good example of the latter situation occurred with a small machining company that was the sole supplier of small turned titanium parts used in race car transmissions. As inflation pushed costs to new highs, competition pounded the company's customer base and kept selling prices low. Its line of credit was stretched, and the company was short of cash. The president warned a major customer that commanded 30 percent of this transmission market that his company needed to reduce its bank debt in order to stay alive. He also suggested that to protect this valuable source of transmission parts, the customer should consider buying 25 percent of the company. The customer agreed, and two months later all short-term loans were paid off and the supplier had $150,000 in cash reserves. It continues to supply these vital transmission parts today.

Allowing customers to invest in your company may not be a palatable alternative. Although it is a viable option under certain circumstances, you probably don't want to be tied to specific customers forever. Economic and market conditions are dynamic, and as conditions change, most companies need the flexibility to shift customers or product lines as needed to maximize market control. It's hard to do this when customers own part of your business. Therefore, a contractual agreement usually stipulates buyout terms for each party.

Supplier Assistance

It is usually easier to convince a supplier to lend to or invest in your company than it is to negotiate new capital from a customer. Actually, supplier financing is just the reverse of customer financing. Every business manager is familiar with using thirty-, sixty-, or ninety-day trade credit. But many times suppliers will agree to terms beyond normal trade credit. A rather unusual arrangement occurred with my Midwest screw machine company. We needed to lay out a substantial amount of cash for raw materials—specifically, a large volume of bars made from a special alloy supplied by a Swedish steel mill—to fill a new order. However, our bank line of credit was exhausted. We negotiated a deal with the Swedish supplier to ship steel bar twice each year, each shipment to be sufficient for six months' production. The steel was stored in a bonded warehouse, from which we could withdraw truckloads throughout the year as needed. The Swedish company agreed to invoice only as we withdrew bars from the warehouse. This allowed us to maintain a six months' supply of critical steel bar inventory without paying anything until it was used.

Another variation of supplier financing was used by a wooden-furniture manufacturer. The purchasing agent contracted with a distributor in California for a three years' supply of specialty hardwood imported from South America at a fixed price for the entire period. As the manufacturer was short of cash, the purchasing agent didn't want delivery until material was needed for production. To achieve better pricing, the distributor took advantage of arbitrage purchasing from its

South American supplier. The distributor also agreed to help the manufacturer conserve cash by holding any excess material in a California warehouse until the manufacturer needed it, with a guaranteed three months' supply on hand. This arrangement saved the manufacturer over $50,000 in interest and inventory carrying charges.

Just-in-time (JIT) deliveries have become a way of life in many industries. No longer willing to carry large inventories, an increasing number of customers are demanding that suppliers finance inventory carrying charges and stocking costs. And most are getting away with it. Supplier financing has become more and more popular in recent years, and if you're not taking advantage of just-in-time deliveries, you are probably missing the boat.

Equity

Large suppliers are generally more amenable to investing in a customer's business than are customers in a supplier's business. And with good reason. Properly structured, such an arrangement can benefit suppliers as much as the company in need of cash. Some of the major benefits are as follows:

- Customers can use the equity contribution to pay long-overdue supplier accounts.
- Suppliers can tie up a customer for future sales.
- Suppliers can lock out competitors' products.
- The investment may appreciate as the customer grows.
- Investors can influence management decisions more readily than creditors can.
- The investment could be the first step in an eventual buyout of the entire company.
- An equity infusion in a valuable customer could ensure continued sales.
- The extra cash could forestall bank foreclosure or other interference with a customer's operations, which would decrease the supplier's sales.

Small companies usually have more leverage in extracting capital from suppliers than they realize. Actually, it's quite simple. Merely hold back on the payment of prior invoices and blame the delay on cash flow shortages, which could very well be true. When business slows down, this tactic is used so frequently that suppliers begin to expect it. There is very little a supplier can do short of cutting off future deliveries.

To ensure a continued demand for materials or services at prices equal to or more than prevailing market prices, more than one supplier has willingly offered to purchase equity shares in a good customer. After all, suppliers who become shareholders have at least some influence on a company's purchase decisions.

Many companies look at equity infusions as a last resort. When all else fails and additional loans become too expensive, outsiders must come through with enough cash to keep the business afloat. The smaller the business, the more impact equity capital has on cash flow, and generally the easier it is to locate sources of extra capital. Of course, the trade-off is selling part of a business, which can be a traumatic experience. Nevertheless, at times you have to take the bull by the horns, as it were, and do things you normally wouldn't consider.

Friends and Relatives

Very small companies may not be able to interest either customers or suppliers. In that case, friends and relatives really are the last resort. If you have to go this route, at least be certain to make the transaction formal with a written contract.

The guidelines in Figure 15.1 should help to minimize family quarrels or misunderstandings.

Figure 15.1
Rules for Staying out of Trouble with Related Investors

1. Make the transaction formal by issuing stock certificates.
2. Execute a written document spelling out the specific date when investors will be paid off so that they know that their money isn't gone forever.
3. Specify what return investors will get—cash returns, appreciation, use of the business facilities or products, free services, and so on.
4. Try to structure the deal so that if the business incurs a tax loss, investors get the benefit of it on personal tax returns (e.g., an S corporation or limited partnership arrangement).
5. Ask for the minimum amount of money needed right now, identify exactly how the money will be used, and then use it for that purpose.

Employees

In addition to soliciting capital from friends and relatives, it's possible to get employees to help bail out a company. The easiest, and perhaps the most beneficial, way is with an Employee Stock Ownership Plan, or ESOP. An ESOP is a tax-qualified employee retirement-benefit plan, similar in many ways to other qualified retirement plans. However, unlike other retirement plans, which restrict the amount of employer securities that can be purchased, ESOPs are authorized to purchase part or all of the stock in the sponsoring company. One of the major benefits of using an ESOP is that the Internal Revenue Service actually helps raise the capital.

The Internal Revenue Code permits two types of ESOPs: *unleveraged* and *leveraged* plans. An unleveraged ESOP is the simplest form. First, company contributions fund the plan. Then the ESOP uses these funds to purchase stock from the company, effectively returning the company's own money. On the surface, this doesn't seem to bring in additional capital. Indirectly it does, however, because contributions to the ESOP are tax-deductible. Since the money is immediately returned to company accounts, no cash goes out the door. In effect, the IRS makes a contribution of about 35 percent!

For example, assume an annual payroll of $1 million. A company contributes 10 percent, or $100,000, to an ESOP. The amount of taxes saved by the transaction is 35 percent of $100,000, or $35,000. The company would not have this cash without the ESOP. Therefore, the IRS has actually put $35,000 into the company. As an alternative to making cash contributions, companies may donate stock directly to an ESOP. These shares are then immediately allocated to employee accounts.

A leveraged ESOP works the same way as an unleveraged plan, except that more money flows into the ESOP. In addition to company contributions, the ESOP may borrow from a bank or other lender specifically to buy shares in the company. Employees get company stock, the company gets the bank's money without booking a loan. Banks generally insist on guarantees from the sponsoring company, but do not require that additional assets be pledged. Annual company contributions pay the principal and interest on the loan, and purchased shares are allocated to employee accounts each year as the debt is amortized.

If you are thinking about setting up an ESOP, be aware that it is an IRS invention. Therefore, the IRS has the authority to change the rules at will. And that frequently happens. Be sure to get competent advice from your tax adviser before taking the first step.

Index